Many of us sense something missing in our busy, active programs, and our overcommitted and often draining "Christianity." That something is depth—the need to go down into our very souls, to rediscover there the deep, deep love of God. Doug Rumford has given us a remarkable guide for our spiritual journeying. *SoulShaping* is full of carefully crafted truths, insights from a wide range of wise travelers, stories of fellow pilgrims, coaching for our necessary spiritual exercises, and godly hope. Don't miss the journey. And take this book along.

LEIGHTON FORD, of Leighton Ford Ministries, author of *Transforming Leadership*

Doug has written a most helpful book for everyone who wants to get his or her soul into shape. It's full of timely, practical advice for spiritual training. It tells, not just what spiritual growth looks like, but also how to pursue it.

JOHN ORTBERG, Teaching Pastor, Willow Creek Community Church

I highly recommend *SoulShaping: Taking Care of Your Spiritual Life.* It is practical, biblical, and filled with experience and application.

RON RAND, Director of UpBuilding Ministries, Inc., author of *For Fathers Who Aren't in Heaven*, Promise Keepers Faculty Member

Advice on developing the spiritual life runs the risk of being either too prescriptive or too theoretical. Doug Rumford has now given us a clear, gracious, motivating manual to help all of us in our journey toward more maturity. Through careful biblical counsel and numerous real-life illustrations, Doug has provided a book useful for both those eager to take their first steps and those well along the spiritual pilgrimage. I will be recommending this book for years to come.

DR. STEPHEN A. HAYNER, President, InterVarsity Christian Fellowship

Doug Rumford has written a helpful book. It is full of sound, practical advice to help us open our spirits to the Spirit of God.

DONALD W. MCCULLOUGH, President, San Francisco Theological Seminary

Underneath all the glitter and veneer, our society is experiencing a tidal wave of hopelessness. As Doug states so well, this is happening because of the widespread neglect of our souls.

Numerous authors have recognized this, but Doug Rumford has approached the issue with a freshness, vividness, and precision that I have not seen for some time. He re-introduces us to a God who is Personal, Passionate, and Present—a God whose love will always find a way to be practical. I think this is what stunned me the most. *SoulShaping* is profound without being esoteric, and Doug makes this wild hope practical without it ever being shallow. He takes us from the "Oh Wow!" of holy awe to a holy boldness, giving us mature tools so that we can take on the challenge of spiritual restoration and growth.

If, like myself, you are deeply concerned about the escalating problems all around us; if you care about your world, your friends, your family, or your "self," this book is a MUST reading. In the midst of all the pain and confusion, there is a Living Promise—a truth that can and will set us free. Rumford knows that this Truth is not just a principle but a Person—One whom he knows at a level few do and about whom he writes with passion, power, and clarity.

TIM HANSEL, Founder/President, Summit Expedition, and Ignite, Inc., author of *You Gotta Keep Dancin', When I Relax I Feel Guilty,* and *Holy Sweat*

This book is extremely timely and relevant to the needs of Christians today. Many are searching for practical guidance for shaping their spiritual lives in the context of a crazy-making world. They are hurried and hassled and don't have a lot of time to discover the spiritual disciplines for themselves. Doug's book provides them with guidance, but it does so in a stimulating, scintillating and soul-serving way. New believers as well as veteran disciples will find it tugging at their heart. Hardly a page goes by that doesn't create a hunger within to know the deeper experience of God's presence.

ARCHIBALD D. HART, Ph.D., Fuller Theological Seminary, author of *Unlocking the Mystery of Your Emotions.*

There is a sweetness about this book. . . . The stories are universal. The questions gently and effectively Socratic. Rumford's guidance toward the answers is clearly Scripture-based. This is a searching and satisfying book.

MAX DEPREE, author of *Dear Zoe* and *Leadership Is an Art*

COLUMBIA BIBLE COLLEGE
2940 CLEARBROOK ROAD
ABBOTSFORD BC

TERM ID: 00F03469   OPER. ID: 1

DEBIT: 5892970000029797561
SALE FROM CHEQUING

$17.64

DATE: 01/02/26   TIME: 19:55:05
AUTH: 445934 - REF: 7580   BATCH: 0247

00 TRANSACTION APPROVED

SoulShaping

DOUGLAS J.
RUMFORD

Tyndale House Publishers, Inc.
Wheaton, Illinois

Published in association with the literary agency of Alive Communications, Inc., 1465 Kelly Johnson Blvd., Suite 320, Colorado Springs, CO 80920.

Editor: Vinita Hampton Wright

Library of Congress Cataloging-in-Publication Data

Rumford, Douglas J.
  SoulShaping : taking care of your spiritual life through godly disciplines / Douglas J. Rumford.
    p. cm.
  Includes bibliographical references.
  ISBN 0-8423-3593-5 (pbk. : alk. paper)
  1. Spiritual life—Christianity. I. Title.
BV4501.2.R82 1996
248.4—dc20   96-20351

Printed in the United States of America

01 00 99 98 97
7   6   5   4   3

To my wife, Sarah
Our souls are knit together in Christ,
woven with His golden threads.

And to our parents
Wayne M. and Marian Moore
Robert K. and Lillian Rumford
Who have often been the Potter's hands,
shaping us in wisdom and love

CONTENTS

DISCLAIMER

The personal stories in this book are true. Many of the stories are told with the permission of the people involved. In many cases, however, the names and identifying details have been altered to preserve their anonymity.

ACKNOWLEDGMENTS

It is a delightful duty to affirm and thank those who've shaped me in the development of this book. Special thanks go to:

Dave Stoop—for encouraging me as an author and being the link to Ron Beers and Tyndale House Publishers.

Ron Beers—for the warm welcome and the vision of treating authors as partners in the ministry of communication.

Vinita Wright—for her editorial intuition and skill, and for cheering me on through those days of doubt when I wondered why I ever thought I had anything new to say.

First Presbyterian Church of Fresno—thanks to the staff, elders, and congregation for coming alongside me in every possible way.

Dr. Howard Rice and Dr. Roberta Hestenes—Those who plant the first seeds rarely hear "Thank you." I want to thank these two, whose input and courses proved to be turning points on my spiritual path.

My family—Dearest Sarah, Kristen, Matthew, Timmy, and Peter, you mean more to me than words can ever say. I love you and thank the Lord for our life together.

ONE

SoulShaping: From Soul Neglect to Spiritual Vitality

The tragedy of it all is that most people die with their best music still in them, still waiting to be released.
IRVING BERLIN, on the death of his dear friend George Gershwin

My soul's house is narrow for you to enter; will you not make it broader? It is in a state of collapse; will you not rebuild it?
ST. AUGUSTINE

Let me know Thee even as I am known. Power of my soul, enter into it and fit it for yourself, so that you may have and hold it without spot or wrinkle. . . . As for the other things of this life, the more we weep for them, the less they ought to be wept for, and the less we weep for them the more we ought to weep.
ST. AUGUSTINE

Religion is the last region for chance desires. Do it as a duty, and it may open out as a blessing. Omit it, and you may miss the one thing that would have made an eternal difference.
P. T. FORSYTH, *The Soul of Prayer*

CHAPTER ONE

Recognizing the Symptoms of Soul Neglect

As David sat down in my study, we moved quickly through the formal greetings. "We need to get down to business," he said, with urgency in his voice. The pressures of his business, which was heavily in debt, the stresses of a young family, and growing conflict with some members of his extended family were pushing him to a breaking point.

"I've always prided myself on being able to 'take it,'" he said. "And I don't like people who whine. . . . But I'm not sure how long I can hold on."

David would tell you that he is a man of genuine faith, with a confidence in God and a commitment to moral principles rooted in the Bible. "I think I believe all the right things, *but where is the power?* Where is the power to get me through this?"

Diane was a single parent in one of those no-win situations. Her teenage daughter seemed bent on testing Diane in every way possible. The constant defiance, the demeaning comments, and now this—pregnant before she was out of high school. "I feel an ache I can't even describe," Diane told me. "It's as if someone has my heart in his fist and is squeezing so hard that it is about to burst. What have I done wrong? And if I've been so bad, why do others have to hurt so much? If I haven't done anything to deserve this, how could God let it happen? How do I get through this?"

Don was one of those guys who found everything going his way. Coming from a strong, loving family had put him far ahead in the area of self-confidence. His winning personality, sharp intellect, and sincere faith were, to be honest, the envy of many people, including myself. That's why I was surprised when he said he really needed to see me. "I just need to talk to somebody who won't say, 'Yeah, right—I wish I had your kind of problems.' You see, my problem is that I don't have many problems—*but I still feel a deep emptiness!* If I had something to blame, it would be one thing. But I just don't get it. Why do I feel this way?"

During my years of pastoral ministry, I've spoken with a number of Davids, Dianes, and Dons, who are wondering where to find the power, not merely to endure life, but to derive true joy and meaning from it. They want to be strong in crisis and to live with purpose. They have the highest expectations of life because they have tasted the promise it holds. That makes it all the more difficult for them when life delivers a kick that knocks the breath out of them.

As we have walked together through the shadows and often very dark valleys, we have discovered a number of principles that have helped us tap into the spiritual vitality God intends for each of us. I used to wish that their questions could be answered easily. But I'm realizing that heart questions such as theirs yield the richest answers when the search takes us deep into God's heart. God wants us to learn our lessons well, rather than race through our days—and dark nights—grabbing a truth here and there. The quest for the answers to life's complex questions can be one of our most satisfying and life-changing pursuits. This quest takes us to the heart of life.

ETERNITY IN OUR HEARTS

This world is a place of soulshaping. It is a place where we can either develop a life marked by values and qualities we know are right and good or slide into a life of inconsistency and regret. It is a place in which all experience, good and bad, happy and tragic, boring and thrilling, can be the raw material for making a life that counts for more. Or it can be a place in which we merely endure our days, worn down by life's disappointments and problems. In short, it is a place in which we are shaped for a richer experience of life or in which we find ourselves poorer and sadder. What makes the difference?

Instinctively, we know that we were created for something more than going through the motions. In the midst of our outward activities, there is an inner process at work. We are searching—for fulfillment, meaning, happiness—for ourselves. We are longing to live life to the fullest! This is not a self-centered pursuit. Becoming the person we were created to be is not only *our* highest reward but also the way in which we will best love and serve others.

Our search for something more out of life usually begins with externals. When we are young, achievements in sports, popularity with others, or academic recognition may drive us. Entry into adulthood presents us with choices about marriage, career, and lifestyle. We often make our choices based upon a set of unexamined assumptions about what "the right way" is.

Often the paths we have fallen into naturally have taken us in the wrong direction. We've confused activity with effectiveness, holding certain positions or titles with personal prestige, accumulating money with security, and sexual encounter with genuine intimacy. We have been so caught up in these pursuits that we haven't really considered what goals we are chasing—and what will happen when we actually catch them! For most of us, there comes a point when we realize that what we've been doing just doesn't bring us satisfaction. We've done what came naturally and still have missed the mark somehow.

And when we realize we've missed the mark, we usually try hard to do more of exactly what we've been doing, hoping for different results. When that fails, we may wander into a dark place of disillusionment and discouragement. Yet this "soul longing" remains, unless we can silence its persistent whispers or dull its insistent ache.

This longing is difficult to name. When he was meeting with me, David voiced it as longing for power. Diane was searching for an explanation, along with relief and strength. Others think of it as a search for peace. Don didn't know what to call it; he just knew there had to be more to life than what he was experiencing.

Through much of our lives we try to name this longing; we also try many remedies to fulfill it. The writer of the book of Ecclesiastes speaks of it as "eternity in the hearts of men" (Eccles. 3:11). Eternity in this case is more than a quantity of time. Eternity is a quality of life that begins now. "Eternity in our hearts" means that we intuitively know that we were made for a life of meaningful relationships, for higher purposes beyond our own success, and for a sense of connection with the Creator and Designer of the universe. It is the longing of the human heart to press to the limits and to squeeze all we can from our experience. We know there is more to life than we can see and much more to our lives than we take time to appreciate. By whatever name, it is this very longing that marks us most truly as human.

WHAT'S SPIRITUALITY GOT TO DO WITH IT?

The purpose of this book is to help us not only understand the first steps of finding fulfillment in life but also to move into the process of personal growth. God designed us with wonderful things in mind! And all our soul-searching leads ultimately to God, God's love for us, and God's purposes. The life that most satisfies is rooted firmly in the soul and is nurtured by faith. This faith is more than a compilation of beliefs, however. Faith is a way of living. There are many ways in which we bring faith to life. Bringing faith alive is our most vital force in daily experience. And we can learn how to apply the principles of faith for practical success in life.

Many of us have had the mistaken idea that spirituality is too complex, too ritualistic, or too advanced for our normal daily lives. These misconceptions have robbed us of the very resources and practices that can bring a sense of control, calm, and purpose to our frantic, overactive, anxious lives. Spirituality transforms daily life into an experience that is more simple and grace filled, a life that matures naturally. Even though spirituality is a rich subject, it is not as complex as we try to make it sometimes. It involves regular actions, but they are not empty rituals. It involves disciplines, but they are not actions designed to earn our salvation or achievement points with God. And spirituality is *not* just for the spiritually advanced—if there could ever be such a category!

One problem with spirituality is that it hasn't been presented in a way that makes sense for it to become a way of life for the "normal person" who is involved in the workday, secular world— who has academic studies and a job or who is scrambling to support a family in a single-parent home. Spirituality has been isolated from "regular life" when it was intended to season regular life with the salt of spiritual energy. Spirituality has been made out to be mysterious—when it was intended to be the light that makes things clear.

True spirituality cannot be a hobby. It is a way of life for those who truly want to follow the Lord. Spirituality is for the person who made an early commitment to Christ (perhaps as a teenager) and felt great enthusiasm for the first few years but who now knows that the fire in her soul burns dimly. Spirituality is for the person who finds himself longing for a sense of significance, especially after tasting the quick-melting joy of success. Spirituality grounds us on the rock-solid foundation of life and escorts us into the richest experiences and expressions of life.

Many people have failed to make spirituality a way of life simply because they haven't been aware of the basic needs of their souls. Neither have they understood the many different roles spiritual activities, or disciplines, play in the care of the soul. Simply put, *spirituality cares for the soul by cultivating a vital connection to the living Lord.* Any "spiritual" activity we undertake must have this connection to Christ as its primary goal. As we abide in the Lord, he pours out his resources and reveals his purpose for our lives.

An athlete whose survival in sports depends on physical conditioning incorporates exercise and training into the daily routine. In the same way, spirituality must become part of our daily conditioning and exercise. It is not cultivated in a vacuum—in a small compartment of time that's disconnected from the rest of life. When we remove spirituality from daily life, treating it more as a hobby than as the spiritual training and conditioning necessary to a truly "abundant" life (John 10:10), we have lost the fire of the spiritual life.

The most powerful evidence for the call to a higher life is the very persistent, deep longing that we experience. Even as physical hunger and thirst point us to the need for food and drink, the longing in our soul points us to the need for spiritual vitality. And if we want to address the deepest longing of our lives, we must first take time to look at our souls, to listen to that voice deep within us. As we do, we have the Holy Spirit to guide and the Word of God, which is "sharper than any two-edge sword, piercing to the division of soul and spirit . . . discerning the thoughts and intentions of the heart" (Heb. 4:12, RSV).

We will progress in our spiritual development as we understand our Creator's plan. The ultimate goal is that we be transformed into Christlikeness. But in fulfilling this larger goal we must deal with some basic questions, such as:

- What does the growing follower of Jesus Christ look like?
- How does a Christian grow spiritually?
- What motivates us to allow our souls to be shaped into the image of Christ?
- What spiritual activities or disciplines can we apply to different life circumstances?
- How do different issues and needs within a person's life affect his or her spiritual growth?

Soulshaping will help you understand spiritual growth and how to practice the specific disciplines of the spiritual life that care for our soul and shape our life inside and out.

We will explore not only the "soul work" we can do but also how our spiritual growth is affected by vision, motivation, natural resistance, and the passing of time.

IS YOUR WELL FULL OR EMPTY?

I was fascinated to learn that the Paris Opera House, best known through Andrew Lloyd Webber's musical *Phantom of the*

9

.
.
.

Opera, sits on three acres of land, and four-fifths of the theater is backstage. There is indeed a subterranean lake, the famous haunt of the phantom. This lake, seven stories beneath the building, is an essential part of the structural design. It is used as ballast, with the water level being raised or lowered to support the varying weight of different scenes that are on the stage. Ciceri, the opera's chief designer from 1824–1847, re-created the eruption of Vesuvius on stage using real stones! Can you imagine the weight? Any other wooden structure would have collapsed. But even as the ocean can support the great weight of a ship, so the lake helped support the excessive strain on the stage. The backstage design ensured the onstage success.

What about the reservoir of life? Each of us is designed with a soul that is like a lake—an inner reservoir—which supports the fluctuating weights and stresses that strain the stage of our lives. To be effective, however, this reservoir must be continually replenished. In this light, it's interesting to reflect on the words of Jesus in John 7:37-38: "'If anyone is thirsty, let him come to me and drink. Whoever believes in me, as the Scripture has said, streams of living water will flow from within him.' By this he meant the Spirit whom those who believed in him were later to receive." Fellowship with Jesus becomes the source of living water. He is the Source of continual refreshment, and we are the catch basins to receive it.

Too often, however, our personal well is dry. David, who came to see me in the midst of business and family struggles, was experiencing this dryness. As the time came to tap the reserves that he needed, the faucet belched out dirty air. Instead of power, he found great weakness. Soul neglect had finally caught up with him.

We experience this soul dryness in many situations. When financial pressures close in on us, we have no sense of promise to prime the pump of faith. When someone criticizes us, threatening our esteem, we can draw only the brackish waters of bitter-

ness that yield an angry response. The words of Jeremiah more
accurately describe our experience: "Thus says the Lord . . . my
people have committed two evils: they have forsaken me, the
fountain of living waters, and hewed out cisterns for themselves,
broken cisterns, that can hold no water" (Jer. 2:13, RSV). God's
response in this passage is more sad than angry. Our reservoir is
dry. Worse yet, we have turned away from the only Source of
living water. Our grief and disgust at seeing dead fish floating to
the top of a polluted lake is like God's response to our forsaking
the care of our hearts.

Our call, then, is to discover God's strategy for releasing the
"streams of living water" which his Spirit provides within and
through us. When we look at our souls, we can locate the boulders
and debris that block the flow of living water that would replenish
our lives. We can also discover the leaks that drain us of vitality.

WHERE ARE YOU NOW?

The needs of our inner lives often go unrecognized
because we don't know how to read the signs. We fail to realize
that many of the problems we face have their roots in soul issues.
What we think of as a problem with another person may in fact
be the sour fruit of our own heart. What we think of as a problem with a job may be a problem with God. The key to effective
living and personal change is dealing with the real issues at soul
level.

There are many symptoms, but we rarely stop long enough to
check them out. Human beings have an amazing tolerance for
misery. How many of us absolutely refuse to go to a doctor to get
the help we know we need? Instead, we tolerate the misery.
While this is true of physical maladies, it is especially true in spiritual matters. People are reluctant to speak with a pastor, counselor, or friend. If we were to reach out, however, another person

could "hold up a mirror" in which we might be better able to see and understand what's going on inside us.

With the physical body there are basic criteria—vital signs—we use to determine the inside condition: heart rate, blood pressure, temperature, and the body's chemistry. There are also certain vital signs of the soul by which we measure spiritual health and symptoms of disease. Before we look more closely at the marks of spiritual health, I want to give you an opportunity to do a self-assessment of your spiritual condition.

SYMPTOMS OF SOUL NEGLECT

In the Psalms, David frequently considered the condition of his soul. "Why are you cast down, O my soul, and why are you disquieted within me?" (Ps. 42:5, RSV). On another occasion he said, "My soul also is sorely troubled" (Ps. 6:3, RSV). On these occasions, he took time to look within, under the guidance of the Holy Spirit, to discern his soul need and God's solution.

Is your inner reservoir replenished with living water, or do you feel that your soul is drained dry? If someone asked you to describe your spiritual condition, what would you say? Don, the man who found everything going his way, used the term *emptiness* to describe his spiritual condition. This is one of ten primary symptoms of soul neglect I've encountered most frequently in my own life and in giving spiritual support and direction to others. These symptoms of soul neglect are meant to be tools for examining your heart, the person you truly are in your soul. The list is suggestive, not exhaustive (it probably tells you a lot more about me than it may tell about you!). An accurate understanding of your particular need or needs will help you know what spiritual disciplines will be most appropriate for your personal soul renewal.

Low-Grade "Depression Fever"

Depression is widespread, especially among spiritually sensitive people. I am not referring now to what we might call "clinical depression," which has psychological and physiological roots. I am referring to a spiritual depression in which a person, feeling fine in most other ways, feels distant and cut off from God. This will vary in its intensity, from mild to severe, but it is an experience dreaded by those who have tasted the goodness of God.

It's ironic that a melancholic streak often passes through those who care most deeply about life. Charles Spurgeon, known as the Prince of Preachers, had a congregation of more than ten thousand in London in the mid- to late 1800s. There was no church in the world larger than that. He was known far and wide for his personal integrity and professional effectiveness. He was a man of deep faith. Yet he knew the darkness of depression. He begins an insightful lecture to ministerial students, entitled "The Minister's Fainting Fits," with wisdom that speaks to all of us:

> As it is recorded that David, in the heat of battle, waxed faint, so may it be written of all the servants of the Lord. Fits of depression come over the most of us. Usually cheerful as we may be, we must at intervals be cast down. The strong are not always vigorous, the wise not always ready, the brave not always courageous, and the joyous not always happy.[1]

There are stories that, after delivering a great message, Spurgeon would go home on Sunday evening and curl up in bed in abject despair!

Biblical servants were no strangers to spiritual depression. Following his thunderous victory on Mt. Carmel, Elijah was afraid and fled for his life. His depression overwhelmed him as he said repeatedly, "I, even I only, am left" (1 Kings 19:10, 14, RSV). His despair grew so desperate that he said, "It is enough; now, O Lord, take away my life" (1 Kings 19:4, RSV). While there are several explanations for this particular depression, one that makes the most sense is intense fatigue from the spiritual battle on Mt. Carmel. *Spiritual service does not make us immune to spiritual depression.* In fact, we are more susceptible. Consider the complaints of Jeremiah, the struggles of Jonah, the affliction that nearly crushed Paul so that he "despaired of life itself" (2 Cor. 1:8, RSV). Since that is the case, we need to learn how to care for our souls in such times.

I use the term "low-grade depression fever" because a low-grade fever is often the indicator of an infection that eludes simple techniques for diagnosis. This depression is best described in terms of coldness and unresponsiveness to spiritual things. Life is blue and blah. The person feels guilty for feeling so dull but cannot find any relief. The courageous ones continue to live the life of faith, functioning out of commitment but without desire. There may be activity, but there's no fire.

Others descend into much darker valleys, where they reject what they used to believe. "I just don't believe that anymore," they say, or, "I used to believe that." They express a deep sense of disappointment that their faith didn't hold up in times of testing or that it hasn't produced what they expected. They usually don't realize that they have neglected many or most of the essential, foundational practices that nurture spiritual vitality. This is not the time to ask a person how much time they've spent in prayer lately, but the answer would be quite revealing.

The writer of Psalm 42 expresses deep depression. "My tears have been my food day and night, while [people] say to me continually, 'Where is your God?'" (Ps. 42:3, RSV). The sadness of depression is not only the sense of having lost touch with God but also of being ridiculed for ever believing in the first place.

14

Depression stems from a sense of loss.[2] The heart knows something is missing long before we are willing to recognize or admit it. Since one of the symptoms of depression is a loss of energy and initiative, we find it nearly impossible to do the soul-searching that can lead us to insight and relief. But it is one of the most important things we can do. We can examine our lives, asking the basic questions: "What have I lost? Is this loss real (such as losing a friend) or imagined (such as not having an opportunity that was never promised to me in the first place)? What am I telling myself about this loss? Why does it affect me so deeply?"

Depression can arise from innumerable sources. It is one of the most common manifestations of soul dryness, usually connected with one or some of the other symptoms listed below.

Busy but Bored

When we are active but exhausted, we may be facing some serious soul trouble. Initially, we thrive on the activity. It is great to have options, adventures, interesting things to do, people to meet, and places to go. We can feel powerful, needed, important. A full calendar tells us that we are in demand.

But it doesn't last. Even the good things we do can lead to burnout. If we assume the goal is happiness, we draw the conclusion that the only way to stay happy is to keep moving—and that soon becomes intolerable. We have a calendar that is full but a heart that is withering, shrinking, unable to care deeply or to experience pleasure fully. We want everything to stop, but we find that no activity is even more frightening than too much. When we've had moments of quiet, the inner ache has been too much.

This was Don's primary complaint. He had everything going for him in life but still felt a gnawing emptiness. He had lost his joy. He was bored with the very life many spend all their energies trying to achieve. Boredom should not be understood to refer to a lack of activity, like children at the end of summer who need to get back to school because they are all played out. Rather, boredom refers to a lack of meaning felt in all the activities we're doing. Henri Nouwen writes:

> While busy and worried about many things, we seldom feel truly satisfied, at peace, or at home. A gnawing sense of being unfulfilled underlies our filled lives. Reflecting a little more on this experience of unfulfillment I can discern different sentiments. The most significant are boredom, resentment and depression. Boredom is a sense of disconnectedness. While we are busy with many things, we wonder if what we do makes any real difference. Life presents itself as a random, unconnected series of activities and events over which we have little or no control. To be bored therefore does not mean that we have nothing to do but that we question the value of the things we're so busy doing. The great paradox of our time is that many of us are busy and bored at the same time. While running from one event to the next we wonder in our innermost selves if anything is really happening. While we can hardly keep up with our many tasks and obligations we are not so sure that it would make any difference if we did nothing at all.[3]

In this condition, a person has little energy for the things of life that used to give pleasure. There is activity without meaning. She may be looking for escapes she never even considered before "just to get some fun back into life." Too often we try to combat this problem with more activity: reading more books, doing more things, being with more people. The condition usually worsens. When we feel trapped like this, the choices seem to be that we either turn our backs on it all or give up our hopes and accept that this is just the way things are going to be.

Loss of Control over Life's Routine

Spiritual vitality can be crowded out of our lives. Another symptom of soul dryness arises when we are overwhelmed by the press of demands, unable to keep all the fires that we've started fueled. Unlike the *busy-but-bored* situation, we are not questioning the meaning of what we are doing. We are, however, overwhelmed by the sheer quantity. There seems to be no time just to "let down" and do nothing. If we stop, we will disappoint either ourselves or others who are counting on us.

Consider your daily, weekly, monthly, and annual schedule. Are you doing the things that really matter to you? Do you find yourself always saying, "Next month, things will be under control," only to find that next month is worse? When you are at work, do you feel guilty about your home life? And when you are home, are you preoccupied with your work?

We were designed for a basic amount of order in our lives. Some personalities need more order than do others. But a loss of order can be devastating to anyone. Studies by sociologist Emil Durkheim showed that there was only one common factor in suicide: a direct correlation to *anomy*, which means, literally, "without law" in the sense of being without order and regularity. Disorder has a negative spiritual effect upon us. For many people, control over the routine is not merely a matter of being "Type A" or "driven"; it is a matter of managing the many demands of life so that the truly important priorities aren't crowded out.

Routine often gets a bad rap, but it is one of "life's economies" for the budgeting of our energy. Routine is not only a time-saver but also an energy saver. It lessens the number of decisions we have to make so that we can conserve our emotional and mental resources for important decisions. It's been said that the average person today makes more decisions in a year than their grandparents made in a lifetime. No wonder it's so tough to keep our lives in order. Options, opportunities, and the multiplying demands weary the soul. Our personal energy drains away, wasted in anxiety.

Loss of Responsiveness to Others

In times of soul neglect, our relationships often bear the strain. We find it difficult to be with people we used to enjoy. Comments or actions you used to overlook now provoke a negative reaction. Even if you control the outward expression, you often find yourself seething on the inside. Spiritual subjects are no longer natural, inviting topics of conversation with others. We are irritable and judgmental toward others, weary of putting up with or overlooking their flaws and habits.

Moses, as close as he lived to God, went through several times of spiritual dryness. Near the end of the journey through the wilderness, he lost his composure with the people. It was a familiar scenario: The people were thirsty, and there was no water to be found. The congregation assembled and complained, blaming Moses and Aaron for leading them into such a predicament again. Moses sought the Lord in prayer, receiving specific instructions for providing water. "Take the rod, and assemble the congregation, you and Aaron your brother, and tell the rock before their eyes to yield its water." But when Moses stood before the congregation, he shouted, "Hear now, you rebels; shall we bring forth water for you out of this rock?" And Moses lifted up his hand and struck the rock with his rod twice. Though water came forth abundantly, the Lord rebuked Moses. Moses' anger had overcome his willingness to obey the Lord (Numbers 20:8-12). Among the many other lessons portrayed here is a strong indication of how spiritual fatigue affects us. In other words, Moses had run out of cope! The demanding thirst of the people had finally parched his own soul.

This soul loss is apparent when we just want to check out of feeling responsible to and for others. Their needs are burdens we don't want to bear. We are tired with what some have called "compassion fatigue." We know we should care, but we can barely bring ourselves to pick up the phone or write the letter. For a variety of reasons, the self and the soul feel depleted. They've run out of cope. Demands and requests are seen as intruders. When we feel crowded, out of control, and over-whelmed, we are soul drained.

My wife, Sarah, and I lived in a cottage that had water supplied by a well. The water was stored in a small holding tank. If we showered too long, that tank drained, and look out! It would start drawing up the rust and gunk from the bottom of the tank and spit it out on us. When your tank is drained and somebody turns on your faucet once too often, the rust, grit, and sludge of your soul spew out, instead of the "streams of living water."

We know we have trouble when little problems get big reac-tions. That's a symptom that our soul is asking for attention. We are being warned that our reserves are too low. If we can't love our brother and sister, it's probably because we haven't taken time to look at the One who loves us best.

Withdrawal from Responsibility and Leadership

A fifth symptom of soul neglect is backing away from responsibili-ties, including leadership. When we see another person begin to resist, refuse, or renege on their responsibilities, their soul is call-ing out for care. A person may be dropping the ball because his arms are absolutely loaded. She may need compassion rather than condemnation to help her manage the burdens she already has. When the inner lake has been drained, it's too low to sup-port the weights of life.

One of my friends stepped out of several significant positions of leadership in the community. He had been on some of the finest boards, making a valuable contribution to worthwhile causes. "I reached a point where I resented those meetings because, while I was doing things to make life better for others, my own world was going from bad to worse." He looked strong and secure on the outside, but his heart was withering from neglect. He couldn't remember the last time he had had quality time with his wife or children without the press of a deadline. "But the real blow was struck when I opened my reading-through-the-Bible-in-a-year guide and saw that I had read the Bible devotionally once in nine months!"

Response-ability is just that: the ability to respond to a need. When our reservoirs are drained, we have all we can do just to manage our own lives, let alone serve others. If we try to fulfill our responsibilities apart from God's power, as I'm prone to do, then they can become a crushing burden.

Everyone has a call from God to serve in this world. Each call is as unique as each individual. Each call, undertaken in the name of Jesus, is spiritual, regardless of the occupation or activity. When you care for your soul, you begin to see your activity in light of that call, and you can experience genuine concern as well as spiritual joy.

Preoccupation with Projects of Lesser Importance

A sixth symptom of soul neglect is a preoccupation with projects of lesser importance. This goes hand in hand with backing away from responsibilities. We keep doing things, but we turn to those things that are less demanding. When you find yourself continually clearing the desk instead of writing a report, or straightening the piles of work instead of eliminating them, or making lists instead of completing them, you may be dealing with a soul problem. Your lack of energy and motivation may be a signal that your inner life needs more attention. If you tend it, you'll then be able to do those other things.

Few people have taken the time to understand the role of the soul in motivation. It's the crucial element. In athletics, coaches spend as much time working on the mental and emotional attitudes of athletes as they do on their physical skills and aptitudes.

My son Matthew and I were in the locker room of a college basketball team before the game. The coach said to the players, "Men, first you've got to win the inner game. Then the outer one will take care of itself." More often than not, it's the attitude that makes or breaks the athletic performance. When our focus is on the important elements of the "inner game," we are less likely to be distracted by the more trivial outer elements.

When we fail to care for our souls, our vision constricts, our hope dims, our energy fades, and we do busywork instead of meaningful work.

Restlessness and Dissatisfaction

A seventh symptom of soul neglect is that of restlessness and dissatisfaction. The loss of contentment is a spiritual problem. The story is told of a man named King Pyrrhus, ruler of Epirus. He planned to invade Italy. He called for Cineas, a philosopher and his friend, to inform him of his plan. Cineas asked him why he planned to invade Italy.

"To conquer it," was the king's reply.

"And what will you do when you have conquered it?"

"Go on to France."

And Cineas asked, "Well, what will you do when you conquer France?"

"Then I will go on to conquer Germany."

"What then?" asked the philosopher.

"Conquer Spain," said the king.

"I perceive," said Cineas, "you mean to conquer all the world. What will you do when you have conquered all?"

"Why then," said the king, "we will return and enjoy ourselves at quiet in our own land."

"So you may do now," said Cineas, "without all this ado."

But Cineas could not divert the king's discontent and desire for conquest. The king went out in battle and was ruined by the Romans.[4]

Restlessness is a symptom of an unmet need. As in many situations, the symptoms may be a long way from the source, confusing us and seeming to lead us in different directions. The king had ambitions for conquest, but beneath them was the desire for rest—a rest of satisfaction and contentment he thought was available only after further conquests. His counselor pointed out that he could already have what he truly sought, but not without an adjustment in thinking.

I'm no expert, but I've heard physicians speak of "radiating pain," which manifests itself in one area of the body but has its source in another area. This can happen with restlessness. Some people bale out of a marriage through an affair, when the need was not for sex but for a sense of significance, which sex can never satisfy. Others go from job to job and place to place looking at the outside world for something that can only be found in the inner world—and that, once found, can make any place a home.

When we live apart from the soul, we find ourselves constantly striving for things that can be ours now if we but stop and receive them from the Lord. Discontent and envy drain our joy, leaving us with bitterness and dissatisfaction. We have lost sight of our own worth, of our blessings. Instead, we look in the wrong places for satisfaction. This makes us especially vulnerable to the next symptom of spiritual neglect.

Resurgence of Unhealthy Habits, Diminished Impulse Control and Diminished Resistance to Temptation

This complex of symptoms is like a decrease in the body's immune system. The white blood cells are the disease fighters of the body. But when the white cell count is down, we cannot defend ourselves. Even so, spiritual vitality defends us against the enemies of life. A low "spiritual white cell count" leaves us open to all strains of "temptation viruses."

When our souls need attention, we may try to satisfy the wrong appetite. We may misread the inner discomfort we feel and do exactly the opposite of what we really need to do. A person out in a snowstorm may become very sleepy. He may not realize it, but he is beginning to suffer from hypothermia. Though he has a long way to go, he may feel an irresistible urge to lie down and sleep. He thinks that if he can rest for a little while, he'll recover his energy. What will happen if he does lie down and sleep? He will die.

When a person feels the need to do something that seems so right but will result in tragedy, it is a sign of spiritual hypothermia. That person is in a desperate situation, wanting exactly the opposite of what her heart really needs.

When a man comes to me and says that he's fallen in love with another woman, who can please him in ways his wife doesn't, I say, "You might as well go to sleep in a snowstorm."

Temptation is a complex, powerful force that has tendrils reaching into all the crevices of our reservoir. Any number of factors can contribute to the germination of the evil blossom in our hearts. Most often, the problem can be traced to a starved spirit which knows that its actions are absurd. But it proceeds in a desperate search for satisfaction.

"I knew it was wrong when I was doing it," a man confessed to me.

"So why did you do it?"

"I don't know," he said in tears and brokenness. "I honestly don't know. But I would give anything to have those days back. I was in such a fog. Now, everything is so clear. Why didn't I give the Lord a chance to stop me?"

We binge on sin when we are starved for grace.

Whether the issue is money, food, or sex—whether in fantasy or action—the warning signs are flashing if we are preoccupied with these, and the soul is in critical need. Vulnerability to temptation is the fever of the soul, not the germ of the disease. The parched desires of soul drought make us crave the closest "relief," even if it is toxic. Falling into sin is abhorrent, but a genuine soul need usually lies beneath the sinful act. We need to focus not only on the sinful act but also on the heart cry behind it.

Guilt and Shame

Guilt has an appropriate place in the human experience. It's meant to be like pain to the body. When you feel pain, you do not savor the pain. No, you go to the physician to diagnose the cause of the pain and find relief. Pain has told you that your body needs attention. Likewise with guilt. Guilt is pain to the soul; it indicates that something is wrong and must be attended to.

A woman who worked for an appliance dealer came for prayer one Sunday. "This is very unusual for me," she said, "but I feel I have to confess something I've done. I know the Lord forgives me, but I just can't get rid of this problem. It's blocking my fellowship with the Lord."

She shared how she had been asked by management to falsify warranty information so they could get refunds on defective merchandise. "At first I protested but then gave in under pressure—they called me 'Miss Goody Two-shoes' and said it was all part of the job. After a while, I did it without even thinking twice. But it's begun to eat at me. I feel so guilty."

Deliberate sin shrinks the soul, wringing vitality from it.

Guilt is an objective state of having violated a law or personal value. Most of us get confused by not understanding that guilt is an indicator, not a cure. Guilt is the God-given, natural response of the human heart to the violation of an objective law. The problem arises when we have recognized that we were wrong but are unable to shake a sense of oppressive sorrow and regret. This kind of guilt immobilizes us, draining every ounce of strength. It casts a dark shadow over all pleasures. It seeks discomfort for penance. It tells us over and over and over that we deserve nothing good, that we deserve to be miserable. This is the "worldly sorrow" referred to in 2 Corinthians 7:10.

A second dimension to guilt is shame. Many of us have not understood that shame is different from guilt. Shame is that sense of lowered self-esteem that accompanies a thought, word, or act that you believed was inappropriate. Shame is the lingering echo of a guilty action. Some have distinguished the two in the following formula: Guilt says, "I did wrong." Shame says, "I am wrong." Obviously, when shame attacks a person's self-worth, it can be very debilitating.

A Hard Heart

This is the most frightening symptom of soul neglect. We see it when we knowingly refuse to do what we know is right or are unwilling to stop doing what we know is wrong. It's as if we stand outside ourselves, spectators in a tragic situation. I remember one father telling me, with tears in his eyes, "I saw myself grab my young son, jerk him off the ground, and spank him as hard as I could—*I didn't want to do it, but I couldn't stop myself!*" As we talked, this father described more than a parenting problem. It had roots at soul level. A process of spiritual carelessness had begun that could be corrected only by intensive prayer and deliberate corrective actions.

Of course, the hardening of a person's heart happens at a level that is difficult for another person to judge. But we must highlight this warning about it: "Therefore we must pay the closer attention to what we have heard, lest we drift away from it" (Heb. 2:1, RSV). Those who do not care for their souls will be less

25

and less able to, unless the Lord intervenes. When dryness reaches this stage, it's like the Sahara Desert of Africa, which just a century ago was a lush region of plants and wildlife. But drought quenched life. Even so, the coming of rain would bring a resurrection.

THE POWER OF AN HONEST LOOK

"Why do I have to bother with all this introspection? I just want to serve the Lord!"

The speaker was a friend of mine who was an imposing presence and whose ministry had influenced many as faithful disciples. But he was soul weary and on the slide to burnout.

"Because if you don't stop and look at what's controlling your soul, it will have its way with you," I answered. "But if you look, you will find freedom. As Jesus said, 'You shall know the truth, and the truth shall make you free.' But first, the truth may make you miserable!"

Far from being a distraction to the deepest things of life, looking honestly at our heart is what puts us in touch with reality. One of the most profound theologians of all time, John Calvin, wrote, "Without knowledge of self there is no knowledge of God." Self-knowledge always points us beyond ourselves. As we consider the mysteries of life, of our hopes and fears, of our darker and lighter sides, of our place in the scheme of things, we begin to think of the bigger questions and answers. The self takes on a deeper dimension—the personal, profound dimension of the soul.

The writer of Proverbs exhorts us, saying, "Above all else, guard your heart, for it is the wellspring of life" (Prov. 4:23). The care of the soul is one of the most practical steps we can take to be effective in all our relationships and other undertakings.

Beneath the surface of daily experience lies an inner world with forces of emotion and motive, hurt and hope, pain and desire, doubt and faith, shame and honor, love and hate—all of which shape the outer, visible life we live. Even as volcanic activity and shifting continental plates have altered the geography of the earth, so these forces determine the landscape of our lives. If left unattended, they can wreak havoc not only for us but also for the people around us, particularly those we love the most. But when we apply God's truth and wisdom to these inner forces, the energy of our "underground" world can be harnessed to produce a life that brings joy to others, unspeakable satisfaction to ourselves, and glory to God.

As we assess the condition of our soul, using the ten symptoms of soul neglect, we are taking the first steps of spiritual renewal. When we have the faith and the courage to take that "inner look," we are able to discover the motives, desires, and fears that have been draining the spiritual life from us. This inner look helps us both to focus on those things that are important and rewarding and to turn away from things that hinder us and waste our time. Self-understanding can begin the process of freeing us from the dark forces that control us. It breaks the hold of those forces that make us do and say the things that hurt us and those we love. Paying attention to our hearts is the first step to valuing ourselves—as God values us—and to setting us free to value and love others—as God through Christ values and loves them.

As I was meeting with Diane, the single parent who had just learned that her daughter was pregnant, one of the first steps that helped her gather strength was looking into her soul to regain perspective and get some sense of God's presence and guidance. (I'll get much more specific about this in later chapters.) She was able to quiet the "maddening noise and confusion," as she described it, which was making any kind of action impossible. This did not solve all her problems, but it was essential to equipping her to take positive steps in a terrible situation.

Another image for looking into our soul is that of rising above or hovering over our lives, much as a helicopter hovers over land or sea. We need to learn how to "helicopter" above our lives. When we can "rise above" our circumstances, we can begin to see the dynamics at work, the possibilities for change, and, above all, the fact that we are not alone. When we "helicopter" up to a new vantage point, the intensity of our emotions decreases, and rather than allowing our emotions to confuse and manipulate us, we can gain some control over them. Is this the kind of personal power you long to have?

We step outside ourselves and examine our heart not only in times of crisis but also in order to avoid crisis. When we are regularly looking at our soul, being aware of what makes us do what we do, we are able to do the "soul work" that leads to a life that is consistent with our beliefs.

FROM SOUL NEGLECT TO SPIRITUAL VITALITY

We've taken the most difficult step on the journey of spiritual renewal: taking a hard, honest look at our own hearts. The funny thing is that when we finally see ourselves in the mirror of truth, the Lord begins to stir those dreams of the hope and freedom he promises. The way of joy passes through the landscape of soul care. God has given us practical principles and activities that will lift us to new heights and open up new depths of life.

The next step is to embark on the path of truth to get help for our neglected souls. Many false voices and deceptive "soulutions" threaten to distract us from God's way. We will look more closely at the major categories of spirituality that are offered by the world so that we can discern what is the biblical way to soul care. We will also see that an improper understanding of the message of salvation can erode all our efforts toward spiritual growth.

Before proceeding to the next chapter, however, I encourage you to process the "Soul-Searching" questions that follow. They will help you better assess where you are on your spiritual journey.

NOTES

1. Charles H. Spurgeon, *Lectures to My Students* (Grand Rapids, Mich.: Baker Book House, 1977), 167.
2. For more information on this view of depression, see Archibald D. Hart, *Feeling Free: Making Your Emotions Work for You* (Old Tappan, N.J.: Fleming H. Revell, 1979).
3. Henri J. M. Nouwen, *Making All Things New: An Invitation to the Spiritual Life* (San Francisco: Harper & Row, 1981), 29–31.
4. Thomas Traherne, *Centuries* (Wilton, Conn.: Morehouse-Barlow, 1960), 11–12.

SOUL-SEARCHING

Questions for Reflection and Discussion

1. Take inventory. I have listed the ten primary symptoms of soul neglect on the ten-point scale, from 1 (Need ISC! i.e., Intensive Spiritual Care) to 5 (Getting Flabby) to 10 (Tip-Top Condition). Mark your self-assessment on the chart.

2. Reflect on the symptom that's of *greatest* concern to you:

   a) When did you begin to experience this symptom? What was happening in your life, both "inside" and "out"?

   b) How did you feel before this symptom began? Were you doing anything differently then? How were your circumstances the same or different?

   c) What steps can you take now to begin to attend to this symptom?

3. Reflect on the symptom that is of *least* concern to you:

   a) Why is this not much of a concern?

   b) Are there any particular steps you have taken to guard yourself from problems in this area?

4. Complete the following sentence: As I consider the subject of soul-searching:

   a) I am excited about doing something I know I need to do.

   b) I feel uneasy about spending time on myself.

   c) I think I must be very careful not to take my eyes off the Lord.

   d) I find much inner resistance to the idea.

   e) I plan to read the book, but don't expect me to do the exercises!

Inventory of Symptoms of Soul Neglect

1. Low-grade "depression fever"

Need ISC			Getting Flabby				Tip-Top Condition		
1	2	3	4	5	6	7	8	9	10

2. Busy but bored

Need ISC			Getting Flabby				Tip-Top Condition		
1	2	3	4	5	6	7	8	9	10

3. Loss of control over life's routine

Need ISC			Getting Flabby				Tip-Top Condition		
1	2	3	4	5	6	7	8	9	10

4. Loss of spiritual connection and responsiveness to others

Need ISC			Getting Flabby				Tip-Top Condition		
1	2	3	4	5	6	7	8	9	10

5. Withdrawal from responsibility and leadership

Need ISC			Getting Flabby				Tip-Top Condition		
1	2	3	4	5	6	7	8	9	10

6. Preoccupation with projects of lesser importance

Need ISC			Getting Flabby				Tip-Top Condition		
1	2	3	4	5	6	7	8	9	10

7. Restlessness and dissatisfaction

Need ISC			Getting Flabby				Tip-Top Condition		
1	2	3	4	5	6	7	8	9	10

8. Resurgence of unhealthy habits, diminished impulse control and diminished resistance to temptation

Need ISC			Getting Flabby				Tip-Top Condition		
1	2	3	4	5	6	7	8	9	10

9. Guilt and shame

Need ISC			Getting Flabby				Tip-Top Condition		
1	2	3	4	5	6	7	8	9	10

10. A hard heart

Need ISC			Getting Flabby				Tip-Top Condition		
1	2	3	4	5	6	7	8	9	10

CHAPTER TWO

Getting on Track for Soul Help

A man who was deeply depressed came to see me. He had a winning personality and was capable in many ways, but he just wasn't happy. He said that he had a problem but he couldn't tell me what it was. I tried to support him in every way possible, but it was like trying to grab the hand of a person who is floating on heavy waves, just out of reach. We couldn't even begin to make the kind of progress he so desperately desired. Was it because he couldn't trust my response? Was it because he was so ashamed? Was it because he had no hope? Whatever the reason, the fear of exposure outweighed his desire for help. To my surprise, he came a second time, after several months had passed, but again, we were forced to speak in generalities. To the best of my knowledge, whatever troubled him then troubles him still.

In the process of soul-searching, awareness alone isn't sufficient to bring the relief we seek or to fill the emptiness we feel. Awareness of our needs is meant to stir us to action in order to meet those needs. But there are countless sources of resistance and uncertainty which can block our progress. One of the most basic obstacles is a lack of confidence that we can find help we can count on. Is there anyone "out there" who hears our prayers? Is there a God who salted our souls with these longings that make us thirst for him? Is there hope that we can really experience a lasting change in our lives? Our greatest fear is that, like the man who came to see me, we will become aware of needs that can't be satisfied, of wounds that can't be healed, or of mistakes we cannot admit.

---

*A*wareness of our needs is meant to stir us to action in order to meet those needs.

As we begin the journey of soulshaping, we need to recognize that there are many approaches to spirituality that, far from satisfying us, can actually lead us into greater dryness. Like mirages in the desert, they promise refreshment when, in fact, they hold no substance. First of all, we need to understand the overall approach to spirituality; the options available include anti-God, human-centered spirituality and New Age spiritualities that compete with biblical spirituality. Second, we need to be settled about the nature of our relationship with God; is it based on what we need to do for God, or is it founded on what God does for us?

We can experience spiritual vitality only when we have come to a proper understanding of God and the nature of the universe. Also, we must understand God's design for relating to us, his creation. If we have mistaken ideas in these two fundamental areas, the entire course of our spiritual journey will be off. It's just like miscalculations on the launch pad; the rocket may get off the ground, but it will soon be drastically off course, requiring monumental efforts for correction.

In my experience with people, I have discovered that even those who think they understand the essentials of the Christian faith often function as practical atheists in their daily lives, reverting to old habits and operating out of distorted assumptions. We need to expose our misconceptions and clearly establish the nature of our relationship and ongoing fellowship with God before we can enter into the fullness of spiritual vitality.

EXPLORING THE SPIRITUAL UNIVERSE

Everywhere we turn, there is some form of "spirituality" out to get our attention and allegiance. Some of them are entirely secular, and others are religious. We are told that everything from the right herbal/organic diet to the right channeler of the spirit world will provide us with the answers and spiritual fulfillment we need. The programs and approaches are too numerous to name and explain, but I want to identify three major categories.

Human-Centered Spirituality

Much of the self-help literature available on bookshelves falls into a human-centered approach to spiritual health. Human-centered spirituality divides further into two types. One type sees the person as self-sufficient, having a built-in reservoir of spiritual energy just waiting to be tapped. This energy recognizes no higher power and no world or existence beyond earthly life. The goal is that I do everything for myself, by myself. Many of the human-potential movements advocate such a spirituality, though they may not say it in so many words. If there is any type of "spirit," it is limited to what is contained in a person. There may be references to "forces" in life, but they are left undefined.

This approach to spirituality is safe and inoffensive because it doesn't support or deny any particular religious tradition. But it leaves many questions unanswered and many issues unaddressed. What does a person do with nagging questions such as: Is there a purpose beyond the individual? Where does our concept of spirit come from? What about our mistakes and differences? Why do some people have more sensitive, "awake" spirits than others? What are the moral guidelines for spirituality, and where do they come from? Thinking people are curious about these things.

The second type of human-centered spirituality has the supernatural component. In this view, spirituality may even be presented as the process of becoming a god or of realizing that you are a god. This is the approach that underlies many pagan mystery religions, some of which have been repackaged as New Age religion. A main concern with this approach is that it is completely subjective. Also, it deals with the supernatural yet has no supernatural authority to speak of. Again, larger questions about purpose and morality remain nebulous.

Force-Centered Spirituality

There are many expressions of this spirituality, including many of the major religions of the world. The individual participates in the life force of the universe, known by various names. The goal of force-centered spirituality is to be absorbed into the force, losing a sense of identity by merging with this life force. This differs from the human-centered supernatural view in that the force, not the human, is the focus. The goal is what I will do for god, or for myself so that I can merge with god.

This approach was popularized in the *Star Wars* movie trilogy. The force was a neutral power and could be used for good or evil, depending on the character of the Jedi knight who was trained to use it. This moral neutrality—the idea that there are no right/wrong absolutes—is very appealing to a lot of people. But if the force is neutral, how can we arrive at any kind of moral code? Who's to say that Darth Vader is evil and Luke Skywalker is good? By what standard do we judge light and dark? The human heart, in fact, has a built-in compass that gives us a natural sense of right and wrong. But force-centered spirituality doesn't deal adequately with this aspect of the human soul.

Other issues are more perplexing. If we really are to become gods, we really have a job on our hands! Are you the kind of god you hope God would be? On the other hand, if our goal is to be absorbed into the rest of the universe, what happens to our individual identities? Do we have no continuing existence as distinct individuals beyond this life?

Christ-Centered Spirituality

In this understanding of the universe, God created the heavens and the earth separate from his own nature and being. Creation is not God, nor is it an aspect of God's being. Humans are spiritual beings who were created not to become a god but to love and enjoy life, which is a gift from God. We will not be absorbed into a nameless force, but we may be embraced by the God with a Name who knows our names. God created human beings in his own image for fellowship and for partnership in the world. Being "in the likeness of God" is never confused with becoming or being God, for unlike God, there was a time when we were not. At some point in time, God gave us life.

To be made in God's likeness means that we have been given the capacity to know God and communicate with him. Being made in God's image also means that we have the freedom to choose our own direction in life. Tragically, as a people we have chosen to go against God rather than with God. When man and woman chose to go against God's command, fellowship with God was broken. We still bear the image of God, but it has been misdirected because we have now become self-centered rather than God-centered.

The goal of Christ-centered spirituality is to redirect our hearts, minds, and lives in accordance with the image of God that has been stamped into our very essence. But that goal cannot be pursued until the basic problems of human separation from God and antagonism toward God are resolved. In other words, we need to be saved from this state of alienation and judgment. We need salvation. We can only develop our spirituality after we have resolved this problem. The question is, how are we saved? How are we reunited with the God who made us?

God has—and has always had—a plan for bringing us back into union with himself. Most of us think we know this plan. But it's amazing how many of us have settled for lesser plans. Let's take an honest look at the four ways in which most people try to achieve salvation.

SALVATION—THE MATHEMATICAL WAY?

How do we reestablish a relationship with God? Why, that's simple! We simply need to do good things, not do bad things, do certain things, or do more things! Human logic has devised a number of methods—all of which seem to have their place, *and none of which are biblical.* Trying to live up to these erroneous views and carry out these misdirected plans drains away our spiritual energy. We live on the basis of inadequate views of God and of ourselves. And the more we "do" according to these human schemes, the less intimacy we feel with God.

First, let's see what faith isn't. I like to call the following, manmade methods of spirituality "mathematical theology."

Salvation by Addition: The Bootstrap Syndrome

I went to lunch with Larry, a man who had been worshiping with us for several weeks. We had a good time getting acquainted. As we neared the end of our meal, I asked him what brought him to our congregation.

"Well, to be honest, I need a break from my church," Larry said. "I have been on the board of trustees for six straight years and chairman twice in that time. My wife and I have taught Sunday school for about ten years and been advisers of the youth group off and on over all that time. She also sings in the choir. It's getting so we can't go to church without somebody asking us to do something more."

"How has this affected your relationship with the Lord?" I asked.

He looked puzzled. "I suppose he's pretty disappointed in me. I've tried to please him, but I just can't keep going on like this."

Larry was facing a spiritual crisis that wouldn't be solved merely by changing churches. Larry and his wife had worked themselves into a pattern of relating to God and God's people that had become counterproductive.

One of the core values we hold most dear is the human capacity for responsibility and productivity. This philosophy, which is often viewed as the engine of American capitalism, is epitomized in the admiring phrase "He lifted himself up by his own bootstraps." We like this image of a person raising himself—through his own, unaided effort—above his former cultural, social, or economic level. Many people have actually done this, and it is admirable. But the problem arises when we take this as a model for our relationship with God and our attaining of eternal life.

In one of the most effective evangelism ministries in this century, the Evangelism Explosion of Dr. D. James Kennedy,[1] the initial conversation with a person is focused on two leading questions: "Have you come to a place in your spiritual life where you know for certain that if you were to die today you would go to heaven?" and "Suppose that you were to die tonight and stand before God and he were to say to you, 'Why should I let you into

my heaven?' What would you say?" The most common response
is, "I've tried to lead a good life," followed by a listing of the evidence of this good life—going to church, being helpful to
others, or working in service clubs, for example.

If "trying to lead a good life" were sufficient for entrance into
heaven, my friend Larry certainly would have made the grade.
Here was a man who sincerely wanted to do what was right. He
felt that he had to be on the board of trustees, teach Sunday
school, and advise the youth in order to please God. At one
point in the conversation I said, "Larry, God doesn't want your
works; he wants *you*. When it comes to salvation, we cannot lift
ourselves up by our own bootstraps."

When we fall into this bootstrap mentality, it's good to remember where the bootstraps came from! As the Lord was preparing
the people of Israel for life in the Promised Land, he warned
them of the danger of presuming that their own efforts could
ever put God in their debt. "When you have eaten and are satisfied, praise the Lord your God for the good land he has given
you. Be careful that you do not forget the Lord your God. . . .
You may say to yourself, 'My power and the strength of my hands
have produced this wealth for me.' But remember the Lord your
God, for it is he who gives you the ability to produce wealth, and
so confirms his covenant, which he swore to your forefathers, as
it is today" (Deut. 8:10-11, 17-18). If it weren't for God, we
wouldn't even have boots! What God does for us always precedes
what we do for God, even as a daughter's birth and nurture by
her parents must happen before she can bear children of her
own.

We must also take very seriously God's assessment of the
human condition. We simply don't hit the mark where righteousness is concerned. The situation is so serious that nothing we do
could ever compensate for our sin: "Yes, all have sinned; all fall
short of God's glorious ideal" (Rom. 3:23, TLB). We fail to live up

to God's standards even in the deepest part of life—the soul: "The heart is deceitful above all things and beyond cure. Who can understand it?" (Jer. 17:9).

Those who think they have led a good life need to read carefully Jesus' clarification of the Ten Commandments in the Sermon on the Mount. "You have heard that it was said to the people long ago, 'Do not murder, and anyone who murders will be subject to judgment.' But I tell you that anyone who is angry with his brother will be subject to judgment. . . . You have heard that it was said, 'Do not commit adultery.' But I tell you that anyone who looks at a woman lustfully has already committed adultery with her in his heart." (Matt. 5:21-22, 27-28).

How have you done so far? Have you been perfect? To be blunt, using the bootstrap metaphor, we do not even have feet! The honest person realizes that we cannot undo the past: We cannot repair a broken heart; we cannot undo a horrendous mistake or take back hurtful words. There comes a time when we must acknowledge that we cannot help ourselves. We have reached the limit of our abilities.

The seriousness of our situation is made most clear by the fact that Christ came to address the human problem with no less than his own life, death, resurrection, and the gift of the Holy Spirit! "The central Christian belief is that Christ's death has somehow put us right with God and given us a fresh start."[2] If that's what it took, we have some idea of the worth God attributes to us. Further, we have some idea of the magnitude of the problem; this problem of human nature is not remedied through simple effort and minimal resources. It takes the very life of God working within us to make change happen.

People who rely on the bootstrap method of salvation have an inadequate understanding of God's standards and of human sinfulness. What about our achievements, then? What good do they do? Our achievements, empowered by God, are the means by which we become the people God can use—and use to the fullest.

Salvation by Subtraction: The Lenten Syndrome

Many people think that the essence of religion is giving something up, subtracting it from their lives. This idea is seen in the practice of giving up things for Lent, the forty-day period before Easter. Meant to be symbolic expressions of fasting based on Israel's and Jesus' experiences in the wilderness, many people stop eating particular foods or doing certain activities as a type of fast.

This is the concept behind the sacrificial system also, which was practiced by the Jews and many other religions. But sacrifice in the Judeo-Christian tradition should not be interpreted as something done to earn salvation. Sacrifice has always been the human response that signifies our acceptance of God's grace and mercy. Sacrifice allows us to express our repentance and our desire for renewed fellowship. But that fellowship is made possible by what *God* has done in establishing his covenant with us. Without God's mercy, our sacrifices would mean nothing.

One problem with this "subtraction" kind of spirituality is that it demonstrates an inadequate view of God. Not only is he often viewed as some mean-spirited god who must be appeased by sacrifice, but he requires that we give up the things that bring us pleasure. He is a god who doesn't like for us to enjoy the good gifts we've been given; he really prefers that we be deprived and miserable.

If a person seeks salvation through sacrifice, eventually he or she will become resentful toward God. We become tired of giving up things, of denying ourselves the simple pleasures of life. So either we continue to subtract good things from our life and harbor a smoldering anger toward the God who requires it or we rebel and throw off all restraints, indulging in anything and everything we want, sort of like the child who rebels against an oppressive parent.

The truth is that God actively seeks our joy:

> *Sing, O Daughter of Zion;*
> *shout aloud, O Israel!*
> *Be glad and rejoice with all your heart,*
> *O Daughter of Jerusalem!*
> *The Lord has taken away your punishment,*
> *he has turned back your enemy.*
> *The Lord, the King of Israel, is with you;*
> *never again will you fear any harm.*
> *On that day they will say to Jerusalem,*
> *"Do not fear, O Zion;*
> *do not let your hands hang limp.*
> *The Lord your God is with you,*
> *he is mighty to save.*
> *He will take great delight in you,*
> *he will quiet you with his love,*
> *he will rejoice over you with singing."*
>
> ZEPHANIAH 3:14-17

The prophet Nehemiah said, "The joy of the Lord is your strength" (Neh. 8:10). Jesus said, "I have come that they may have life, and have it to the full. . . . I have told you this so that my joy may be in you and that your joy may be complete" (John 10:10; 15:11). We are continually exhorted to receive the good things of God with gratitude and thanksgiving (1 Thess. 5:16-18). God does not begrudge our enjoyment of life. Subtraction is not the way to his heart.

There's a second major problem with subtraction as a means of salvation. As much as we may sacrifice and as virtuous as we may feel about it, what we give up cannot begin to compare with all that must be removed from our lives. What are we to do with all the unworthy attitudes, words, and behaviors that are so offensive to a holy God? It's impossible for us to *subtract enough* of what is wrong to stand in righteousness before God. If we rely on our sacrifices to be enough, then we make a mockery of Christ's ultimate sacrifice. To think for one moment that giving up television or chocolate—even both!—for forty days is a means of salvation is to cheapen our salvation to the point of worthlessness.

And what could we ever give up that would be equal to what God gives us in Jesus Christ? Once we begin to understand the vast treasures that are ours in God's mercy, we can never make the mistake of equating our subtractions with paying God back. As the hymn says:

> *We give thee but thine own,*
> *Whate'er the gift may be:*
> *All that we have is thine alone,*
> *A trust, O Lord, from thee.*

We do not subtract things from our lives to get God's attention; we surrender them to free ourselves from distraction. But even this comes after, not before, what God has done for us.

Salvation by Division: The Holy Compartment Syndrome

A third strategy people try for securing salvation is to limit religion to one compartment of their lives—a compartment they can keep respectable and in order. People who "divide" life into manageable parts take comfort in maintaining some superficial actions of "doing the right thing." These people divide life into "sacred" and "secular" and assume that the two never meet or mingle.

The man who cheats in business but gives a "donation" from the ill-gotten profits sees nothing wrong. The couple who live together outside a marriage covenant but weekly attend church sense no inconsistency. Using this system, a person can do one or two "spiritual" things well and feel virtuous and quite all right in God's sight.

The division approach is based on an inaccurate view of life in this world; it draws false distinctions between the many aspects of life that do affect each other. We are whole people, and what we do in one area of life affects all the other areas. But if we divide up our life, cutting God and spirituality out of parts of it, we often find ourselves lonely and impoverished in those very places where we most need the Lord's wisdom and assistance.

One day, I went to the home of a couple who had visited our congregation. After getting acquainted, we began to discuss spiritual matters. As we talked about the Bible, the man made it clear that he thought the Bible was "just another book, filled with errors and contradictions." As I shared an outline of the gospel with them, again the man spoke up and said that he didn't "buy this born-again stuff" and that Jesus was "just a good person who showed us how to live." They attended our church sporadically a few more times but soon stopped coming altogether.

Sometime later I was in the grocery store when Sally, the wife of this man, came over to talk with me.

"It's so good to see you, Doug. My husband and I were just talking about calling you."

"What's on your mind?" I asked, truly curious about what could have stirred their interest in me after our difficult discussions nearly a year before.

"John just found out that he's never been baptized. We were wondering if you could baptize him."

My mind was racing. "Has John changed his outlook on things?" I asked, as tactfully as I knew how. "Last time we talked, we had some differing ideas about the Bible and the necessity of receiving Christ as Savior."

45

"No, I don't think anything has changed. He just wants to be baptized. His sister and brother were baptized, so he thinks it's important for him. His parents had just moved after he was born and they forgot to have him baptized."

"Well, if you could give me a call, I'd love to visit with you again, to explain the meaning of baptism and see how we can proceed."

For a number of reasons, we were unable to make contact with each other for about three weeks. Finally, I called and spoke to Sally.

"Thanks for calling, Doug, but we don't need to get together. We got John baptized at another church last week."

I was dumbfounded and frustrated. It was clear that baptism had a certain importance to John, but it did not indicate the central orientation of his life, as the Lord intends it to indicate. Baptism was a compartment, separate from the rest of Bill's life and beliefs.

At its worst, this "division" approach promotes hypocrisy as a person goes through the religious motions in one area of life while contradicting them in other areas. Keeping God-things in one compartment of our lives is a most dissatisfying way to live. Either we find ourselves pulled back and forth between different worlds or we go through rituals and activities halfheartedly. Even more serious, however, is the fact that God will not settle for a partial life. He gave his Son's whole life for us. He wants our whole life in return.

Salvation by Multiplication: The Supersaint Syndrome

There is an almost universal tendency for the most earnest Christians to revert, unconsciously, to busyness and activity in order to please God. The activity may be undertaken with joy initially, but it degenerates to obligation and duty. It is easy to fall into the productivity trap. For one thing, as we put our faith in Christ, we gain a new sensitivity to others' need for salvation. As we read God's Word, we grow in our understanding of our responsibility to express obedience in all areas of life. We see that we are called to feed the hungry (including the junior- and senior-high youth groups!), visit those in prison, work for change in society, sing in the choir, teach Sunday school, have daily family devotions, and so on and on and on! Before we know it, our calendars are full, and our lives are empty!

Keith Brown, pastor of First Presbyterian Church in Bethlehem, Pennsylvania, went through a difficult period as a youth pastor. He was extremely effective but found himself so overwhelmed that he began to go into a deep depression. In an interview I did with him for *Leadership* magazine, he confessed, "I used to view God as a perfectionist who was never quite satisfied with my achievements. It took me quite awhile to learn that God really isn't happy when we're working ourselves to death." George McCausland, a Methodist pastor in Pittsburgh, helped Brown come to this understanding. "The greatest moment in my life," he told Brown, "was when I resigned as manager of the universe."[3]

We are all liable to fall into this situation if we lose sight of the continuing role of God's grace in our lives. Grace (which will be defined more completely later) applies not only to the first steps of faith, but is also designed to sustain us for our entire spiritual journey.

Believers in the early church also lost sight of this fact. They began to rely on ritual, whereas today we turn to productivity; but the result is the same: Our faith suffers, and we fail anyway. Paul chided some Galatian believers who fell into the multiplication trap; we do well to heed his words today: "Are you so foolish? After beginning with the Spirit, are you now trying to attain your goal by human effort?" (Gal. 3:3).

We also need to admit that we may unconsciously overestimate our own ability and value. If someone asked you, "Do you earn more of God's love as you do more?" you would probably deny it. Yet this very assumption may be deeply ingrained in your heart and habits. We need to be reminded over and over again that God's love is rooted in his own promise, not in our performance.

We need to be reminded over and over again that God's love is rooted in his own promise, not in our performance.

Because of [God's] kindness, you have been saved through trusting Christ. And even trusting is not of yourselves; it too is a gift from God. Salvation is not a reward for the good we have done, so none of us can take any credit for it. It is God himself who has made us what we are and given us new lives from Christ Jesus.
(Eph. 2:8-10, TLB)

If this tendency toward multiplication is not recognized and corrected, a person is likely to end up exhausted and dissatisfied, without a trace of spiritual vitality. Even as Keith nearly broke down trying to be the "manager of the universe," so we run the risk of trying to do far more than we were ever meant to do. We need to stop and heed the counsel of the psalmist:

> *It is in vain that you rise up early*
> *and go late to rest,*
> *eating the bread of anxious toil;*
> *for [the Lord] gives to his beloved sleep.*
> PSALM 127:2, RSV

The spiritual life is based solely on what God has done and continues to do for us in Christ. As we begin to explore the exercises, practices, and disciplines of this spirituality, we must not see them as our efforts to reach God or to earn his favor. They are given to make us more open to God, who constantly reaches down to us. Never was this made more clear than in the coming of Jesus Christ.

GOD'S ARITHMETIC: CHRIST PLUS NOTHING EQUALS EVERYTHING!

The basis of salvation is what God has done for us in sending his own Son, Jesus Christ, to secure our salvation. The wonder of this message is often lost on us, especially if we have heard it a number of times. What Christ has done, however, came home in a fresh way to me when a friend told me about an incident from summer youth camp.

One afternoon at a senior high summer camp in upstate New York, a group of inner-city youth left their cabin and went off with their counselor for some fun and adventure. When they returned, they found one of their friends stealing money from their suitcases. Having caught the young man red-handed, the counselor said, "Let's figure out how to handle this right here and now." They set up a "cabin court," tried the young man, and found him guilty. The challenge was to choose a punishment that "fit the crime." After considering a number of creative options, the boys sentenced him to take a cold shower (and even in the summer that snow-melt water is cold!) with all of his clothes on for three minutes. Then he'd have to stay in those clothes through dinner.

The young man was escorted to the shower. They ran the water until it was as cold as possible. Then, just as they were about to throw him in, the counselor stepped in and took the shower in place of the youth! When the three minutes were up, he got out dripping wet and took all the boys back to the cabin. They tried to get him to dry off and change clothes, but he refused.

"What's with you?" the guys asked.

"I'm just doing for him something like what Jesus did for all of us. Jesus took our place so we wouldn't have to suffer the punishment for our sins. I took that cold shower so our brother here wouldn't have to suffer."

Jesus had never made as much sense to them as he did in that moment.

"If that's what Jesus is like," said one of the guys, "I want to know more."

True spirituality is stimulated by a growing vision and deepening understanding of the wonder of God's work in Jesus Christ. He took our place and received the sentence of death that is charged against each of us. More than a cold shower, he endured the cross so we wouldn't have to. The wonder of the gospel is not only that Jesus Christ secured our freedom but that he secured our adoption as full members of God's royal family. John Calvin captures the sweeping implications of Christ's work, describing it as a great exchange:

> This is the wonderful exchange which out of his measureless benevolence he has made with us:
>
> that becoming the Son of Man with us, he has made us [children] of God with him;
>
> that by his descent to earth, he has prepared an ascent to heaven for us;
>
> that by taking on our mortality, he has conferred his immortality upon us;

that by accepting our weakness, he has strengthened us by his power;

that receiving our poverty unto himself, he has transferred his wealth to us;

that taking the weight of our iniquity upon himself (which oppressed us), he has clothed us with his righteousness.[4]

Perhaps you've seen yourself in one of these four "mathematical" methods of salvation. If so, it's time to be clear about your relationship to God and how Jesus figures in. Maybe you think you understand the basics of salvation, but don't be too sure. The "basics" are where we are most likely to slip up.

Spirituality is not a subject to be mastered, but a relationship to be savored. As we consider the soul, it is tempting to treat it as a subject separate from ourselves, instead of realizing that at its heart, it's about knowing and loving God—pure and simple. How do we respond to the person and work of Jesus Christ? We receive the grace-given life by faith and respond through a grace-shaped life energized by spiritual discipline. This begins with a vision for the life that is ours in Christ. That is the focus of our next chapter.

NOTES

1. D. James Kennedy, *Evangelism Explosion* (Wheaton, Ill.: Tyndale House, 1970).
2. C. S. Lewis, *Mere Christianity* (New York: Macmillan, 1952), 57.
3. Douglas J. Rumford, "How to Say No Graciously," *Leadership* (fall 1982): 94.
4. John Calvin, *Institutes of the Christian Religion,* ed. John T. McNeill, vol. 2, bk. iv, chap. xvii (Philadelphia: Westminster Press, 1960), 1362.

SOUL-SEARCHING

Questions for Reflection and Discussion

1. Which comment best describes your experience of spiritual growth:

   a) *I am a new explorer:* I have never given much attention to Bible study and prayer.

   b) *I am a frustrated veteran:* I have ridden the roller coaster of on-again, off-again Bible study and prayer.

   c) *I am an experienced explorer, venturing into new territory:* I have begun to explore some of the spiritual disciplines and have found them intriguing.

   d) *I am an amiable skeptic:* I identify with those who have many questions and suspicions about spirituality, but I am open to considering it.

2. When have you felt most spiritually alive? What was happening in your life at that time? Were there any spiritual activities, practices, and/or relationships that were especially energizing? What were they, and how did they support you?

3. When have you felt least spiritually alive? What was happening in your life at that time? Were there any activities, practices, and/or relationships that were draining your spiritual vitality? What were they, and how did they affect you?

4. Which of the three approaches to spirituality (human-centered, force-centered, or Christ-centered) best represents your background? If you have changed from one approach to another, how and when did that happen?

5. Review the "Mathematical Methods of Salvation." Which, if any, best describes your spiritual tendency? How has this affected

your spiritual life? How has the material in this chapter affected your understanding of salvation?

6. Spiritual growth is guided by our heart's desires. Since this book surveys a broad range of topics, some subjects will be of more interest and importance to you now than others. What is your heart's desire right now? It may help to complete one or more of the following sentences:

a) Lord, I want to grow in the area of _____.

b) Lord, for years I have struggled with _____. Now is the time I want to do something about it. I hope you will use this study to _____.

c) I believe the key to my spiritual growth right now is _____.

CHAPTER THREE

Vision: The Secret to Getting beyond Good Intentions

🌿 JOURNAL KEEPING

W E have already seen the high cost of soul neglect. So why do we resist doing those things that keep our souls healthy? Why do we ignore our relationship with God?

Too often we see spiritual development as an obligation, a duty to be borne in spite of our natural desires. And as we begin to explore the subject of spiritual growth, we may fear that it will add one more burden to our already overextended lives. Yet true growth will eliminate the unnecessary burdens. In fact, cultivating spiritual maturity is a great clarifier, bringing us freedom from the trivial tasks that drain us and helping us focus on the tasks that renew us most.

Spiritual change begins when we take our desire for a better life and harness it to God's deep love for us and to our own discipline. But one element must be present before we are able to follow through on our desires, or our disciplines.

A DEFINING VISION

H is brother had always been a bit of a dreamer. If someone new came along, he was one of the first to check
him out. This time Andrew was sure this was the One. "Come on,
Simon," he insisted, "I'm not fooling this time. He's the One!"

Simon walked out to meet the man, but before he could say
anything, the man began speaking to him: "So you are Simon,
son of John? I have a new name for you. I'm going to call you
Cephas" (which means "Peter", the rock). "Now," Jesus continued, "come with me."

Simon looked at the man for quite some time without speaking. A new name? Only a father could change a name! *What
could this man see in me,* Simon wondered, *that would make him call
me that?* One thing for sure: He'd stick with him until he could
figure it out.

Jesus' renaming of Simon as "Peter" gives us one of the most
vivid examples of vision as the key to faith, growth, and life. Jesus
meets the wavering Simon and renames him Cephas, or "Peter,
the rock." Why? Not to describe Simon as he was but to hold out
the hope of what he would, by Jesus' touch, become. Why didn't
he rename all the disciples, you ask? We aren't told. But what
Jesus did with Simon he does with all of us. The book of Revelation holds out this hope that the Lord has a new name for each
of us (2:17). What name might the Lord give you?

PICTURING AS NOW WHAT WILL BE

God has often used vision to nudge us toward redemption:

- The vision of a new nation through which all nations of the
  earth would be blessed drew Abram from the comfort of his
  homeland to journey to the land of God's choice.

- The vision of worshiping the true God in freedom and prosperity carried Moses and the Israelites through the wilderness to the Promised Land.
- The vision of a glorious temple for the worship and honor of God guided David's life in his later years.
- The vision of a world that needed to hear the good news of Jesus Christ fueled the mission of the early church.

Vision means that we see through the eyes of the Holy Spirit who we are to become and how we are to live in Christ. *Vision* can also describe the clear perception of a destination or goal that is valuable to us. George Barna writes, "Vision for ministry is a clear mental image of a preferable future imparted by God to His chosen servants and is based upon an accurate understanding of God, self and circumstances."[1] He continues:

> The objective is not to acquiesce to a preordained future but to create the future. The vision is the means to define the parameters within which the future will emerge. Realize that the future is not something that just happens; it is a reality that is created by those strong enough to exert control over their environment. The future is not a "done deal" waiting for response. The future belongs to God and through Him to those who are driven to shape it.[2]

We should allow Barna's perspective to jar us loose from our complacent resignation to "our lot in life" so that we give God an opportunity to open our eyes to something more, much more, than we could ever have imagined. The fact is, people who have been captivated by a great dream have attempted great things for God.

Vision is *picturing us NOW what will be.* Through meditation on God's Word, prayerful dialogue with God, and the examination of our hearts, we begin to see that we were made for something more. This longing for something more is what stirs us to action.

VISIONS OF GLORY FOR OUR EVERYDAY LIVES

We have every encouragement from God's Word to "think big" when it comes to considering the future—not only our heavenly future but our earthly experience as well.

Marian, my mother-in-law, was walking with a friend along a Florida beach near her home. As they were soaking up the sea breezes and warm sun, her friend said, "Isn't it wonderful how God splashes his glory upon us?" This friend, who truly loves Jesus Christ, was talking about more than the beauty of nature. He was referring to the privilege of participating in the very life of Christ as his followers.

Splashes of glory—the phrase is close to that of a passage which describes our being changed "from one degree of glory to another" (2 Cor. 3:18, RSV) or, as another translation says, "And we, who with unveiled faces all reflect the Lord's glory, are being transformed into his likeness with ever-increasing glory, which comes from the Lord, who is the Spirit." God's goal for our lives is no less than that we be conformed to the image of Christ, sharing in his glory. To be like Christ is to cultivate his character and conduct through intimate fellowship with God. The spiritual life is not simply a matter of the imitation of Christ but of the formation of Christlikeness within us.

Jesus' Glory

In the beginning of John's Gospel, John describes Jesus' incarnation in terms of glory. "The Word became flesh and made his dwelling among us. We have seen his glory, the glory of the One and Only, who came from the Father, full of grace and truth" (John 1:14). This glory was concealed throughout most of Jesus' earthly ministry, though you could argue that it was manifested in the power of his miracles.

Still, the only true glimpse of glory comes at Jesus' transfiguration (Luke 9:28-36). This passage, which echoes with Old Testament imagery, describes Jesus' change in appearance: "As he was praying, the appearance of his face changed, and his clothes became as bright as a flash of lightning." Other translations say "dazzling white." Peter, James, and John "saw his glory."

Even more fascinating is the fact that Moses and Elijah appeared in glorious splendor, speaking with Jesus about his "departure, which he was about to bring to fulfillment at Jerusalem." The word for "departure" is the Greek word *exodus*. Even as God's glory was revealed in the saving acts of delivering the Jews from Egypt, Jesus' glory is revealed in the great exodus secured by his death and resurrection, leading us from the captivity of sin and death into the glorious splendor of life, abundant and eternal, with God!

The glory that is Christ's is now ours through faith in him! Paul speaks of this as "the mystery that has been kept hidden for ages and generations, but is now disclosed to the saints . . . the glorious riches of this mystery, which is *Christ in you, the hope of glory*" (Col. 1:26-27, italics added).

Jesus' Glory Given to Us

Do we appreciate the unspeakable privilege that is ours in Christ Jesus? It should also cause us to stop and consider our own daily experience of life. Most of us would say that we are leading subnormal lives, with occasional flashes of glory in the midst of dreary days and nights.

To be honest, most of us have no clue what living in "ever-increasing glory" would look like in our lives. In fact, such a concept can de-motivate and discourage us, presenting an ideal that intimidates us because we do not understand it. *What does a life of glory look like?*

There are countless aspects to our ever-increasing glory. Paul does not describe the specific degrees of glory, but it isn't difficult, with the help of God's Word and some meditation time, to see just a few "glory stages" in our lives.

We experience, first of all, the glory of new birth. When we put our faith in Christ, we receive a new identity as children of the Lord of life. If God is King, we are royal heirs! As a prince or princess, each of us shares in the honor of our divinely royal family.

We experience the glory of awareness, having been given the capacity to look at all of life with new, enlightened eyes.

Our lives are glorified by new ideals. We see life with hope, as we've never imagined. We also see that change in our own lives is possible. The fruit of the Spirit brings all sorts of new glory into possibility.

As we grow in this new life, we experience the glorious increase of love for other people. Our hearts are big enough to see others as valuable in the eyes of God. We have compassion for their struggles in life, and hope for their transformation. We are more willing to make ourselves available and vulnerable, experiencing the rewards of deeper relationships.

We experience the glory of knowing God's power in our weakness and failure. We experience the wonder of God transforming failure into spiritual victory.

We glory in using our gifts for God's service.

Picture a life in which
Joy carries you through the day,
and laughter comes as naturally as breathing.
You are not lured by that which would destroy you
but are drawn to that which builds you up;
You can trust yourself—
having control over your thoughts and words,
over your responses and reactions;

You live above the distractions and deceptions of the world,
being a nonanxious, very real presence to others around you;
You have no need to hide;
You can look others in the eye, valuing them for themselves alone,
not for what they would give you;
You find courage to face every conflict honorably
and strength to fulfill every responsibility faithfully;
You endure suffering with courage,
able to live with the questions.
You can admit when you are wrong:
You can say, "I'm sorry," and begin again,
and are gentle with yourself,
renouncing the chains of shame and self-condemnation.
You are connected to God, who created you as you,
and are becoming all that God created you to be.
You are at peace in all circumstances:
celebrating God's faithful provision in times of abundance,
trusting in quiet contentment in times of want.
You are free to serve others willingly,
without thought of or need for thanks.
You have the freedom to live for an audience of One.
Picture such a life—
For it is meant to be yours.

This is a picture of a life splashed with glory. Life in Christ is not a list of dos and don'ts or shoulds and oughts that we anxiously check or belligerently ignore. It is a process of fulfilling the deepest longings of our hearts. This progress from one degree of glory to the next is a fantastic invitation, not a court summons!

An essential question in spirituality is: How do we change? Possessing a list of things to do will not help us actually do those things. Something has to kick us into gear. That something is vision. A clear picture of who we are to become in Christ, combined with exercises that make sense to us and that we can put into practice, can accomplish in a matter of months the dramatic changes we may have been struggling after for years.

FREE TO CHOOSE A FREER WAY

Let's say your good friend is also your insurance agent. There's been a robbery of your home, and you call your agent, very upset. She assures you that everything (less the deductible) will be reimbursed. She says you need to make an inventory, and the company will get you the check in no time. "I can vouch for you guys," she says.

As you go through the inventory, you see that you've lost nearly all your valuables—but the thieves didn't find a very valuable diamond and ruby bracelet you had bought your wife with the incredible bonus you received that one year. (For the sake of illustration, I'll address you, my fine reader, as a husband. Nothing sexist intended!) You still have the receipt—for five thousand dollars! The insurance company could never really know that it wasn't taken . . . so you list it as stolen. You tell your wife and she protests strongly; then, she begins to think of the financial pressures your family is under and agrees not to say anything.

Your agent takes the inventory. "Wow, they really hit a gold mine here! Good thing you had listed all this stuff with me in advance." You get the check.

Some months later, you're getting ready to go to the annual Christmas formal dinner dance, the city's social event of the year. Your wife takes out the bracelet. "Wait—you can't wear that! We're sitting at the table with our insurance agent! She'd recognize it."

"Great," your wife responds. "When can I ever wear this again? It's not exactly a charm bracelet for grocery shopping! What good is it? Every time I look at it now . . ."

She stops and looks at you. Tears fill her eyes. You look at each other. "How did we get into this mess? How will we get out?"

What are the consequences of that choice? Were they limited to the "insurance company compartment" of your life? How many lives did that choice touch? We see here the principle that Adam learned: One wrong act begins to control and interfere with all other aspects of life. The fraud "reigns" in your life. The treasured bracelet that used to be a prize of accomplishment and a symbol of love is now evidence that could convict you in a court of law! You are not free to wear it openly for the admiration of your friends; you have to hide it—even from your children. What if they see it and say something? You are ashamed of yourselves and each other. And the insurance money, which you spent to buy a new sailboat . . . every time you see the boat, you can't help but remember. You see, our actions either set us free or bind us. Since Adam and Eve, this has always been so.

This kind of soul-neglected, unglorious living is filled with shame and frustration and the need to hide. *The first "free choice" of doing what we want to do results in our losing the freedom to do things we most value, losing our self-respect, and losing honesty in our relationships.*

Jesus Christ has come to break this self-destructive cycle of choosing the wrong way. Through faith in him, we gain new options for responding to old temptations. He came not merely to secure a new place for us in heaven but to give us the power to make different choices on earth now. These new choices are the expressions of holiness.

Let's imagine that you made a different choice, one based upon the mind of Christ and the freedom to do right. Same situation, same temptation. But when the idea of falsifying the insurance claim comes to mind, you consider it for only a moment, then push it away in horror. You say to yourself, *My agent trusts me. This is not what Jesus would want me to do. And I could never ask my wife to be part of such a deception.* You complete the inventory without the false claim and turn it in.

"By the way," you tell your agent, "the burglars missed that great bracelet I gave my wife. That was worth more than all the rest put together! Praise the Lord, eh?"

Now—how do you feel? You feel like a million bucks! You cannot buy this feeling for any amount in the world, let alone for five thousand dollars. You have won a personal victory that makes you feel like a king! You are free. Your esteem has grown, and what the Bible calls "the old man" has lost more influence over you.

When pictured this way, the invitation to spiritual change and growth has a powerful influence on our orientation toward life. The week following a sermon in which I used the parable of the bracelet and the insurance agent, a man from our congregation called me.

"I want you to know it's working," he said.

"What's working?" I asked.

"Your preaching. After your sermon on the bracelet and insurance fraud, my older daughter and son went out after church for fast food. The cashier gave my son three dollars too much change. When he showed my daughter, she said, 'You've got to give it back.' At first my son objected, but then she said, 'Remember the bracelet?' So he gave it back!"

"That's great," I started to say, but he interrupted me.

"Wait. There's more. Later that week, my daughter's car engine got messed up—beyond repair. She needed to get another car, but we are not able to co-sign for her. She talked to me after dinner one night. It seems that there was a woman at work who could 'exaggerate' her part-time hours so that she could qualify for a loan. She asked me what I thought she should do. I just looked at her and said, 'Remember the bracelet! Every time you get in that car or make a payment, you will remember that you cheated to get it.'"

"How did she respond to that?" I asked.

"She winced, then smiled, and walked thoughtfully away. She's doing all right—and praying for a cheaper car!"

As we pursue the path of holiness, the way of a healthy, thriving soul, we will make good choices for ourselves and find that we are living in a freer way. Our mind can be clearer, swept clean of all the clutter that goes with dishonesty, resentment, and so forth. But this process is not always as simple as it would seem. As we grow, we must learn how our soul progresses and make room for times of seeming dormancy as well as growth.

SEASONS OF THE SOUL

Spiritual life is a living thing; it is not mechanical. We so easily forget this in the midst of a world driven by technology. We are so accustomed to controlling our external environment that we become impatient when our inner environment goes off course. The soul will not be manipulated like a thermostat or turned on and off like a switch. If we are going to cultivate true spiritual growth, we must respect the natural movement of the spirit. Rather than thinking of your present spiritual state as a *condition*—something that's set in its ways—think of your spiritual life in terms of seasons, which have their distinctive qualities, yet much variance within them.

Are you in a spring of new beginnings? Spring is a messy season, filled with sudden warmth and dreary days as winter gasps its last breath. Days of clouds and rain alternate with dry, sunny ones. The overall feel, however, is one of refreshment, expectancy, and renewed vigor. Spiritually, spring is a time when our love for God is stirring anew. We are excited about new opportunities and are ready to consider undertaking new commitments to ourselves and to others. We've had enough of the status quo; we are longing for a richer, more meaningful life. It's time to risk sowing new seeds.

Summer is the season for cultivating. We begin to see the fruit of our labors, as well as those things that "didn't take." Early summer is often a time of thinning out overplanted crops. We may have tackled many new projects in the spring and now need to step back and reevaluate what stays and what needs to be released. We also think of summer as a time of easing up a bit from the rigorous schedule of the rest of the year. Vacations vary our pace and bring brief adventures. We may want to experiment with a new discipline or spiritual activity, setting a limited period of time for the project. The primary characteristic is that we are in a growing season, feeling no urgency to change.

Fall, in the best of circumstances, is the season of harvesting fruit. The energy of spring and the discipline of summer now bring tangible changes to our lives. We hope it will be a season of thanksgiving as we savor the faithfulness of God and the satisfaction of work done well in his strength. We see the truth of the principle that "life adds up." There's no doubt, however, that fall can be a discouraging season if we are looking for fruit and find a poor crop. We may find ourselves in situations that demand resources we haven't taken the time and effort to cultivate. The threat of a spiritual famine can be devastating. We may have to take some extraordinary measures to secure the resources we need. We will find that God's mercy is ever present. This may not come, however, without a bittersweet sense that the recovery of our spiritual health requires some immediate, significant action.

Winter is a time of dormancy in anticipation of a new awakening. As with the other seasons, winter has its positive and negative nuances. Winter can be a delightful season, resting from the rigors of fall. Telling stories with friends around crackling fires, enjoying the falling snow that blankets the earth in beauty and brings a hush over all activity—these can be the gifts of winter. In this season, we may take stock of our lives, gather with our friends, and tell the stories of God's faithfulness. We may take time to muse, with no urgency for action. Action will come with spring. The ground is resting, and so are we. Yet winter can be harsh: cold, barren landscapes, darker days, longer nights. If we are in a bleak winter, God seems faraway indeed. Talk of his presence is a harsh mockery of our emptiness. Of all seasons, winter requires a grace spark of memory to ignite at least a small spiritual fire to sustain us through the season. It may help to remind us that the first day of winter has the fewest hours of daylight. From that day on, the days get longer and brighter. The best strategy may be to stay put, conserve your energy, and realize that you must walk by faith, not by sight.

These are not once-for-all seasons. We experience each of them many times over. And as we consider our vision for spiritual growth, we need to take into account the season we are in. Upcoming chapters of this book will describe various spiritual disciplines—exercises designed to move us consistently closer to Christlikeness. But not every discipline is for every season. Following is a story about vision and transformation. Allow yourself to be caught up in the story; put yourself in Ezekiel's place. Then use the questions at the end to help you evaluate your spiritual season before you proceed to a plan of action.

THE TRANSFORMATION OF EZEKIEL

The renewal of Israel-in-Exile started with a vision given in the most desperate circumstances. The nation of Israel had steadily declined since the death of King David. The seeds of decline had been sown in David's reign with his sins of adultery with Bathsheba and the murdering of Uriah, her husband. Several of David's own sons had turned against him. Then, soon after the crowning of Solomon, the nation divided. After Soloman's death, Rehoboam became king of Judah and Benjamin, in the south and Jeroboam became king of the ten tribes of the north. Spiritual apostasy made the people of God vulnerable, and political powers eventually overran both the northern and southern kingdoms. Ezekiel had been captured and exiled to Babylon, nine hundred miles away from Jerusalem. He brought the word of God to interpret the judgment that had fallen upon Judah. Then, beginning in chapter 36, he began to bring a message of hope. This hope is pictured in the vision of the Valley of Dry Bones in Ezekiel 37. Though this vision was supernaturally given, the principles of the visionary process can nurture our spiritual growth.

The hand of the Lord was upon me, and he brought me out by the Spirit of the Lord and set me in the middle of a valley; it was full of bones. He led me back and forth among them, and I saw a great many bones on the floor of the valley, bones that were very dry. He asked me, "Son of man, can these bones live?"

I said, "O Sovereign Lord, you alone know."

Then he said to me, "Prophesy to these bones and say to them, 'Dry bones, hear the word of the Lord! This is what the Sovereign Lord says to these bones: I will make breath enter you, and you will come to life. I will attach tendons to you and make flesh come upon you and cover you with skin; I will put breath in you, and you will come to life. Then you will know that I am the Lord.'"

So I prophesied as I was commanded. And as I was prophesying, there was a noise, a rattling sound, and the bones came together, bone to bone. I looked, and tendons and flesh appeared on them and skin covered them, but there was no breath in them.

Then he said to me, "Prophesy to the breath; prophesy, son of man, and say to it, 'This is what the Sovereign Lord says: Come from the four winds, O breath, and breathe into these slain, that they may live.'" So I prophesied as he commanded me, and breath entered them; they came to life and stood up on their feet—a vast army.

Then he said to me: "Son of man, these bones are the whole house of Israel. They say, 'Our bones are dried up and our hope is gone; we are cut off.' Therefore prophesy and say to them: This is what the Sovereign Lord says: O my people, I am going to open your graves and bring you up from them; I will bring you back to the land of Israel. Then you, my people, will know that I am the Lord, when I open your graves and bring you up from them. I will put my Spirit in you and you will live, and I will settle you in your own land. Then you will know that I the Lord have spoken, and I have done it, declares the Lord.'"

First, God's vision confronted Ezekiel with the stark reality of a world dead apart from God. It is difficult to imagine a picture more bleak than a valley (the lowest place) of bones (the last remnants of a human being), indeed a great many dry bones (indicating the most extensive tragedy). Ezekiel is led to walk back and forth among them. The parched ground crunches sharply beneath his feet as he steps gingerly over skulls, trying not to trip over tibia and fibula, getting scraped by a sharp rib bone. . . . It's almost too much to take. And the bones are dry, very dry; this catastrophe has long been unremedied.

Such conditions can dishearten the best of us. We would dread the Lord's inquiry, "Son of man, can these bones live?" The whirl of possible responses: *They are so dry—yet all things are possible with God. . . . There are so many—but God's power is infi- nite. . . .* "O Sovereign Lord, you alone know." Ezekiel's response, interpreted by many as a diplomatic dodge, is truly a confession of faith. He does not have certainty in what God plans to do, but he does have faith in what God *can* do. Ezekiel's uncertainty does not disqualify him from ministry. Instead, it helps him con- front his own assumptions. As we face the stark reality of our spiritual and personal condition, we may indeed lack certainty that God can do anything with us. We don't let this deter us. Instead, it compels us to search more deeply. In the search, the Lord plants the idea of something new.

Having seen the harsh reality and been challenged to envision a glorious possibility, Ezekiel is asked to take the next step in faith. He is commanded to prophesy to the bones. The vision and the command of the Lord provide the energy to risk obedience. Can you imagine how foolish it would feel to be preaching to the dead? The situation is not inviting; the market survey has given no hopeful indicators. The barren landscape threatens to smother any sound. But into this barrenness Ezekiel speaks. Though it makes no sense, though he can barely believe it will do any good, he acts out of sheer obedience to God. And the bones begin to stir.

I've often wondered what Ezekiel did when the bones began coming together. Did he stop preaching in awed silence? Or did loud whoops of amazement spring from his lips? Whatever his reaction, it is clear that the obedience of one led to the blessing of many. The risk of appearing foolish in response to God's Word will lead to things the mind of woman or man could never imagine.

Now a stranger thing happens. Ezekiel is standing in a valley of corpses! The bones have come together, and the skin and muscle have covered them. But they lie there lifeless. We can imagine Ezekiel watching, like a person standing at a casket, expecting any minute to see an eyelid flicker. But nothing. Nothing.

How often we begin with a flourish, exulting in the grace and power of God. We feel responsive to his touch. We see his work in others' lives. We begin to feel as though we've really got this thing together. Then . . . nothing. Just plain nothing. We may begin to doubt that anything really happened, or we may begin a frantic search for more techniques to keep things going. What did we do wrong? Is there something we missed? Has God deserted us? Is there something wrong with these people?

The answer lies in God alone. Though by the grace of God there were initial results, the Lord makes it clear that the entire work of revival is his work! Trying to do spiritual things without the Holy Spirit is like a mortician dressing corpses. They may look lifelike, but there is no life in them. There is no life apart from breath.

Ezekiel is commanded to turn his attention from the breathless corpses to the breath of God. He is invited to pray boldly. In the name of God, he commands the spirit to come and enter the corpses, and "they came to life and stood up on their feet—a vast army."

We see here the final purpose of the vision: an army for battle. This army will be equipped to take back that which was lost and hold it secure for the future. "'Then you will know that I the Lord have spoken, and I have done it,' declares the Lord."

WHAT MADE THESE DRY BONES LIVE?

In this amazing story, *a vivid picture of a new reality inspired a new level of obedient action.* Let's review the process:

- Start with the honest recognition of dryness apart from God.
- Let God stir a new dream.
- Take the risk of stepping out before there's any evidence to support your dream.
- Be ready for the disappointment that will remind you that God is in charge.
- Pray boldly for the Holy Spirit to breathe life into all you do.
- Expect to see God bring resources together that will accomplish greater works for his glory.

Most of us think of spiritual wholeness as being free from sin. But our restoration to spiritual wholeness is best understood in terms of recovering a vision of who we are in Christ. The defeat of sin in our lives is but one aspect of the much larger process of being shaped into the image of our Lord through the power of the Holy Spirit.

Such a goal is both inspiring and daunting. Many people who have eagerly begun have fallen short through discouragement and exhaustion. As we affirm that God's Word is true, we ask ourselves some basic questions: What does it take to keep at it? What are the biblical principles that unlock the energy that will change us? The next chapter explores how we grow and where spiritual exercise fits into the process. God does not give us high hopes in Christ without providing a way to see those hopes become reality!

THE JOURNAL: THE SOUL'S SKETCHBOOK

In my experience of looking into my soul and growing spiritually through the various spiritual disciplines, I've found the journal to be a most effective tool. I've used journaling with many of the people who have come to me for spiritual help and direction. Since I have seen how beneficial the spiritual journal can be, I recommend it highly.

You may not be a person who feels comfortable keeping a journal—or doing writing of any kind. That's OK. Many of the world's Christians, especially in earlier centuries, were illiterate and couldn't have kept a journal if they had wanted to! A journal may not work for you as it would for me or another person. However, let me encourage you to read the following section, which explains the benefits of journal keeping and gives some simple advice about it. You may find that journaling is something you *can* do that will greatly help in the renewing of your soul. Or you may find that it is not so important to you right now; if so, read about it, file it away, and proceed to the "Soul-Searching" questions at the end of this chapter.

One of the first instructions God gave to Moses after the Exodus was to "write these things in a book" (Exod. 17:14). Recalling the mighty acts of God was an essential element for sustaining the people's vision of God. What about our own "holy histories"? A personal journal is an invaluable tool for preserving a record of God's work and the application of his truth in our lives.

Personal Benefits

A journal is like a spiritual diary, with an emphasis on the condition and responses of the soul rather than a chronology of events, which is characteristic of a traditional diary. The journal is a place to reflect on our moods, our personal disciplines or lack thereof, our temptations and failures, our answered prayers, and biblical insights. My own use of a journal evolved from keeping a notebook of insights gleaned from my personal Bible study. I prize those moments of illumination. The thrill of discovery is a gift from God. How is it that when a person prays for illumination and receives it, he or she can let that precious truth slip away like writing in the sand that the tide erases? Trust it to paper—not to memory. Over a period of time, I began to include prayer requests and answers, problems and hurts, and hopes and plans for the future. Initially, writing came in surges, but over time it has become more regular. Each person discovers a pace that fits.

A journal gives us insight into our own growth.   Our confidence comes from knowing where we've been and where God is directing us. In his *Confessions,* Augustine wrote, "I want to call back to mind my past impurities and the carnal corruptions of my soul, not because I love them, but so that I may love you, my God . . . that the bitterness may be replaced by the sweetness of you." As we reflect on our spiritual pilgrimage, we gain understanding of the dynamics of spiritual life: the obstacles, the predictable crises, the doubts, and the means of grace to overcome these things. The preservation of these insights and the memory of God's faithfulness promote an attitude of praise and thanksgiving.

A journal helps us clarify our priorities.   Life always seems at least a step or two ahead of us. It's easy to lose control. I often turn to my journal as the key to unlock the shackles of the time trap. Reflection enables me to sort out what's important. The commitments that clamor and crowd in on me lose some of their urgency in the light of my basic goals and values. On the other hand, a clear perception of the important matters awakens a new resolve to get on with it.

A journal also helps in problem solving.   Conflicts and disappointments are part of growth. Sometimes we are put in the lonely position of having nowhere to turn for guidance. Writing crystallizes issues. As the dust settles and specific details become clear, prayer and careful thought often open a way to reconciliation and progress.

Ministry Benefits
A journal stimulates accountability.   One of the unrelenting thorns of the Christian life is the discrepancy between what we talk and how we walk. As we discipline ourselves to what the Puritans referred to as "the self-watch of the journal," we constantly reset our course to walk in the way of Christ.

A journal leads us toward authenticity, the ability and willingness to let others enter the home of our hearts.   Honesty in a journal generates the courage to be open and vulnerable in our relationships. People can listen and respond best to the person who is a fellow traveler. Respect and a ready ear are given to the one who understands from his own experience the thickets and loose stones on the trail.

A journal sensitizes us to the hurts of others; it develops empathy.
Somewhere I read the story of a ten-year-old boy who was asked
by his mother, "What's empathy?" The little boy responded,
"Empathy is your pain in my heart." Human struggle is demo-
cratic. The pain, doubt, frustration, and anxiety that we feel are
common to all. This realization enables us to provide genuine
support as we counsel and guide others to wholeness in Christ.

*A fresh and vital ministry springs from creativity, another benefit of jour-
nal keeping.*   Jesus was creative in his preaching, teaching, and
healing. Truth passed through the prism of his life and burst
into a spectrum of applications. As we learn to trust our insights,
a creative power builds momentum; ideas begin to propel themselves into our consciousness. Frequently, the seeds of sermons
or particular actions are planted when we break ground with a
journal.[3]

Write It Down

A favorite motto of my ministry is "Write It Down." I firmly
believe the proverb that "even weak ink is more powerful than
the strongest memory." When someone tells me of answered
prayer, an exciting evangelistic encounter, or an insight into
Scripture, I urge them to write it down. As a result, many people
in our congregation, especially among the leaders, have begun
keeping journals. A new appreciation has grown for the fact of
God's activity in the details of our lives.

The journal is also a tool I've used in counseling. When
people are caught in a particular problem or are unclear concerning God's will, I often encourage them to prayerfully talk it
over—in a journal—with the Lord. This proved so helpful to
one woman that she frequently counsels her friends to do the
same. One day this woman learned that her nephew was dis-
traught over the death of a teenaged friend in a boating accident. As she consoled him, she suggested he talk it out with God

on paper. He did, and it helped him immensely to recognize his grief and renew his faith in the Lord.

I suggested to a college student considering a call to the ministry that he begin to keep a journal. After more than a year of study, he commented to me recently, "You know, one of the best things I ever did was start my journal. As I read over it, I see God's hand shaping my life."

NOTES

1. George Barna, *The Power of Vision* (Ventura, Calif.: Regal Books, 1992), 28.
2. Ibid., 48.
3. There's no right or wrong way to keep a journal. The basic principle is: Does it help me better understand the Lord, myself, and others? Here are seven principles that can set you on the road to developing your own style.

Trust the Holy Spirit to guide you. I always begin with prayer. Often the journal entry is entirely prayer. The Lord searches our hearts and directs us to the most important matters.

Work with feelings and perceptions. The journal should not be a chronicle of dates and events. The important thing is how you felt, what you perceived about a particular event.

Trust your own insights. If they are wrong, that will become apparent in the process of writing. A proper sense of independence and personal authority is healthy. After all, who, besides the Holy Spirit, is a better authority on yourself than you?

Anything goes. Be completely free in your journal. Write it for your eyes only, not to impress someone who may someday read it. It is private; no one is looking over your shoulder. You're free to go with God over the landscape of your soul.

Be honest.   Don't fool yourself with pious talk; if you feel lousy, say it. We are free to be honest because, as has been said, "The One who knows me best, loves me most." In honesty, we will see both the light and dark sides of our souls. The point is to accept them and take God with us as we explore them.

There is a natural tendency to what I call "spiraling."   This is my own term for going over the same ground again and again. The center of the spiral, the issue, may be the same, but our understanding of it is continually deepening and progressing like the widening loops of a spiral.

Discipline yourself to write positively.   The aim of the journal is to generate the energy to be an overcomer. State the facts, record your negative feelings honestly; but then seek out the promises of God that apply to this situation.

   This material first appeared in the article "Keeping a Personal Journal" by Douglas J. Rumford, *Leadership,* (winter 1982): 156–157.

SOUL-SEARCHING

Questions for Reflection and Discussion

1. One of the most effective ways to help us cultivate our personal vision is to put ourselves in the future and look back. So picture yourself at a testimonial dinner in your honor. The most important people in your life are there to share what you are like and what you have done. Who are they? What do they say about your character? What do they say about your behavior?
Example: Your sibling says, "The thing I most appreciate about you was the way you changed from being so easily rattled and upset when things didn't go your way to being steady and firm in your convictions and commitments, no matter what the cost." This could be what Andrew would have said to Simon Peter if they had had such a testimonial!

2. Another way to cultivate a vision is to reflect on the question, When do I feel most alive? What does this reveal about the deep desires and dreams of my life?

3. To help you understand which spiritual exercises might be most helpful to you at this time in your life, spend some time thinking about what "spiritual season" you are in. Provide as many specifics as possible that lead you to this particular response.

_____spring of new beginnings

_____summer of cultivation

_____fall of harvesting fruit

_____winter of dormancy, awaiting a new awakening

4. One of the greatest frustrations of the spiritual life is being overwhelmed by all the needs. We take comfort in the principle that "life adds up." A little bit done each day adds up to significant progress over time. With this in mind, rank the areas of soul need you would like to consider. This will help you focus

on a manageable goal as you develop your "soulshaping" plan. Which need do you most want to address at this time?

____I am looking for guidance in a major life decision.

____I need spiritual stamina.

____I am looking for victory over temptation.

____I sense that I am preparing for a new challenge.

____I long for a deeper sense of God's presence.

____I need something to cling to when God seems far away.

____I need comfort and restoration for recovery after being hurt.

____I need assurance of forgiveness for recovery from guilt.

5. Get a spiral notebook and begin your journal with your first draft of a personal spiritual vision.

CHAPTER FOUR

Unlocking the Energy That Will Change Us

SANDRA was one of the sharpest students in the college fellowship. Her enthusiasm, winsome personality, and grasp of the Bible made her an ideal dorm leader. She was very open about the fact that she was contemplating going into full-time Christian service, but she wasn't sure whether it would be through the church or overseas missions. Her leaders knew that whatever she did, she'd be effective. Then, at the end of her junior year and into her senior year, she began to miss some of the events she always attended. People who phoned to check in got a rather cool reception. "I was just busy with some other things, that's all," Sandra would reply. By the middle of the year, she was hardly ever around her old friends. "I'm just tired of things," she'd say.

A patient faculty advisor finally solved the mystery. Had Sandra fallen into some terrible sin? It turned out that at a summer conference prior to her junior year Sandra had made a commitment to study the Bible for an hour a day, pray an hour a day, and share her faith with one new person a week. At first things went well, but as the weeks passed she couldn't sustain the pace with school and her part-time job. When she failed to meet these commitments, she felt she had no right to go ahead with her ministry career plans. And being around others just reminded her of her failure.

THE FAILURE OF INSPIRATION

Think of all the projects you've begun that lie waiting to be finished, of all the books with white flags of surrender halfway through. Think of your To Do lists. How many things get added and never crossed off? How many lists do you have? I even have lists of my lists!

For those who've tried to develop and maintain a spiritual care plan once or twice, this fear of failing to follow through may stand in the way of their trying again. None of us likes the pain of failure. We'd rather not even attempt it than look at the partially completed Bible study booklet or open our journals to the latest entry, dated weeks or months earlier. How can we begin again if we lack the confidence that we can do better on follow-through? We want to know how we can get beyond the initial burst of enthusiasm—that impulsive commitment that may be driven by the emotion of the moment—in order to make the sustained commitment that Eugene Peterson has called a "long obedience in the same direction."

GROWTH IS NATURAL—ALMOST!

Every living thing grows, seeking its greatest potential. Growth happens involuntarily at the physical level in most situations. As I write today, my yard is unmowed. I have often wished someone would breed a grass that would reach a certain height and stop. (It may already be on the market, but I haven't heard about it!) Living things grow naturally. Nothing within a tree says, "That's enough for now; no more leaves!" Granted, there are physical limitations that affect growth, but the energy of life will seek to overcome them. In spite of the second law of thermodynamics, which says that everything tends toward disorder, God has put a life force within creation that moves living things toward growth.

But the human heart, mind, and spirit do not grow involuntarily. Unlike other creatures, people take a conscious role in their own development. Other animals are moved by instinct; Gods wants us to make choices that will link us to him in the partnership leading to our transformation. We will remain spiritually underdeveloped unless energy is infused into our system. If a person doesn't learn to read, that ability will not develop automatically. If a person doesn't hear or study a language other than her native tongue, she won't be able to speak it automatically. And if a person doesn't seek the things of the Spirit and the kingdom, those things won't be found automatically.

HUMAN EFFORT, HEAVENLY HELP

In one of the more intriguing verses in the New Testament, Paul writes, "Therefore, . . . work out your salvation with fear and trembling, for it is God who works in you to will and to act according to his good purpose (Phil. 2:12-13). This passage captures the dynamic interplay between divine empowerment and human effort. The picture here is one of making the most of a treasured gift. Even as a person with musical skills can develop them to the maximum through practice or allow them to lie dormant through neglect, so we can make the most of God's gifts to us or allow them to lie dormant.

Discipline is the effort we invest for the return we value most.

How do we "work out" our salvation? By the activities, the disciplines, and the intentions we call spirituality. While we can do nothing to save or redeem ourselves, we are given the means for participating in the fullest expression of God's love and power in our lives. As we go along, it becomes very clear that grace—God's love and power—sustains us. Yet coasting all the way to heaven is a seriously inaccurate perception of grace's work in our lives. We are on our way to Christlikeness, but we take the steps ourselves, empowered by God's gracious Spirit.

Having begun with the Spirit, we do not continue in our own energy. But we do actively contribute our own energy as the Spirit empowers us. This is no easy concept to articulate with theological accuracy! Divine grace and human responsibility together form an age-old paradox. We can sum it up this way: Believe and follow, and don't worry about discerning the boundary between God's power and human energy. We might as well try to mark the exact dividing line between the water molecules of the Mediterranean Sea and the Atlantic Ocean or between those of the Indian Ocean and the Pacific. Somehow, these two energies merge.

THE LINK BETWEEN DESIRE AND ACHIEVEMENT

Somewhere I heard the phrase, "If you keep doing what you're doing, you'll get what you've got." It could be rephrased to say, "If you keep neglecting what you need to do, you'll keep missing what you want." I realize that I have often expected my life to improve but have done nothing differently that would

cause a change. I've relied on wishful thinking, hoping that outward circumstances or fast-fading bursts of inspiration would
make something happen. Inspiration and wishful thinking are
unreliable fuels for the engine of life. I remember, as a young
boy, coming home from my first visit to the Ice Capades, convinced that I wanted to be a championship skater. I was so
inspired that I even went skating the following month at Cincin-
nati Gardens, on the very ice the champions skated on—twice!
Needless to say, Olympic committees and Ice Capades officials
never called!

Inspiration—the feeling of emotional excitement—is not
enough to sustain us on the long journey of spiritual growth. Neither is spiritual growth sustained through information—knowing what to do and how to do it. What we lack is motivation.

Which has contributed most to your lack of success: not knowing the right information or not doing what you know? In my
own life, the greatest problem is the failure to do what I already
know.

My goal in this book includes not only new information concerning the development and disciplines of the spiritual life,
that is, the *content* of spiritual growth, but also an emphasis on
the *process* of spiritual growth. How do we unlock the energy to
do what we already know to do?

What unlocks the energy that can change us? Inspiration may
be the spark that lights the fires of determination, but discipline
keeps them burning. Inspiration may energize movement in a
new direction, but discipline keeps us on the road. Building on
the momentum of vision, discipline taps the energy reserves
stored within the soul, moving us toward the goals we value most.

If discipline is seen as an end in itself, it is as dry as dust. It is
just plain hard work. A vision must be attached to the discipline.
For example, coaching young children in the fundamentals of a
sport is most successful when they see the connection between

practice drills and game situations. The vision of winning the game helps them go through the practice over and over again.

My friend Bill knew he had to watch his cholesterol and lose a few pounds, but he never seemed to get around to it. Then, as I stood by his bedside while he was recovering from quadruple bypass surgery, he made an insightful comment: "Doug, I used to think that eating well was a nice thing to do but not all that important. Now I realize it's an investment in life."

Most of us need an emotional push into action, not merely the knowledge that something should be done. We must learn to live for our vision, not our impulses.

We must learn to live for our vision, not our impulses.

Our goal in spiritual vitality is to make the investment in life before—long before—we need spiritual heart surgery. Or, returning to our image of our inner well or reservoir, we need to keep the water flowing in on a regular basis. This investment is best motivated *not* from a negative threat but from a positive, heart-stirring vision, such as the glorious destiny we've already begun to consider. Seen in the context of vision, discipline means forgoing what we want for the moment, for the sake of what we want from a lifetime.

SOUL REFLEXES—THE RESOURCES THAT SUSTAIN US

In one of my first skiing lessons, the instructor said, "A muscle needs to repeat an action about two hundred times to remember what it's supposed to do. The idea of practice," she continued, "is to build muscle memory. Do it right, again and again, and your muscles will gain the habit you want. You'll begin to react without effort, without even thinking. If you've learned the wrong way, however, it will take even more repetition for your muscles to unlearn the bad habit and develop the right one."

Spiritual discipline, then, is developing *soul reflexes* so that we know how to live. We discipline ourselves to develop *soul memory* in normal times so that we'll be equipped for the times of high demand or deep crisis.

Consider the practice of prayer. Many treat it as the last resort instead of the first response. When faced with a crisis, are you more apt to call someone to talk it through, get a book to read, run the other way, or stop and spend an extended time in prayer? Without discipline, we are most likely to look every which way but up! Those who develop the holy habit of extended daily prayer, including exercises of listening to God, are able to "be still and know that [God is] God," even when chaos and noise envelop them.

Let's take a more difficult one: dealing with character reactions, such as anger. A man who was trying to get control of his temper told me that one of the most effective tools in his transformation was the simple process of praying five minutes a day for the people who irritated him the most. "It's really tough to hold those people up before the throne of mercy and then treat them with no mercy!" he said. He also spent time exploring the roots of his anger through meditation on God's Word and reflection on his past. His intentional discipline brought new freedom to his life.

One of our deepest desires is to be able to count on the strength we need for the demands of life. The Bible promises, "As your days, so shall your strength be" (Deut. 33:25, NKJV). All of us have known times when strength beyond ourselves sustained us. Mercy like a rushing river has carried us along. But we have also known times when we've looked within and found dryness; our strength is sapped. If we have been neglecting the soul-strengthening exercises of spiritual disciplines, we will be too weak to stand.

Regular practice nurtures our confidence in God and our confidence in his promise that "greater is He who is in you than he who is in the world" (1 John 4:4, NASB). The mind and heart have to be trained to believe this, in spite of appearances to the contrary. Discipline enables us to walk by faith because we've been over ground like this before. We've tested our limits, anticipated our places of vulnerability, and, above all, begun to know the riches for living that are ours in Christ.

---

*D*iscipline develops the reflexes in our souls.

As the saying goes, the only thing that spills out of a glass is what is already in it. When life jostles you, what spills out? A gracious response or anger? Appreciation or cynicism? What are your automatic responses in life? What would you like them to be? Do you have a vision for the person Christ would have you be at home? At work? When you achieve your highest goals? When you fail? When others fail you? The answers to these questions will help guide you in the cultivation of the soul reflexes you most value.

GROWTH DELAYED?

As followers of Jesus Christ, we want to see change in our lives. But change is hard, often discouraging, work. We expect immediate results—and lose heart when they don't come. If you base your effort on immediate results, you will rarely do anything long enough to see what you need to see in order to keep you going. If you understand "the delay factor," however, you may keep at your goals long enough to see results beyond your highest expectations.

An intriguing example of the delay factor is demonstrated in exercise physiology. Progress in physical exercise is not noticeable immediately. At first, we feel tired and sore. Is it worth it? Is it working? We're tempted to quit, but if we keep going consistently for six to eight weeks, a series of changes happen "all at once" in the body, giving us new vitality.

Kenneth H. Cooper, M.D., in his book *Aerobics,* reports one of the most famous and amusing experiments demonstrating this. A researcher set a weight on the floor, tied a rope to it, ran the rope over a pulley fastened to the edge of a table, then sat on the other side of the table and looped the rope over the middle finger of his right hand. Then, in time to a metronome, he began lifting the weight. The first time and for many weeks thereafter, the best he could do was twenty-five lifts before his finger became fatigued. To expand the experiment, he had a mechanic in the building lift the weight occasionally, and the mechanic always beat him.

One day, about two months later, the researcher began his usual lifts but found his finger wasn't tired at twenty-five. He kept going and ultimately reached one hundred. He suspected what had happened and brought the experiment to a rather unorthodox conclusion. He invited the mechanic in again and made a small bet that he could best him. The mechanic accepted and lost.

What the researcher suspected, of course, was the vascularization of his finger muscles; more blood vessels had opened up, creating new routes for delivering more oxygen. They apparently didn't open up one at a time, but *a network at a time.*

There is other evidence to support this conclusion. People begin conditioning programs, agonize for months trying to get the oxygen where it's needed, then *boom!* almost overnight, the exercise becomes relatively effortless. Athletes report similar "plateaus of progress," improving not only day by day but in quantum jumps. Scientists call this "the training effect."

Here's the key principal: *The process of change doesn't follow the logic of our expectations: It may not come gradually but all at once— following a time of persistent effort in which we saw no progress!* Spiritual conditioning bears many correlations to physical conditioning. After sustained discipline, with apparently little fruit, our spiritual lives suddenly respond and deepen with increased vitality and sensitivity to God's presence and direction. I know a man who tried for several years to start reading the Bible every morning. He would start and stop, start and stop. Then, he started again and has been reading and praying daily for several years with no sign of stopping. I have seen the same dynamic with people who have made a goal of tithing and with others who have made a goal of sharing their faith with new people.

The important thought to remember is that while a level of change may finally come "all at once," it is not without effort. It is the fruit of persistent effort. The haunting question: How often have I quit just before the change was about to kick in?

Blessed are those who keep at it—they shall see change!

The greatest tragedy in spiritual growth is stopping just before the benefits would have begun to show. It's like cultivating a field, then leaving it just before the plants emerge from the soil. Why would we desert the field? Because we couldn't see anything happening. Much was happening underground, out of sight, but we did not have the means for perceiving it. We didn't understand the delay factor.

---

*T*he greatest tragedy in spiritual growth is stopping just before the benefits would have begun to show.

Our spiritual growth and personal development do not proceed at an even pace. We move in stages of rapid progress and then consolidation of our gains. We see this principle not only in the training effect from aerobics but even in botany. If you look at the stump of a tree, you see the annual growth rings, like the circles on a target. These rings show how much growth the tree added each year. What most people don't realize is that the tree adds that growth in the first six weeks of spring. The rest of the year, the fiber is hardening. Such is often the case in the spiritual life. Personal maturity and mastery come from continuing through the periods of growth and hardening, the climaxes and plateaus. Most people do not gain mastery because they become discouraged by the plateaus, instead of seeing them as places to prepare for the next stage.

THE POWER OF COMMITMENT

We need to remind ourselves again that discipline supports a goal we value. It supports our commitments. Our lives are shaped by commitments. When a child is born, many parents make a commitment to God through baptism or dedication that shapes their priorities. In the marriage ceremony, a man and a woman make a commitment that they will stand by each other "in plenty and in want, in joy and in sorrow, in sickness and in health." In school, sports, careers, and relationships, we make commitments that determine either the narrow boundaries or the broad expanse of our lives.

Commitments have power to make or break our lives. I recall a quote from an architect who said, "First we build our buildings, then our buildings build us." The same can be said of our commitments. We make our commitments, then our commitments make us. Once they are chosen, many other choices follow as a matter of course.

What kind of commitments are shaping your life? Is life just happening to you, or are you shaping a life that is life indeed? If we want to become all we were created to be, we need to discover how to tap the power of a committed life.

If we are dissatisfied with life, an inventory of our experience will most likely reveal two things: First, we are investing ourselves too much in things that are unworthy. Second, we are not truly invested in worthy commitments.

Commitment can unlock the energy of life. The decision to invest yourself in a valued course of action satisfies your mind, energizes your will, and engages your emotions. A commitment must be worthy of the name. It is an investment of your life energy and personal resources in proportion to the value of the object.

As we've already considered, initial effort may meet with minimal, even unpleasant results. God has designed us so that the resources develop and circumstances adapt to support the commitments we make. You have probably experienced this in your own life on numerous occasions but may not have appreciated the principle. One man I know made up his mind to go back to school to finish his degree. He had a full-time job and a young family, but he was committed, seeing it as the best way to provide for his family's future security. He succeeded wonderfully. Now he looks back, after more than ten years, and marvels that he did it. How did he succeed? Commitment! The resources developed and circumstances adapted to support a choice he truly believed in. Examples could be multiplied, but the best ones come from looking back over your own life.

God has designed us so that the resources develop and circumstances adapt to support the commitments we make.

LULLS AND BREATHERS AND HOW THEY
AFFECT OUR COMMITMENTS

Demas was a man who showed tremendous promise. He had joined the movement wholeheartedly, even going on the road to spread the message. No one knows what he had given up, but whatever it was, he was one of the few who paid that price. The chief spokesman of the group, a man named Paul, would later write from prison that Demas and Luke, known for writing the New Testament Gospel that bears his name, were detained with him. About six years later, however, Paul would write, "Demas, in love with this present world, has deserted me." He had made a good start and even endured imprisonment for the cause of his faith, but he failed to see it through.

Before considering the process of making specific commitments (the promises to ourselves which we call goals), it's wise to be prepared for two predictable dynamics that affect discipline and commitment. The first is the *lull*. Between inspiration and imple mentation, there can be a significant lull when nothing happens. This downtime can be of varying lengths, depending on the factors causing it. False starts, life circumstances, inner resistance, and unbelief are all factors that take the wind out of our sails. Usually we don't recognize a lull at first. But once we do, it can help us see our life more clearly. We see the "comfort" of life without discipline, but we also become aware of the cost—the cost of opportunities lost, of progress delayed, of growth stunted. We also gain a clearer understanding of the changes we really need to make. Do not be afraid of the lull. But be aware of it. A lull is simply the gap between the information we receive and the action we take.

The second is the craving for a *breather,* when you weary of the rigors of discipline. You want to ignore the alarm clock, to "veg,"

93

.
.

to do something absolutely meaningless, to sleep in, to stay up late, to watch a frivolous movie—anything that has absolutely no value whatsoever. You are just plain tired of doing anything that counts. My advice: Relax and take a break. Your heart may be saying there are other needs to meet. It may be that you've been keeping a pace too intense for the long haul. This was Sandra's problem after making her intense commitments at the summer conference. A time of rest and readjustment put her back on a more productive track.

When you take a breather, it is wise to make a note on your calendar to reevaluate after whatever period of time you feel is best. Just tell yourself that you will probably get back to it. My personal experience is that my breaks do not last as long as they used to because I am learning to manage the intensity of my discipline: The more intense it is, the more we will need to break. After you have rested, try to find a sustainable pace.

You will gain renewed momentum as you see the fruit of your discipline. That fruit may be a while in coming, but it will come. With this in mind, let's take a look at what spiritual disciplines really are and how the Holy Spirit uses them to mature us into genuine Christlikeness.

SOUL-SEARCHING

Questions for Reflection and Discussion

1. As you consider your own follow-through style, are you more of a burster, who jumps on a project and goes at it intensely at first, losing energy and interest rather quickly? Or are you more of a plodder, who starts slowly but sticks with it until completion? How does this affect you in your spiritual life?

2. In what areas do you find it easiest to discipline yourself? Why? What areas are most difficult? Why?

3. What soul reflex(es) would you most like to develop at this time? How does your desire fit with the vision of who God is calling you to be? Specific ideas will be offered in the next chapters for how you can develop various soul reflexes, but what do you think would most help you now?

4. List at least one goal in each of the following areas:

- spiritual growth in my personal life
- spiritual growth with my family and friends
- spiritual growth in service to God and others
- spiritual growth in my vocation (if applicable)

Pick one goal that excites you the most. If this goal were fulfilled right now, how would you feel? What would your life be like? Take some time to describe it, as if you were writing a letter to a dear friend. Try to boil it down to one descriptive sentence, filled with emotional words that are true to you. Read it each day for at least a week, tinkering with the wording until it expresses a passion of your heart. Make it a matter of prayer, and see what God does as we proceed.

CHAPTER FIVE

Spiritual Exercises: What, How, and Why?

H OW *do* we develop a lifestyle of freedom and fulfillment?

How do we become more and more like Christ, God's Son and model for all who would live as God's children?

In short, how do we shape our souls?

SPIRITUAL DISCIPLINES: SOUL-SHAPING TOOLS

The exercises that get our souls in shape are frequently called "spiritual disciplines." These are the intentional activities we practice for spiritual growth and service. Roberta Hestenes defines a spiritual discipline as "an act or behavior which is deliberately chosen and intentionally practiced in order to focus on God and grow in obedience in the Christian life."

As we explore the area of spiritual disciplines, we should keep in mind that spiritual vitality resists the mechanical use of methods and techniques. As with any relationship, love and respect—not manipulation—guide the deepening life. *Spiritual vitality grows out of our relationship with the Lord Jesus.* We must remind ourselves again and again that "God [gives] the growth (1 Cor. 3:6), that "unless the Lord watches over the city, the watchman stays awake in vain (Ps. 127, RSV). Our efforts will not merit God's favor or earn us special blessings.

But spiritual exercise can help put us in a place where we are more receptive to God's grace and goodness. Even though the process of spiritual growth is in many ways mysterious, *there are steps we can take* to develop spiritual sensitivity—a sense of God's presence and a deepening awareness of the spiritual reality that exists in all of life and experience. *There are steps we can take* to align our disoriented and dissatisfied lives with God's purposes. *There are ways* in which we can put ourselves in touch with God's power.

While most books on spirituality describe specific disciplines and delve into the principles of spiritual growth, they are usually silent when it comes to the ultimate goal of the process. Often, they do not answer such key questions as: Why am I practicing this particular discipline? Where does it fit into the rest of my life? We can accumulate all sorts of books on spirituality, but without a vision of what we are trying to achieve, the effect is the same as if someone handed us a box of tools and said, "Here, go build something."

In *SoulShaping,* not only are we learning about how to exercise spiritually, but we are also setting before us a vision of where it all leads. We will make sense out of some of the complexities of the spiritual life and aim at becoming Christlike in specific ways.

FOUR AREAS IN WHICH OUR LIVES ARE SHAPED

In my years as a Christian, as a preacher, counselor, and pastor, I have discovered that there are four areas in which our lives are shaped—either by the world or by God through Jesus Christ. Probably we could describe spiritual growth in many ways, but let's keep it simple! Any spiritual exercise that will benefit us is going to fall into one of these four areas, and they are easy to remember.

Presence: Making the connection with God.　　The central experience of the spiritual life is *the practice of the presence of God.*[1] Every activity in the spiritual life either leads to or flows from a living relationship with the Father, the Son, and the Holy Spirit. Our spiritual life is sustained by a growing relationship with the Lord as we learn to connect and communicate with him in the routine as well as the exceptional experiences of life.

However, many things stand in the way of our making this consistent connection. God's presence is often hidden from us because of the many evils and distractions in this world. Our lives are busy, anxious, and centered on ourselves. And most of us have never really learned how to look for God in our daily experience. The fact is, God is always with us. But we must learn how to heighten our own awareness of his presence and his work in and around us. Then we can actually behave and believe like people who have God with them every moment. This awareness requires some practice on our part. There are specific spiritual exercises that will increase our ability to practice the presence of God. These exercises are the subject of part 2 of this book.

Perspective: Seeing life as it truly is.　　The world offers many different views of life—and those views shape us, with hardly any work on our part. But the only true perspective of life is God's perspective. And we are able to see with this perspective only as our minds are renewed.

We fail in our thinking before we fail in our behavior. Likewise, God has designed us so that change begins with understanding. Am I living in terms of God's big picture? Or have I been "magnifying minors and minimizing majors"? A biblical outlook brings life's complexity under control. We are able to step back from the details and see the larger forces at work.

Understanding and obeying the Word of God are crucial to spiritual growth. Our view of life has too often been shaped by the "wisdom" and opinions of this world. We reorient our thinking and change our lives by allowing God's Word to challenge and correct us and conform our minds to the mind of Christ. Specific spiritual disciplines that shape our souls through God's Word are the focus of part 3.

Power: Drawing on the resources of God. One of the primary purposes of the spiritual disciplines is to detach us from the normal power sources of worldly life so that we draw on God's power. The resources of spiritual vitality (which we obtain through the Holy Spirit, who dwells in us) make it possible to fulfill God's highest purposes for our lives.

The life to which Christ calls us is impossible in our own energy and resources. Like the disciples in Gethsemane, we too often find that "the spirit is willing but the flesh is weak." Spiritual exercises are like electrical lines that tie us into God's spiritual generators. His power at work in us is able to do more than we could ever dare ask or imagine.

When we live in God's power, we can triumph over evil. The fallen world threatens our spiritual progress by distracting and

---

Spiritual warfare is aimed at our destruction. We need to be armed in mind and spirit, equipped with practical strategies for victory.

---

confusing us. The desires of our sinful nature are also battling the nudgings of God's Spirit within us. Spiritual warfare is aimed at our destruction. We need to be armed in mind and spirit, equipped with practical strategies for victory. In part 4 we will explore our weak spots and consider the disciplines that are most helpful in strengthening these weaknesses.

Purpose: Expressing God's will in our activities and relationships. God's purposes for us are to serve in his kingdom through the exercise of our spiritual gifts and to cultivate the fruit of the Spirit, or Christian character. We were created "a little lower than the angels" in order to be partners with God in the establishment of his rule in life. The practices that shape our souls enable us to live out of our gifts instead of the compulsions of our sin nature, and to act out of our God-given passions instead of imposed obligations.

The practices that shape our souls enable us to live out of our gifts instead of the compulsions of our sin nature, and to act out of our God-given passions instead of imposed obligations.

Our souls take shape according to the direction we are going and the purposes that motivate us. As we align ourselves with God's purposes—what he designed us to do and to be from the beginning of creation—our lives will take on the beautiful shape of Christlike people, who show the world what God is like. In part 5 we will discuss the various spiritual exercises that shape us according to God's glorious purposes.

SOUL-SPECIFIC SPIRITUAL EXERCISES

The exercises of the spiritual life are not a hodgepodge of optional activities for the spiritually advanced. They are the tools God has developed to help us mature in these four areas, as beloved children and valued servants of God. Our failure to see the specific purposes of the disciplines in relation to these four dimensions is one of the most prevalent reasons for our inability to sustain them and profit from them. It's like the beginning piano student who tires of scales and other technical exercises. "I just don't see the point," she says. The wise teacher will immediately try to make the link between the scales the child finds so boring and the music the child longs to play. Once we see the link between exercise and the end result, we can embrace the exercise, our hearts behind the work.

Not all spiritual exercises aim toward the same purpose. As in a physical fitness program, certain exercises move us toward certain goals; we work the cardiovascular system through aerobics, and we work the various muscle groups through specific weight training.

Again using the analogy of physical exercise, some disciplines are "broad range," addressing most of our spiritual needs. Jogging, for example, is an excellent cardiovascular exercise which also builds strength and endurance. Bible study and prayer are the aerobics of spiritual fitness, building both stamina and strength. Study and prayer are essential exercises that support and supply all the other disciplines. We will see that some disciplines focus primarily on personal intimacy with God, while others shape our relationship to the world, and still others build us up in the ways we function in the body of Christ.

Spiritual exercises also need to be tailored to the person and right for the spiritual climate he or she lives in. For example, while the spiritual discipline of a simple lifestyle is not impossible for a high-level executive, it could impede her ability to share her faith with friends who would view her "scaled-down" life as religious fanaticism. On the other hand, that same executive may practice weekly fasting or attend an office Bible study. One person may be most drawn to spiritual reading, while another comes alive through a discipline of quiet service. The joy of the disciplines, properly understood, is that God has provided a spectrum for the full range of human personality and preference.

To determine which disciplines are best for our particular soul condition, we can ask questions such as:

- What spiritual season am I in?
- Which disciplines best suit the need I am feeling now?
- What exercises will help me if I am looking for guidance?
  —for spiritual stamina?
  —for victory over temptation?
  —for a new challenge?
  —for a deeper sense of God's presence?
  —for something to cling to when God seems far away?
  —for recovery after being hurt?
  —for recovery from guilt?

If we don't understand the soul-specific nature of the disciplines, we may do things that are actually counterproductive. Seek wise counsel, especially if you find yourself "going backward" in the course of practicing a discipline. For example, fasting is not wise for a person who is depressed. The loss of food will aggravate the sense of loss that fuels the depression. What this person needs is a recovery of energy—spiritually and physically. Likewise, intensive confession is not wise for a person who has an overactive "conscience" and much misplaced guilt to begin with. It would be more healthy for this person to read the stories that convey the no-matter-what-you've-done-I-love-you nature of God's acceptance. The thief on the cross is a great example. His simple admission of guilt was all that was required. Confession is bearable only in the tropical climate of grace. Such exposure in the frigid places of judgment brings a devastating heart chill.

Ironically, in times of special need we are often drawn to those disciplines that are least helpful. Back to the physical analogy: Hot packs may be great for relief from muscle ache, but a hot pack applied immediately after a muscle injury will complicate the problem because it brings more blood and swelling to the tissues. A cold pack reduces blood and fluid accumulation, reducing the stress on the strained or torn tissue. If God seems far away, extensive Bible reading may not be helpful; I would recommend spiritual reading of biographies or inspirational literature combined with times of prayer and conversation with a spiritual mentor, often called a spiritual director. For the person who is overwhelmed by perfectionism, I would recommend a fast from spiritual activities and a good, long dose of recreation and diversion from the heavy issues of life. Those who are on the edge of burnout—finding themselves "out of cope" and emotionally drained—should step away from disciplines of service and take some time to renew themselves in nondemanding ways.

When used wisely, spiritual disciplines enhance our lives in ways we could never imagine. It is time for worn-out, burned-out believers in Jesus to rediscover the energy, joy, and productivity encompassed in his statement: "I came that they may have life, and have it abundantly" (John 10:10, RSV).

Spiritual growth means weaving faith into every aspect of life. We are not only saved by faith, but we also learn to live by faith in our character development, our relationships, our careers, our recreation, and in every other way.

There is one more resource we need to understand before we begin to look at the process of transformation through spiritual exercise. That is the resource of the Holy Spirit.

TAPPING THE WELLSPRING OF THE HOLY SPIRIT

As we enter the spiritual life, it is imperative that we do so through the Spirit of the living God. The lure of self-improvement and personal development is enough to take us a fair distance on the road of spirituality. But if we undertake it in our own effort and for our own ends, the road will soon become rough, leading us finally into an arid wasteland. Too few books on the spiritual disciplines begin with an emphasis on the Spirit. The Spirit cannot be an afterthought or an appendix. The Holy Spirit is essential in the awakening and sustaining of our desire and discipline.

The Holy Spirit plays a number of roles in our spiritual development. The work of the Spirit is mysterious: "The wind blows wherever it pleases. You hear its sound, but you cannot tell where it comes from or where it is going" (John 3:8). We cannot reduce the Holy Spirit's work to a formula or limit the Spirit to only certain activities and functions. But there are a few things we do know, because the Bible has told us, about how the Spirit works in our lives and what he does.

Breathing God's Life into Us

The Hebrew and Greek words for spirit (*ruach* and *pneuma*) are the same words for breath and wind. God breathes his life into us through the Spirit. We see this clearly in Genesis 2 as the Lord breathes life into the man made from dust. The Spirit actually gives new life to us.

Our lives can be changed simply by learning spiritual respiration. We learn to inhale the power of the Lord and exhale our anxiety and inadequacy. We break our habits of self-reliance by reminding ourselves that God "is able to do immeasurably more than all we ask or imagine, *according to his power that is at work within us* (Eph. 3:20, italics added). Even as deep breathing oxygenates our blood to relax and energize our bodies, so spiritual deep breathing renews and empowers us for life. The power of God is at work within us. Our task is not to somehow get more of the Spirit for ourselves but to surrender more of ourselves to the Spirit.

Translating God's Voice into the Language of Our Hearts

A primary work of the Spirit is softening our hearts to hear and respond to God's Word. As we read and hear the Word of God, the Spirit interprets and applies it to our lives. But the Spirit also guides and directs our lives in many ways that are so natural that we may miss them. The Spirit may inspire us with the thought to call a person or write a letter. The Spirit may arrange our schedules and activities so that we encounter people we need to see or who need to see us. These "divine appointments" have an infusion of grace we often miss. Spirituality sensitizes us to the many movements of God in our lives and world.

The Spirit also interprets us to God. "In the same way, the Spirit helps us in our weakness. We do not know what we ought to pray for, but the Spirit himself intercedes for us with groans that words cannot express. And he who searches our hearts knows the mind of the Spirit, because the Spirit intercedes for the saints in accordance with God's will" (Rom. 8:26-27). As we walk the journey of faith, muffled cries of pain, sighs of longing, and gasps of embarrassment do not go unnoticed. They are conveyed to our listening Lord by the Spirit.

Instructing Us in Kingdom Values

The Spirit renews our thinking, reorders our priorities, and reshapes our values. The values of Christ are the inverse of worldly values: losing your life to save it; becoming last so you can be first; loving your enemies and praying for those who persecute you; going the extra mile for one who forces you to go the first mile. Jesus' ways are the opposite of our natural instincts. As we study God's Word and prayerfully consider our circumstances, the Spirit often leads us to creative responses that surprise us.

Enlarging Our Vision

In Genesis 1, the Spirit broods upon the waters, giving form and order to that which is formless and void. The creative activity of the Spirit is evident throughout Scripture. We see it in the inspiration of prophets and in the ongoing inspiration of people in the service of the Lord. As Moses was preparing to implement God's plans for the tabernacle, the Lord said, "See, I have chosen Bezalel son of Uri, the son of Hur, of the tribe of Judah, and I have filled him with the Spirit of God, with skill, ability and knowledge in all kinds of crafts" (Exod. 31:2-3). The Spirit reveals what God is doing in the world, inviting us and equipping us to participate.

Awakening God's Gift and Call

The awakening of Gods' gifts and call may be the result of an enlarged vision, or it may follow as a matter of daily obedience. God has equipped us to be partners in the coming of his kingdom. He has endowed each of us with gifts for the service of others. The Spirit's role in this is necessary, and the Scriptures are quite clear about it. When the Lord was preparing to ascend into heaven, he entrusted the ministry of witnessing to his resurrection and the proclamation of the gospel to his disciples—with the provision that they were to wait until they received the power of the Holy Spirit. Their task could not be accomplished in human power.

The magnitude of the task is captured in a well-known story that tells how Jesus, after the Cross and the Resurrection, returned to his glory, still bearing the marks of his sufferings. One of the angels said to him, "You must have suffered terribly for people down there."

"I did," said Jesus.

"Do they all know about what you did for them?" asked the angel.

"No," said Jesus, "not yet. Only a few in Palestine know about it so far."

"And," said the angel, "what have you done so that they will know about it?"

"Well," said Jesus, "I asked Peter and James and John to make it their business to tell others, and the others to tell still others, until the farthest person on the widest circle has heard the story."

The angel looked doubtful, for he knew well what poor creatures people are. "Yes," he said, "but what if Peter and James and John forget? What if they grow weary of the telling? What if, way down in the twentieth century, people fail to tell the story of your love for them? What then? Haven't you made any other plans?"

And back came the answer of Jesus, "I haven't made any other plans. *I'm counting on them.*"2

Not only does God count on us, but he has done all that is necessary to ensure that we have the abilities required to fulfill his expectations.

Sustaining Us in the Risks of Obedience

As we step out in obedience, we will find ourselves in circumstances where only God's power can make the difference. We will be asked questions too deep for our ordinary minds to handle. At times such as these, we recall that Jesus gave us the Spirit for this very purpose.

"When you are brought before synagogues, rulers and authorities, do not worry about how you will defend yourselves or what you will say, for the Holy Spirit will teach you at that time what you should say" (Luke 12:11-12).

Shaping Us into the Image of Christ

God is forming us into the likeness of his Son through the Spirit's work within us. He is transforming every aspect of our lives to conform to the model of Christ. This task will continue until Christ's appearing. "Dear friends, now we are children of God, and what we will be has not yet been made known. But we know that when he appears, *we shall be like him,* for we shall see him as he is" (1 John 3:2, italics added). No one who has sincerely sought this transformation believes it is possible in their own human effort. The power of the Lord working within us brings the deep changes that God desires.

Earlier, we explored the fact that our souls are like reservoirs, needing a supply of living water. Jesus takes this image a step further when he says, "'If anyone is thirsty, let him come to me and drink. Whoever believes in me, as the Scripture has said, streams of living water will flow from within him.' By this he meant the Spirit, whom those who believed in him were later to receive. Up to that time the Spirit had not been given, since Jesus had not yet been glorified" (John 7:37-39). The Holy Spirit is like an artesian well, bubbling up within us. As we practice the spiritual disciplines, relying on the Holy Spirit, the waters flow more and more freely with cleansing, healing, and revitalizing power.

FREEDOM IS THE FRUIT OF DISCIPLINE

The person who has invested the time and effort to master a task opens doors that others who haven't been disciplined will rarely see. The trained athlete has the greatest freedom in the contest. The trained musician has the greatest freedom in singing or instrumental performance. The disciplined student has the greatest freedom with her material. The disciplined disciple has the freedom to face life unafraid, confident that he can trust God and that he has also developed the skills to sustain him no matter what the circumstances.

This view of freedom is far different from what the world defines as freedom. The world defines freedom as the ability to do what you want when you want, without any restrictions. But this kind of lifestyle will bring a person into captivity. The person who uses his freedom to indulge his appetites soon becomes the slave of those appetites. The one who uses her freedom to avoid responsibilities soon finds herself with increasingly limited options in life.

Freedom, for example, is not demonstrated by eating as much food as you want, but by being able to say no to food. Freedom is not spending as much money as you can (going way beyond a wise credit limit); freedom is living in contentment within your means. Discipline gives us the freedom of spirit to live with or without because we are not dependent on outer circumstances.

Discipline means freedom to face life with confidence. Discipline develops "spiritual reflexes" before you need them. When Joe Frazier was the world heavyweight boxing champion, he revealed something of his own personal philosophy of life. He said: "You can map out a life plan or a fight plan, but when the action starts, you're down to your reflexes."[3]

Discipline means freedom from one of the most discouraging attitudes in life: regret. One simple sentence that has helped me keep at spiritual discipline is: *Discipline weighs ounces; regret weighs tons.*[4]

I have never regretted physical or spiritual exercise. I have never regretted eating only one plate of food at a buffet (though I'll admit that's a little harder!). I have never regretted getting up early and getting started on the day. I've never regretted making a financial sacrifice to help another. When you feel yourself begin to flag in your spiritual exercise, try saying to yourself, *I don't want to regret this tomorrow.*

Physical exercise gives us the freedom of flexibility and stamina. We can keep a fairly full schedule without undue fatigue. We know our limits, but we also know our capabilities and how far we can push ourselves. We appreciate the gift of health and do what we can to enjoy the freedom of feeling good.

Spiritual discipline gives us the freedom of experiencing God's presence and knowing God's general will and direction for our lives. We learn which options are not good for us. We know what situations are most conducive to our spiritual health. We live by priority, not impulse. Responsible living gives us great flexibility to say yes to new opportunities because we have done the important things.

Discipline allows us to play without guilt. When life is in order, anxiety has fewer closets to haunt. A plan puts things in their place, with a realistic perspective. The wondering, the burden of feeling there are things I ought to be doing now—it's very draining, isn't it? A wise plan spreads out the work, portioning it according to our strength, with a pace that includes rest and recreation.

Discipline sets us free to make the most of life. When you have so many options, discipline is essential in order to make the best choices. When you want to maximize life, discipline is essential. To "go with the flow" means you drift through life, wherever the current takes you. That may be fine for a lazy afternoon, but it spells disaster as a philosophy of life.

Discipline makes life manageable and lessens the burden of living. It is the most practical means for helping us discern the important from the less important. It guides us to focus on the activities and priorities that bear the return we value most.

I had been going to the fitness center two to three times a week for about four weeks. I vividly remember getting up one dark winter morning and thinking, *I just don't think I can do this three days a week for the rest of my life!* It was a particularly disheartening thought, thinking of doing this for at least thirty-five or forty more years! Somehow, I got up and out to the gym. As I was riding the exercise bicycle I was musing over this sobering idea, when I thought of all the meals I eat in a week, in a month, in a year. What if someone took us into a warehouse filled with all the meals we had to eat in a lifetime and said, "OK—start eating!" Even those who delight in food would be daunted, even nauseated! It was never meant to be seen all at once. It is a daily matter. Daily bread, daily discipline.

NOTES

1. Brother Lawrence, *The Practice of the Presence of God* (Old Tappan, N.J.: Revell, 1958), 15.
2. William Barclay, *The Letter to the Romans* (Philadelphia, Penn.: Westminster Press, 1955), 243.
3. Mark Landfried, *This Service of Love* (United Presbyterian Church in the United States of America: Synod of the Trinity, 1978), 52.
4. Jim Rohn, "How to Be a Bigger Winner," *Success Strategies* cassette tapes (Niles, Ill.: Nightingale-Conant, n.d.)

SOUL-SEARCHING

Questions for Reflection and Discussion

1. When have you been most disciplined? Why?

2. How would you describe your level of discipline?

   a) I am a self-starter, ready to go.

   b) I do okay when I need to.

   c) Somebody needs to hold my feet to the fire.

   d) Discipline? Forget it! Things work out nicely for me without a lot of bother.

3. Based on your assessment of the Symptoms of Soul Neglect from chapter 1, in what area do you feel the greatest need or desire?

   a) To experience the sense of God's presence

   b) To gain God's perspective on life

   c) To discover and pursue God's purpose for my life in terms of character and gifts

   d) To experience God's power by detaching myself from the world's power sources and attaching to God's

4. What's your vision for spiritual vitality in this area? In other words, if you grew "from glory to glory" in this area, how would you descirbe your new life in the next year or two? Be as specific as possible.

5. Review the benefits of discipline described in the chapter. Which of them would be most valuable to you right now? Why?

   a) Discipline means freedom to face life with confidence.

   b) Discipline means freedom from one of the most discouraging attitudes in life: regret.

113

c) Spiritual discipline gives us the freedom of experiencing God's presence and knowing God's general will and direction for our lives.

d) Discipline allows us to play without guilt.

e) Discipline sets us free to make the most of life.

f) Discipline makes life manageable and lessens the burden of living.

PART TWO

Making the Connection: God's Presence with Us

SOULSHAPING AT A GLANCE

Exercises That Increase Our Awareness of God's Presence

- 🌿 **Repentance**
- 🌿 **Confession**
- 🌿 **Preview**
- 🌿 **Review**
- 🌿 **Prayer**
- 🌿 **Worship**

Exercises That Help Us See Life with an Eternal Perspective

- 🌿 Bible study
- 🌿 Meditation
- 🌿 Spiritual reading

Exercises That Free Us from Evil's Power and Connect Us to God's Resources

- 🌿 Fasting
- 🌿 Silence
- 🌿 Solitude
- 🌿 Battling temptation
- 🌿 Prayer for spiritual battle

Exercises That Direct Our Lives toward Kingdom Purposes

- 🌿 Building character
- 🌿 Building relationships
- 🌿 Spiritual direction
- 🌿 Spiritual friendship
- 🌿 Stewardship
- 🌿 Spiritual service through spiritual gifts

As I sat in Miller Chapel at Princeton Seminary following a week of study in spirituality, I was overcome by the presence of the Lord. We were gathered for a closing worship service with Dr. Howard Rice, professor at San Francisco Theological Seminary and Moderator of the United Presbyterian Church (USA) for 1979–80. Howard had been stricken by multiple sclerosis about eight years earlier and was seated in a wheelchair. As he preached, he visibly portrayed the power of God in weakness.

The service concluded with anointing for each of us. As others began to go forward, I was ambushed by tears. I sobbed and wept. At first I was honestly surprised by my response. Then I kept hearing in my mind, *These are the tears I forgot to cry*. Later, I wrote in my journal:

> I had an overwhelming sense of my unworthiness. As I watched others receive the blessing from Howard, seated in his wheelchair, the grace and love of God were too much for me, a sinner. As I sobbed, Earl and Virginia put firm hands on my shoulders the touch of Christ came through them and I knew again the forgiveness that is mine forever. As I regained composure and went forward, I was determined to receive the blessing and celebrate it with a smile.
>
> Howard anointed me with a fragrant oil, first making a cross on my forehead: "Doug, may the blessing of the Lord pour over you." Then he proceeded with further anointing as he pronounced the blessing:
>
> "May your ears hear what is right
> May your eyes see what is true
> May your lips speak God's Word

May your hands do God's work
And may the Lord bless you and make you strong in his service."

I sat for a long time in the silence, soaking in the nearness of God. This was the first time I ever felt overwhelmed with an experience of God's presence. It was far greater than I ever would have imagined.

Spirituality, simply put, is living in the continuing knowledge that God is with us. The symptoms of soul neglect trace their roots to the loss of this assurance. When we forget God, neglect God, or doubt our connection with God, our spiritual energy drains away. We fall prey to spiritual depression and boredom. We fail to keep our priorities in order, and we find ourselves indifferent to spiritual things and vulnerable to our weaknesses.

When we forget God, neglect God, or doubt our connection with God, our spiritual energy drains away.

God's presence is not limited to outwardly spiritual activities, such as worship, prayer, and Bible study. True spirituality seeks to discern God's presence and the Holy Spirit's activity in all of life's experiences: in our relationships, careers, schooling, finances, politics, and recreation, to name some of the major ones. For the Christian, there are no compartments in life which are labeled spiritual and nonspiritual—sacred and secular. Every facet of life is shot through with glory. And every part of our life cries out for redemption. Our spiritual vitality increases as we learn to:

- recognize the presence of God at all times
- give voice to the Word of God in all conversations
- draw on the resources of God in all situations
- express the will of God in all relationships

These are the four primary dimensions of soulshaping, covered in parts 2 through 5 of this book. But let's be realistic. The sense of God's presence is rarely as vivid as I have described in the opening of this section. We may be blessed with a specific occasion when God seems tangible to us, but most often his presence is more like that of our vital organs: We know they are sustaining our lives, but we aren't acutely aware of their moment-by-moment function. We can, however, exercise spiritual disciplines that will make us more aware of and more sensitive to the movement of God in and around us.

Growing on the inside—taking care of our soul—can be lonely business. We need early on to learn how to experience God's presence. Spiritual practices that focus specifically on God's presence are the focus of part 2. These include:

- our initial encounters with God and our response of faith,
- confession and our experience of forgiveness,
- prayer, and
- worship—both personal and in the family of faith.

Your "soul life" must be rooted in your relationship with God, not in techniques or gimmicks. Christ in you is where it all begins.

CHAPTER SIX

Who's Looking for Whom?

I seem to recall from my reading in the legends of King Arthur that Merlin, the wizard, followed an unusual course in training the young Arthur. Merlin was a "shape changer," having the capacity to change himself into different beings, including animals. In Arthur's early years, Merlin would change Arthur into different creatures so Arthur could learn life from different perspectives. But there were times when Arthur, as a human, was facing difficult times alone, with no knowledge of Merlin's presence. He didn't know that the eagle flying overhead had his sharp vision trained on the young lad, discerning his every move. He didn't know that just out of sight was a bear, ready to protect him in time of danger. He didn't know that Merlin was in the shape of the eagle and the bear. Merlin was there all the time, but Arthur didn't know it.

"He was there all the time; I just didn't see it." I heard these words recently from a person talking about his experience with

God. We were discussing a time of deep darkness, when this man felt that all hope was gone—and that God was long gone from his life. But prayer, counseling, God's Word, and the support of loving friends had brought him through the valley. Now, looking back, he can clearly see the hand of God.

God's presence is a fact, but our *experience of God's presence* is a skill that we cultivate. We develop the sense of God's presence through learning to pay attention to the spiritual reality that is present in every moment and every activity of life.

GOD IS THERE ALL THE TIME

We do not have to coax God to be present with us. Scripture makes it abundantly clear: "I will never leave you nor forsake you" (Heb. 13:5, NKJV) is a message stated, implied, and demonstrated on every page of Scripture and in the testimony of God's people across the ages.

One of the most convincing and intimate expressions of God's desire to be with us comes from the opening chapters of Genesis. God formed the heavens and earth; the sun, moon, and stars; the birds, fish, and animals—all by the power of his word; he spoke and they came to be. But in the creation of humankind God moves from his throne of almighty power to the place of a loving Creator hovering over a precious work. In the Creation account of Genesis 2, God takes the dust of the earth, shapes it into a human being, and breathes his own breath into that human being. It's difficult not to picture God on his knees, taking the dust of the earth into his almighty hands with the tenderness of a parent and the skill of a master craftsman shaping the finest porcelain. Our creation is presented as a loving, intimate act.

In the fellowship that followed creation, conversation between God and humankind was direct and natural. In one of the most poignant passages of the Bible, the Lord is "walking in the garden in the cool of the day" or, as the New Revised Standard Version translates, "at the time of the evening breeze." He is looking for the man and woman, seeking the delight of fellowship following the deeds of the day. We can picture this idyllic scene: the beauty of the garden, the fragrances of flowers, the sweetness of the fruit, the soft breezes, and the joy of anticipating conversation with God. But this day the man and the woman had chosen to disregard God's command and go their own way by eating of the fruit of the tree of the knowledge of good and evil. Their instinctive response to disobedience was to hide from God. Yet God still sought his creatures. The intimacy was broken but not lost.

The Genesis account shows clearly the cost of disobedience: The man and woman came under the curse, along with the serpent, and were dismissed from the Garden. But it is also clear that *they were not dismissed from the presence of God. His presence was not limited to the Garden!* The fullest experience of his fellowship, with all its joy and innocence, was lost, but not the possibility of God's being with us in the midst of our fallen existence. Indeed, the Scriptures are the record of God's continual seeking after us.

God doesn't merely tolerate human beings; he deeply loves us and desires fellowship with us. Psalm 139 pictures the Lord's intimate and complete knowledge about us, including his active involvement in knitting us together in our mothers' wombs. His continuing care for his people is again presented in most intimate terms in Isaiah 49:15-16: "Can a woman forget her nursing child, and have no compassion on the son of her womb? Even these may forget, but I will not forget you. Behold, I have inscribed you on the palms of my hands" (NASB). We're not simply creatures God tolerates or anonymous citizens of his vast kingdom. We are members of his own household. "For you did not receive a spirit of slavery to fall back into fear, but you have received a spirit of adoption. When we cry, 'Abba! Father!' it is that very Spirit bearing witness with our spirit that we are children of God" (Rom. 8:15-16, NRSV).

As we seek to reconnect with God, we can be confident that that sense of God's presence is not a rare treat which must be earned. Nor is God's presence an exceptional experience for the few. It is the reality for all who will receive it. The goal of the spiritual life is not trying to get God's attention, overcoming his disinterest. Spirituality is about awakening our own deadened awareness; we make the vital connection with the God who already deeply cares about us.

Spirituality is about awakening our own deadened awareness; we make the vital connection with the God who already deeply cares about us.

PROOF THAT GOD HAS NOT DESERTED US

The clearest evidence of God's care is seen in one of the names given to the Messiah: Immanuel, "God with us." This phrase was first given to Isaiah when Israel was experiencing severe threats, wondering if God had deserted them altogether. The promise given to Isaiah was fulfilled ultimately in the coming of Jesus Christ. He came to reveal God's presence in the thick of life. The name—and the reality of God's presence—came to have a new meaning far richer than could have ever been imagined. Jesus Christ, God Incarnate, lived the human experience, from the routine of daily life to the monstrous tragedy of betrayal, rejection, humiliation, and crucifixion. Yet even in death, God did not desert us, for Jesus Christ was victorious over death. When Jesus met his disciples after the Resurrection, he emphasized the principle of presence. He told them, "I am with you always, even to the end of the age" (Matt. 28:20, NKJV). Even with his ascension, his physical departure did not mean spiritual abandonment. He would send the Holy Spirit to be present, indwelling every believer—the living presence of God within all who believe.

God *wants* to be with us. God *desires* to be found by us. When we hide out of guilt, God comes looking for us. Even more, Jesus Christ is true to his promise: He *is* with us! We don't undertake spiritual exercises in order to convince God to reveal himself to us. *We undertake these activities in order to come out from hiding and to peel away the layers of our own callousness and insensitivity, so that we become aware of the God who is with us always.*

Spirituality is experiencing the presence of God and living out of that experience in daily life. Don't equate the word *experience* here with emotion. Experience is a sense that goes deeper than emotion; it could be explained as an inner assurance. It's a confidence in which you move, not an emotion that moves you. Sensing God's presence is rarely experienced as goose bumps.

When Do I Sense God's Presence?
Cultivating the sense of God's presence can begin with asking yourself a very simple question: When has the presence of God been most real to me? This begins to show you how you're made. Some people find the presence of God in silence and solitude. Others experience God most in the midst of a worshiping congregation. Others, in the midst of practical service. Others experience God when they read the Bible or books that explore the things of faith. I sense God's presence when I take time to "graze" in his Word, when I listen to inspirational music, when I backpack in the mountains, when I read and reflect, when I worship, and when I'm in ministry, watching God touch others' lives. When do you experience his presence? If you can search

your heart and find those times when you most notice it, you'll begin to cultivate those experiences.

THE FIRST AND MOST IMPORTANT STEP

The first step toward experiencing God's presence is renewing your friendship with God through faith in Jesus Christ. I touched on this earlier, but it must be emphasized as the central purpose of spirituality. We are to be reunited with God before anything else makes sense. Apart from this, all our efforts and activities will produce no lasting fruit.

Too often we get sidetracked into activities, forgetting why we are involved with them in the first place. We are also tempted to seek the benefits that come from these activities without connecting with the Lord who designed them. In and of themselves, spiritual exercises will have a positive (though limited) effect, apart from direct connection with God. They make good sense. That's why there are so many human-centered expressions of these activities: relaxation techniques, using the imagination for visioning, chanting mantras, and holistic medicine, to name a few. These are merely stepchildren, developed out of the spiritual dynamics God has woven into our nature. They can never, however, fulfill the deepest longings of our hearts or the highest purposes of God.

If we want genuine, lasting spiritual vitality, we must surrender our lives to Jesus Christ as Savior and Lord. This is the first step, not the destination! There is much more to spiritual health than escaping from the judgment of eternal separation from God in order to receive the assurance of eternal life. In fact, in Jesus' last prayer with the disciples, he says, "Now this is eternal life: *that they may know you*, the only true God, and Jesus Christ, whom you have sent" (John 17:3, italics added). The purpose of salvation is not simply eternal life, but a relationship with God— Father, Son, and Holy Spirit—for all eternity!

In a way, our spiritual exercises here are rehearsals for heaven. They attune our lives to the reality beyond this fallen world. They bring us glimpses of glory and tastes of splendor. Time and effort invested in cultivating God's presence bears fruit that will abide. As Paul reminds Timothy, "Physical training is of some value, but godliness has value for all things, holding promise for both the present life and the life to come" (1 Tim. 4:8). But there is no promise without the first step. It's like marriage: once the commitment is made, the relationship can develop in ways that cannot be experienced without that commitment.

The Surrender That Brings Victory

My friend and fellow pastor Jon Glover tells of working with a man who was a long way from any connection with God. For six years, Willy had been suicidal because of the loss of his family through divorce. During that time he tried to kill himself on several occasions. On one occasion, he deliberately rolled the eighteen-wheeler that he drove for a living. In another attempt, he defied a policeman in a patrol car when the officer told him to pull over and stop. He hoped that the officer would shoot him as he fled. Soon seven police cars were chasing him, but no one tried to shoot him.

Then Willy's despair took a different turn. Willy is now charged with first-degree murder, and the state is going to push for the death penalty because of the allegations that he had lain in wait to murder his estranged wife and her lover. She died instantly, but her boyfriend recovered from his wounds.

When Willy was put in jail after killing his wife, he was suicidal in the extreme. Guards put him in "the hole," where he stayed for several days. Later Willy was put into a regular cell with other inmates. He started doing Bible studies. He committed what was left of his life to Christ. After two interviews with him, the chaplain said he was convinced that Willy was sincere in his profession of faith in Christ.

In the second interview, Willy began by saying, "You know, Chaplain Glover, how people prepare themselves for what they want to do in life? Like you going to school to become a chaplain or a reverend? Well, I'm preparing myself to die."

He is a totally different person from the violent, drug-saturated man he once was. In the confines of a county jail, one of the most difficult places in the world to show the virtues of Christ, Willy is doing just that—accepting the taunts of those who claim that because of his gentleness and willingness to back off from a confrontation, "He couldn't crush a grape."

Willy's story is a powerful example of God's touching a down-and-out life. But we are all in a type of confinement apart from the freedom God gives. What unlocks the door? My experience and the stories of countless others have led me to see four primary elements that are part of connecting with God.

We must wake up to our deepest need.   Willy saw that he had no hope apart from God. Others may not be in situations as desperate, but they see that life is missing the central ingredient. They have the clear sense that no matter how much they have, it's never enough; or that no matter how little they have, there's something that would put it all together.

We must hear the story of God's love in Christ.   There can be no surrender until we've heard clearly of the awesome love of God, who surrendered his Son to death on our behalf. Once this is understood, our next steps are motivated by what God has done for us, not driven by fear of what we must do for God.

We must believe God's promises for our lives.   Moving from intellectual assent to trust is a long step. But when, in the mystery of God, the Holy Spirit moves us to trust God, the promises of God become keys that unlock not only the cells of our needs but also the jail of the old life as well.

We must surrender ourselves to God.   Along with yielding control of our lives to God, this surrender means letting go of lesser things. Unlike the surrender of a defeated warrior, which means disgrace, our surrender means grace. Unlike the surrender of a defeated army, which means captivity, our surrender means that we are liberated from the captivity of sin and evil, from futility and anxiety, from loneliness and isolation. We are free from the pressures of this world in order to be free for the pleasures of God. Perhaps one of the best pictures of surrender is that of a person hanging over a cliff, desperately grasping a fraying rope. He can't pull himself up, but to let go means to fall to his death. Then a person comes along who is able to reach over the edge and pull the desperate man to safety—if the man will surrender the rope and take the rescuer's hand.

By faith, we let go of the fraying ropes of life in order to take hold of God. We give what we know of ourselves to what we know of God. I hasten to add that surrender is a process that spans a lifetime. But it begins with a choice to let go of whatever is keeping us from taking firm hold of God.

I was speaking with a man and his fiancée in preparation for their wedding. He had lost his first wife nearly a year before, after a prolonged illness.

"I had not been a churchgoer for many years, but following the funeral, I felt the need to reconnect with God," he told me.

As we talked, he said, "I have to tell you something. I have never been one to pray much, especially for myself. But in a message several weeks ago, you asked us to consider God's promises and pray for him to do one thing for us that week. I have been facing a crisis in my business partnership. It has kept me awake at night for months. Well, Beth and I began to pray about it—and on Thursday, the crisis was resolved!"

"That's fantastic! Praise the Lord," I replied.

"I had never thought I could know God the way you talk about him. I don't think I really know God. He answered my prayer . . . but I don't really know him."

I was about to speak when he said, "Doug, let me ask you this: What does it mean to be born again? Is that something that needs to happen to me?"

Within the next few minutes, Ron heard the story of Jesus, believed God's promises were for him, and was praying to surrender his life and trust Jesus Christ as his Lord and Savior. God had shown Ron his love in many ways, and Ron was finally able to see that God had been there all the time. He took the first step after realizing that God had been walking with him all along life's way.

One of the greatest barriers to experiencing God's presence is our failure to understand that God is a seeking God. "For thus says the Lord God: Behold, I, I myself will search for my sheep, and will seek them out. As a shepherd seeks out his flock when some of his sheep have been scattered abroad, so will I seek out my sheep" (Ezek. 34:11-12, RSV). Jesus makes this same point time and again (see Luke 15). God goes after us!

The great gospel song says it best:

> Amazing grace—how sweet the sound—
> That saved a wretch like me!
> I once was lost, but now am found—
> Was blind, but now I see.

Take it on faith, not on feelings: God is with us. Now, begin to ask yourself: What difference does that make?

Don't let God's presence be something you sense only occasionally. Look around: The Lion of the tribe of Judah is there, ready to spring to your aid. Look up: The One who will raise us up on eagles' wings is circling, his eyes ever upon us. God is there! God is here!

SOUL-SEARCHING

Questions for Reflection and Discussion

1. Have you ever experienced God's presence in a special way? Where were you? What was happening in your life at that time? How did that experience affect you?

2. If you have never had what you would call a vivid experience of God, how do you sense his presence? Are there specific suggestions from this chapter that intrigue you, holding the promise of greater intimacy with God?

3. Review the examples of God's presence in the chapter. When do you sense God's presence? How often do you participate in experiences that impart the sense of God's presence?

4. If you knew that God was present with you moment by moment, how would it affect every choice you make?

5. Have you taken the "first and most important step" of trusting Christ? If so, describe how it happened.

6. If you are "on the journey" but aren't sure you've taken that step, can you identify where you are?

    a) I'm just now waking up to what my deepest needs are.

    b) I'm learning the story of God's love in Christ and what that means to my life.

    c) I'm beginning to trust and believe that God's promises are for my life.

    d) I am ready to surrender to God.

7. What is one particular step you could take to cultivate a new sense of God's presence?

CHAPTER SEVEN

Freeing Ourselves from Yesterday

🌿 REPENTANCE
🌿 CONFESSION

O N an early December morning, we stood at a new grave. A dusting of snow powdered the headstones. The faintly shining sun did little to warm the deep chill inside us. The winter wind was biting, but not as deeply as the grief. We were here to bury Nathaniel, the ten-year-old, severely disabled son of Nancy. Across from Nancy and her vibrant daughter, Brittany, stood Nancy's former husband, Cliff, with his second wife on his arm. Cliff had left his wife and two children shortly after Nathaniel's traumatic birth.

I ached inside. When he was still married to Nancy, Cliff had been confronted about his behavior and his responsibility toward his child. But he turned a cold shoulder—and a cold heart resulted. At a time like this, I knew Cliff was in deep pain, like the rest of us. But the thought came into my mind, *This father could have been a hero. But instead, he ran away.*

We will experience many setbacks along the way of spiritual restoration. One of the most powerful forces that interrupts our sense of God's presence is our ongoing battle with sin. We are caught in the tension between the objective truth that God has pronounced us pardoned (1 John 1:9) and the fact that we are still disobedient to God in thought, word, and deed (1 John 1:8). This is not as hard to understand if you compare spiritual birth and growth to biological birth and maturation. A newborn baby is already fully human in identity but not yet fully grown. In the same way, we who have been born anew by faith have begun a process of spiritual maturation. By faith in Jesus Christ, we have been released from sin's penalty and can be called saints! But we are not fully free from sin's lingering power in our lives (Rom. 6:11-12). Because Christ Jesus paid our debt in full, we no longer live under the threat of condemnation, but we are still involved in the lifelong process of transformation into the likeness of Christ.

As we grow in the knowledge of God, we become more sensitive to all the ways in which we naturally resist God. It seems that the harder we try to follow God, the more we defy him. The more we know about ourselves, the more readily we echo the words of the apostle: "I do not understand my own actions. For I do not do what I want, but I do the very thing I hate. . . . For I do not do the good I want, but the evil I do not want is what I do" (Rom. 7:15, 19, RSV).

While this struggle with sin deeply distresses us, it is, in fact, a sign of spiritual health. Our judgment is being restored, and our conscience is being renewed. We have a new standard by which we evaluate life's situations. I came to understand this in a new way one cold winter day in Connecticut. We were visiting friends who have a beautiful white dog. She looked so clean and bright curled up by the roaring fire. After a great meal, we all decided to go for a walk through the snow (to make room for dessert!).

The dog came out with us. As she romped around, I was surprised how drab and dirty she looked against the newly fallen snow. Without the contrast of the snow, the dog looked fine. But when a different standard was held up, my idea of white was shown to be far below the ideal.

As we come to know God's Word and begin to examine our hearts according to its standards, we become aware of the gap between our calling and our behavior as disciples. We are aware both of the presence of our *destructive* thoughts, words, and deeds and of the absence of *holy* thoughts, words, and deeds. In fact, the good that we fail to do can often be more distressing than our mistakes. This heightened sensitivity often causes us shame; we feel unworthy of God's favor, and we become unwilling to be in God's presence. Even though we may understand that God does not leave us when we sin, we live as if this were the case. God is grieved when we sin, but he remains with us, the ever present Father, Helper, Healer, who seeks to restore us to spiritual health (see Eph. 4:30).

WHY DO I FEEL GUILTY?

What is guilt, exactly? In terms of theology, guilt is my condition after I have violated God's ways. I have sinned, and I am therefore guilty; *guilt* describes me in a totally objective way. *Guilt is a fact*, regardless of feelings, and we deal with it through repentance, confession, and trust in the sacrifice of Christ. In people whose consciences still have some sensitivity to God (and that includes most people), the condition of being guilty produces feelings of guilt. So guilt is an objective condition that leads us into feelings, which are subjective. This is why two persons can commit the same sin, and one feels acute guilt while the other barely recognizes that he or she has transgressed. The extent of our guilty feelings is determined by many factors—family background, the surrounding culture, our general sensitivity to spiritual things, and the consequences of past experiences.

We can think of guilt as the fever of the soul. When we feel guilt, we know we have acted against God, ourselves, and others. Our guilt announces the problem. It is like the warning light on the dashboard of a car. At this point, many people descend into deep depression, chiding themselves and creating a number of punishment scenarios, including the assumption that God has deserted them. Persistent wallowing in guilt feelings leaves people discouraged and spiritually drained.

Guilt, however, is not intended as punishment. Guilt's purpose is not atonement, as if we could make up for our sin by the misery of a guilty conscience. When you have a fever, you seek medical help. You neither ignore the fever nor focus on it alone. You treat the root cause, and the fever takes care of itself. God's strategy in guilt is to stir us to get help, drawing us to himself.

Psalm 32 exhibits the intense discomfort of guilt fever, forcing David finally to face the infection of his sin in committing adultery with Bathsheba and murdering her husband, Uriah, as a cover-up.

> *When I declared not my sin, my body wasted away*
> *through my groaning all day long.*
> *For day and night thy hand was heavy upon me;*
> *my strength was dried up as by the heat of summer.*
> *I acknowledged my sin to thee,*
> *and I did not hide my iniquity;*
> *I said, "I will confess my transgressions to the Lord";*
> *then thou didst forgive the guilt of my sin.*
>
> PSALM 32:3-5, RSV

Guilt is meant to drive us into the arms of mercy. Psalm 51, the sister of Psalm 32, shows us the ointment of grace applied to the self-inflicted wounds of sin. When we run to God's mercy, our guilt is removed and the healing begins. "Cleanse me with hyssop, and I will be clean; wash me, and I will be whiter than snow. . . . Restore to me the joy of your salvation and grant me a willing spirit, to sustain me" (Ps. 51:7, 12).

Not all feelings of guilt are the result of real guilt. False guilt feelings arise from an oversensitive or misdirected conscience. These, likewise, are a call for help; often the best help for an oversensitive conscience is clearer teaching on God's grace and forgiveness.

Guilt feelings also arise from the darts the evil one shoots into sensitive hearts. The name *Satan* means "adversary." We learn that one of his primary activities as an adversary of the people of God is finger-pointing. He is described as "the accuser of the our brothers, who accuses them before our God day and night" (Rev. 12:10). We see an illustration of this in Job 1 when Satan stands before the Lord and questions the faithfulness of Job: "Does Job fear God for nothing?" With that question, we see how the evil one "lives down" to his other name, "the devil." The Greek verb *diaballo* is the root of the primary New Testament word for "devil," *diabolos*. This root in the Greek means "to split, to divide." The devil's main objective is to split human beings from God, from others, and within themselves. One of the keys to discerning the difference between real and false guilt is that in false guilt, Satan points at us to tear us down. In true guilt, God points us to Christ to build us up.

The greatest danger arises when we don't manage our guilt in the right way. Instead of running to God for forgiveness and help, we give in to despair. In C. S. Lewis's *The Screwtape Letters,* Screwtape, a master demon, or devil, is writing letters of instruction to his apprentice nephew. At one point he addresses the issue of shame and guilt:

There is, of course, always the chance, not of chloroforming the shame, but of aggravating it and producing Despair. This would be a great triumph. It would show that he had believed in, and accepted, the Enemy's forgiveness of his other sins only because he himself did not fully feel their sinfulness—that in respect of the one vice which he really understands in its full depth of dishonor he cannot seek, nor credit, the mercy. But I fear you have already let him get too far in the Enemy's school, and he knows that Despair is a greater sin than any of the sins which provoke it.[1]

The true use of our sensitivity to our recurring sin is best illustrated by Paul: "Here is a trustworthy saying that deserves full acceptance: Christ Jesus came into the world to save sinners—of whom I *am* [note the present tense, italics added] the worst. But for that very reason I was shown mercy so that in me, the worst of sinners, Christ Jesus might display his unlimited patience as an example for those who would believe on him and receive eternal life. Now to the King eternal, immortal, invisible, the only God, be honor and glory for ever and ever. Amen" (1 Tim. 1:15-17). He acknowledges his continuing sin but focuses on God's boundless grace. The whole situation is transformed by grace from a temptation to despair to a catalyst of worship!

WHAT DOES CONFESSION ACCOMPLISH?

The story is told that Frederick the Great, king of Prussia, visited a prison and talked with each of the inmates. There were endless tales of innocence, of misunderstood motives, and of exploitation. Finally the king stopped at the cell of a convict who remained silent. "Well," remarked Frederick, "I suppose you are an innocent victim too?"

"No, sir, I'm not," replied the man. "I'm guilty, and I deserve my punishment."

Turning to the warden, the king said, "Here! Release this rascal before he corrupts all the fine, innocent people in this place!"

Confession releases the power of truth, and the truth sets us free. I have sometimes used what I call the "Dracula principle" to explain the power of confession. The vampire Dracula possessed incredible powers in the darkness of night, but he lost all his demonic, destructive power with the coming of dawn. This is a fascinating parable of the effect of life-draining sins in our lives. When we refuse to confess our sins, they gain increasing power over us. Our greatest hope lies in following the counsel of John. In his letter he writes that God is light, like the dawning and noonday sun. When we walk in that light, sin's power is destroyed. If we dwell in darkness, it is given new power. "If we claim to be without sin, we deceive ourselves and the truth is not in us. If we confess our sins, he is faithful and just and will forgive us our sins and purify us from all unrighteousness" (1 John 1:8-9).

Confession is the appropriate response to guilt. Confession does not earn God's forgiveness; it makes that forgiveness real to us. When we cling to our sin, refusing to admit our need, God's grace is like an antiseptic, healing ointment—that's still in the tube. Confession does not create our forgiveness, even as a check does not create money you don't already have in your bank account. It releases what we already have.

Confession simply means *to agree together,* from the Latin, *com-* (together) and *fateri* (acknowledge). When I confess my sins to God, I agree that I have violated his standards and that I have been wrong in doing so. Confession probably has much more to do with our growth than with any need God has to hear us admit our sin. God has made a choice to forgive us, based on Christ's atonement for our sin. By confessing, though, we let go of our sin and renew our commitment to live God's way.

Guidelines for Confession

There are three basic types of confession.

Immediate confession. We make this confession just as soon as we recognize that we have sinned. Simple prayers that focus on letting go of the sin are most effective. "Lord, forgive me. I surrender this sin and its consequences to your grace and mercy. Guard my steps and deliver me from evil." Such a prayer moves us beyond merely acknowledging that we have done wrong. It guides our focus to the means God has given us to repent and be transformed.

End-of-day confession. As we prepare for bed, a few moments in prayerful reflection on the day will bring our sins to mind. Here again, we agree with God that we have lived in ways unworthy of citizens of his eternal kingdom, unworthy of his royal children. Then we release them with prayers of thanksgiving and praise for God's infinite mercy.

Whole-life confession. This type of confession focuses on releasing significant life-pattern sins. This often occurs in seasons of crisis and/or spiritual awakening in an individual's life and in community-wide revivals. This confession is a liturgical tradition undertaken with a spiritual director, in which a person moves systematically through the stages of her life, asking God to bring to mind any sins she has committed so that she can confess and release them. It is a powerful, demanding exercise, not to be undertaken by the fainthearted. But seeing God's mercy cover all our sin can be one of the most liberating experiences of the soul.[2]

I was talking with a man who went through a whole-life confession with a spiritual director. He described the process, which took an entire day. He was asked to write his sins by decades, beginning with his earliest childhood memories. Before beginning, his spiritual director (mentor) prayed for the Spirit to open his memory for the sake of releasing God's grace into his past. Then the man was given a period of time to record all the sins he could remember committing during a ten-year period: birth to ten; eleven to twenty; and so on. After time alone in prayer and writing, the man would meet again with his director and read what was on the paper, adding any other sins that came to mind as they talked. A very simple prayer concluded each segment: "O Lord, I confess these sins to you. Forgive me in the name of and for the sake of Jesus Christ." The man then put the paper in a metal brazier and burned it. Then he would undertake the next decade. When he had gone through his entire life, they read together Psalm 19:12-14:

> *Who can discern his errors?*
> *Forgive my hidden faults.*
> *Keep your servant also from willful sins;*
> *may they not rule over me.*
> *Then will I be blameless,*
> *innocent of great transgression.*
> *May the words of my mouth and the meditation of my heart*
> *be pleasing in your sight,*
> *O Lord, my Rock and my Redeemer.*

Then they took the ashes outside and scattered them across the lawn.

"Now, regather your papers and read them to me," instructed his spiritual director. The absurdity of the request was immediately apparent. "Such is the grace of God," said his director. "When these sins come to mind—and they will—remember this moment. They are ashes, consumed by holy fire, covered by the blood of the cross of Christ, and scattered on the winds of the Spirit."

Some people, primarily of the Protestant tradition, may resist this practice as "smacking of Roman Catholic legalism," concerned that the confession may be viewed as a means of merit through the mediation of a priest. This is *not* what has happened here. A whole-life confession, as with any other confession, is not a means to earning forgiveness. It is a means to experiencing the presence of God through the grace that covers all our sins in Christ.

What If You Keep Remembering Your Sins?

Many of us have been taught that we haven't truly forgiven ourselves or been forgiven by God unless we can obliterate the memory of the sin. If we look at it this way, it is then deeply troubling to have the memory of a sin come to mind. If a sin is truly forgiven, why can't it be forgotten? Because forgetting would deprive us of the two greatest lessons of sin: the lesson of our continuing need for God and the lesson of God's continuing flow of grace, transforming sin into a means of growth. We remember our sin, not for punishment, but for the sake of learning from our mistakes. If we didn't remember the pain of being burned, we might continue to toy with fire.

I have spent so much time dealing with confession and forgiveness because my experience leads me to believe that this is the single most significant boulder damming the living waters of spiritual vitality in the lives of most believers. An anemic theology leaves them shackled by the chains of guilt and shame. The truth sets them free to live in the vibrancy of grace. As a result of this liberation from sin, new gratitude gives us energy to continue our journey with God and our process of soulshaping.

HOW IS REPENTANCE DIFFERENT FROM CONFESSION?

A Sunday school teacher asked her class what was meant by the word *repentance*. One child spoke up, "It is being sorry for your sins." "No," said another child, "it's also being sorry enough to quit."

In recent reports of revival on college campuses, one of the most profound testimonies of change has been the public confession of sin accompanied by acts of genuine repentance. The students have brought items such as drugs and damaging books, magazines, and music CDs to the chapel services and thrown them into huge trash bags. They have also sought reconciliation in relationships and made restitution in cases of stealing, and confession to professors in cases of cheating. Such actions reveal that God is at work, setting people free from the materials and practices that have drained their lives of spiritual health and energy.

It is difficult to decide whether repentance precedes confession or if confession comes first. My own sense is that the awareness of sin stirs confession and repentance simultaneously. I have explored confession first because I find that the ointment of grace rejuvenates the soul and motivates the deep longing for change that is repentance.

Repentance *(metanoia)* literally means "a change of mind." It describes a decision of the will to turn in a different direction. We could say that repentance verifies our confession. If we don't change our direction, the confession has offered little more than a few moments' relief, not life change.

We see this process of public confession followed by specific acts of repentance in Ephesus, following the preaching of Paul. "Many of those who believed now came and openly confessed their evil deeds. A number who had practiced sorcery brought their scrolls together and burned them publicly. When they calculated the value of the scrolls, the total came to fifty thousand drachmas [well over ten thousand dollars, with a drachma being the standard wage for a single day]. In this way the word of the Lord spread widely and grew in power" (Acts 19:18-20). The bonfire of books not only gave physical light to the city, but it shone as a beacon of truth. Like a lighthouse in a storm, it showed the way home for many people lost in dark, dangerous waters.

The essence of repentance is agreeing that God's grace is sufficient not only for the past but for the present and future choices we will make. Again, repentance is best served not by a dogged exercise of willpower but by yielding to God's spirit and cultivating a vision of the kind of person God is calling us to be in Christ. Repentance says, "Lord, I know you want to transform me. You are awakening in me this desire to change. I can do better for you, for myself, and for others. So work in my heart, by your Spirit."

Repentance is most effective when we are fed up with our sin. When we see how we are being cheated by sin, deceived by trifling trinkets when we have the right to heavenly treasures, we cry out for power to live as new creatures.

BREAKING FREE FROM SIN THROUGH REPENTANCE AND CONFESSION

Many years ago I met a man who had broken free from sexual temptation by one very specific act of repentance.

"I had a collection of 'adult' magazines," he said, "which I kept for a while, even after becoming a Christian. I tried not to look at them, but I had nearly every issue they published, and—I know this sounds ridiculous—they were valuable as collectors' items. I didn't want to burn them or just throw them away. But the Lord wouldn't let me alone. I continued to struggle until I finally threw out the whole batch."

Repentance is a process of allowing God to search our hearts and set us on a different course. For some, it means throwing things away. For others, it means breaking the control of habits that distract them from God's grace and presence. For others, it means making a decision to tell themselves the truth for the first time in their lives and get the help they need.

Guidelines for Repentance

Repentance happens in two distinct steps and is reinforced by a third.

Choose to renounce the sinful behavior.   Even as the Ephesians burned their scrolls and Eric discarded his magazines, so one who repents makes an intentional break with sinful items, habits, behaviors, and actions. This can be done with a simple—yet extremely powerful—prayer in which one says, "In the name of Jesus Christ, I confess and renounce the sin of [fill in the specific sin]. I declare that I no longer desire to participate in this in thought, word, or deed. I rely upon the grace and indwelling power of the Holy Spirit to set me free and conform me to the image of Jesus Christ."

Choose a new behavior that honors God, others, and yourself.   Eric committed himself anew to his marriage and to Bible study. Recall the parable of Jesus that warned against halfway repentance. He told of the spirit that was cast out returning to the 'house' (i.e., the person) he had left and finding the house clean and swept and put in order, but nothing had been done to fill the house with the protection and power to resist the evil spirit—so it returned with seven other spirits. "And the final condition of that man is worse than the first" (Luke 11:26). It isn't enough to part with sin—we must embrace God to be safe!

Make yourself accountable.   For breaking the toughest sin patterns in our lives, we need to rely on other people for support and accountability. We may choose one person or a small group. But it's important that we realize we cannot go it alone. I have two friends who have developed what they call a "provoking friendship." They have taken to heart the message of Hebrews 10:24: "Provoke one another to love and good deeds" (NRSV). They ask each other several simple questions: "Is there anything you have done today that has dishonored Christ? Is there anything that God has called you to do that you have refused to do? And finally, have you lied to me?"

"Just knowing that we're going to ask each other those questions each day or once a week has the power to quench many temptations," said John. "I can chart specific changes in my thoughts, words, and conduct to when Jeff and I began asking each other these questions."

Guilt is one of the most powerful forces cutting us off from the sense of God's presence. As we deal with it head-on through confession and repentance, we see how it becomes a doorway to grace and a catalyst for change. But other forces besides guilt drain us spiritually and distract us from taking care of our souls. In terms of sheer power over us, anxiety is next in line, and it is the topic of chapter 8.

NOTES

1. C. S. Lewis, *The Screwtape Letters* (New York: Macmillan, 1954), 138–139.
2. I believe that God, in his mercy, allows much of our sin to remain hidden from our view lest we be totally overwhelmed. See Isaiah 6:5; also the references to hidden faults, in Psalm 19:12, and faults we cannot detect, in 1 Corinthians 4:3-4.

SOUL-SEARCHING

Questions for Reflection and Discussion

1. This chapter described guilt as "the fever of the soul." What does that mean? What is the spiritual role of guilt in our lives?

2. How would you describe your experience with guilt?

   a) I am very sensitive to guilt, often struggling with feeling unforgiven.

   b) I occasionally wrestle with guilt, but I'm not deeply troubled by it.

   c) Guilt? What's that?! I really don't think about it much.

3. What is the difference between genuine guilt and false guilt? Can you give an example of an area in which you have experienced false guilt? How have you (or could you) release that false guilt in a healthy way?

4. What is the purpose of confession? How would you rate your practice of confession in your relationship with God? In your relationship with others? Are there any specific steps you would like to take now?

5. How does repentance affect the way we deal with sinful habits?

6. Is there a specific area in which you would like to change direction? How would you complete the following steps recommended in the chapter:

   a) What sinful behavior do you need to renounce? Be as specific as possible.

   b) Choose a new behavior. Describe your new behavior to yourself in as much detail as possible. (Remember, the key to change is vision, not simply willpower.)

   c) How will you be accountable for this life change?

CHAPTER EIGHT

Living beyond Worry

🌿 PREVIEW
🌿 REVIEW

THE phone rang at 2:05 A.M., jarring me from a deep sleep. "Pastor Rumford?" began a man's voice.

"Yes?"

"Were my sister and her husband at church this evening?"

I told him that in the midst of having a dinner and service with over three hundred people present, plus children's and youth activities, I honestly couldn't recall seeing them, but that wouldn't be unusual.

"Well, they took our son with them, and they never came home. We haven't heard from them."

I was stunned. This man was talking calmly—but I could hear the emotion in his voice, with his wife making comments in the background. I couldn't imagine what situation could account for the disappearance of this wonderful family. I gave him the name of one person I knew who is close to this family and would most likely have seen them, and we prayed for God's grace and mercy in this situation.

After hanging up, I called a member of our church staff, who said she hadn't seen them. I hung up the phone, and a fearful chill gripped my heart. My wife, Sarah, was awake, so we prayed and tried to go back to sleep. What could have happened? My mind ranged through possible explanations, none of which were pleasant.

Finally, I just said to the Lord, "Lord, I cannot do anything about this, but you can do everything. So it's up to you. You love that family. Be their shepherd." I felt some relief. Shortly, I was asleep.

The first thing on my mind as I awakened a few hours later was this family. I called their home from my office and got an answering machine. I left a message and hung up—baffled. A few hours later, Sarah called.

"It's good news," she began. "They are all right. Just as they were heading down to the church, they got a call on their cellular phone that one of their dearest friends, who lives in another city, had been killed in an accident. They dropped off the children with a relative and drove to be with their friend's widow. The relative thought they had called the other child's parents to let them know she was keeping the children for the night. Everyone's fine, and they are deeply sorry about the misunderstanding."

What looked like a horrific crisis was simply a communication problem! Now, before you spend too much time trying to figure out how this particular mix-up occurred, just think about the response you felt as you started reading this story. Were you calm and confident that everything was fine? Or were you concerned that something had definitely gone wrong? Most of us respond in the latter way, anticipating the worst.

Lewis Thomas, scientist-philosopher, described us best when he said, "We are, perhaps, uniquely among earth's creatures, the worrying animal. We worry away our lives, fearing the future, discontent with the present, unable to take in the idea of dying, unable to sit still."1

Worry interrupts our sense of God's presence. It chokes off the breath of the Spirit. The word *worry* is derived from an Old English word *wyrgan*, which means "to strangle, to choke." It was used to describe the attack of an animal that would tear, bite, or snap, especially at the throat. It could also be used to describe shaking or pulling with the teeth, e.g., a dog shaking its victim.

These images lend us valuable insight as we consider the effect of worry on the human spirit. When we allow ourselves to be caught in the jaws of worry and anxiety, our spirit is choked, our energy is drained, and our enthusiasm is stifled.

Anxiety overwhelms and distracts us, turning our attention from confidence in God to concern with what we can or cannot do about our circumstances. We increase our spiritual energy when we bring worry under the dominion of the Spirit. We do this through what I call the twin disciplines of preview and review. As with all spiritual exercises, these move us from mere knowledge into tangible action. We will consider several specific steps we can take on a daily basis to release our cares to God and thus cultivate confidence in his power and purposes for us.

DEVELOPING THE HABIT OF EXPECTATION

Previewing is the practice of spiritual preparation by which we intentionally remind ourselves of God's presence and promises *before* we enter specific situations. This practice is illustrated frequently in the Scriptures, as God prepared his servants for specific tasks. Some of the most vivid examples occur with the prophets. My favorite is the time when the king of Syria set out to ambush Elisha because the prophet kept warning Israel of Syria's battle plans. One morning, Elisha's servant arose and looked outside to see an army of Syrians surrounding the city. When he reported this threat to Elisha, the prophet was calm. "Fear not," Elisha said, "for those who are with us are more than those who are with them." He then prayed that the servant's eyes would be opened to see the spiritual reality in the midst of the earthly crisis. "So the Lord opened the eyes of the young man, and he saw; and behold, the mountain was full of horses and chariots of fire round about Elisha" (2 Kings 6:15-17, RSV). Elisha, a spiritual veteran, had learned to expect God's help, and the heavenly army was already visible to him!

The point is to learn to "see" the spiritual reality at work in the midst of all our daily activities. Our experience may not be as dramatic as that of Elisha and his servant, but it can be just as real.

---

*T*he point is to learn to "see" the spiritual reality at work in the midst of all our daily activities.

If This Is the Day the Lord Has Made, What Will It Be Like?

I suggest that you rise fifteen minutes earlier than usual and go to a place where you can pray and meditate with your calendar and journal. Look at the day ahead, asking yourself, "How would this day be different if Jesus were physically present with me?" What people will you see? What projects will you work on? What appointments do you have? What difficult situations will you be facing? What are you really looking forward to doing? Bring these, one by one, before the Lord, picturing him literally present with you. As you do this, you will find yourself bathing these situations in prayer. You will also discover ideas and options you had never considered before. And I believe you will enter your day with a refreshing sense of anticipation and expectancy, with the prayer request that Jesus Christ make his presence known in all things.

This can also be practiced in the midst of the day. When I have a difficult phone call to make, I often preview the conversation. I anticipate it in order to script it with Christ. I ask, "Lord, what do you want me to say, and how do you want me to say it? Give me the opening line. How do I start this conversation?" This kind of preview has made a tremendous difference in my life. I remember calling one woman who had expressed some strong criticism toward a staff member. I kept putting off the call because I didn't want to face the anger that I thought would come. When I finally could delay no longer, I took a few minutes for this kind of prayer. As I pictured Jesus making the call, I knew—I'm not sure how, but I just knew—that this person was having a very difficult time this very day. I switched gears from calling as an "administrator" who had to deal with a "customer complaint" to being a pastor calling a person in need.

"I can't believe you called today," she said when I called. "This is one of the worst days of my life. I never thought it would be this bad." She went on to tell me that her former husband was getting married that day and that her grown children were all attending the wedding, leaving her desperately alone. We talked and prayed; then as the conversation was coming to a close, I mentioned that I knew she had a concern about a staff member. "Well, I think we can work things out. I think I overreacted— with all that's been going on emotionally these past few months. I'll give him a call next week." Words cannot express the power of God in the midst of that phone call. I shudder to recall my own hard feelings and frustration as I had contemplated calling her, until I took time to prayerfully preview the conversation with the Lord.

I have seen this process work in counseling, church meetings, community activities, and family situations. Our prayers invite

God to be more active in the midst of ordinary things. We then go through our days with a holy curiosity, looking for the signs of God's presence. David and Karen Mains use the term "going on a God hunt" to describe this active expectancy that searches for God's activity in each day. Where did you see God today, and what did he do?

---

*W*e then go through our days with a holy curiosity, looking for the signs of God's presence.

Guidelines for Preview

Give yourself an additional fifteen minutes at the start of the day with your Bible, journal, and calendar. This may be before or after your devotions. The value of doing this at the beginning of the day is that it sets the tone for all you will encounter.

Focus on today's plans only. Jesus exhorted us, "So do not worry about tomorrow, for tomorrow will bring worries of its own. Today's trouble is enough for today" (Matt. 6:34, NRSV). Though Jesus' emphasis here is trouble, this is wise counsel for all aspects of planning. Consider what relationships you will be in today: at home, at work, at school, traveling, shopping, and in the neighborhood. Consider your responsibilities and appointments. What does today hold—to the best of your knowledge at this time?

Invite Jesus to walk with you through your day. See him alongside you in conversations, meetings, and activities. How will you interact with others in light of Christ's presence in, with, and through you? Write in your journal any insights or ideas that come to you. In the midst of this process, I have gotten ideas for solving prob-

lems or how to process a difficult issue or things I can do with
my children that I hadn't thought of before. I have also had
names of people come to mind that I hadn't thought about for
some time. I write them down and try either to call them or to
drop them a simple note. It is a powerful blessing to call or
write, saying, "You came to mind as I was praying this morning.
Just want you to know I care."

Surrender yourself and your plans to the Lord.   This activity must
be guided by the counsel of James:

> *Now listen, you who say, "Today or tomorrow we will go to this or
> that city, spend a year there, carry on business and make money."
> Why, you do not even know what will happen tomorrow. What is
> your life? You are a mist that appears for a little while and then
> vanishes. Instead, you ought to say, "If it is the Lord's will, we will
> live and do this or that." (Jas. 4:13-15)*

Our primary goal in this time of preview is to make ourselves
available to God. We give our day to him, asking him to
"redeem the time" (see Eph. 5:16; Col. 4:5). We make our best
plans but yield to God's sovereign direction of our lives. We
trust him to bring divine appointments to us throughout the
day.

As you practice this simple exercise, the sense of God's presence and guidance will come more easily throughout the day.
You will hold your schedule more loosely and be looking for
God not only in what you planned but also, more important, in
the interruptions. As Dietrich Bonhoeffer writes:

> We must be ready to allow ourselves to be interrupted by
> God. God will be constantly crossing our paths and cancel-
> ing our plans by sending us people with claims and peti-

tions. We may pass them by, preoccupied with our more important tasks, as the priest passed by the man who had fallen among thieves, perhaps—reading the Bible. When we do that we pass by the visible sign of the Cross raised athwart our path to show us that, not our way, but God's way must be done. It is a strange fact that Christians and even ministers frequently consider their work so important and urgent that they will allow nothing to disturb them. They think they are doing God a service in this, but actually they are disdaining God's "crooked yet straight path" (Gottfried Arnold). They do not want a life that is crossed and balked. But it is part of the discipline of humility that we must not spare our hand where it can perform a service and that we do not assume that our schedule is our own to manage, but allow it to be arranged by God.[2]

LOOKING BACK IN ORDER TO SEE AHEAD MORE CLEARLY

We can begin our day by previewing situations in which we ask God to help us and expect to see him work. But what happens when we're settling at the end of the day? This is a perfect time to look back at the day with a view to seeing how God worked—what we looked for as well as what we didn't anticipate. This practice is not only good for day's end but over longer periods of time. The people of Israel built review into their songs, their prayers, and their worship. The Passover feast was given to command the people to a yearly remembrance of God's mighty works (Exod. 12:12). This practice formed the basis for all their annual festivals. It was David's review of past deliverance that gave him the confidence to endure present difficulties. When he faced death at the hands of the Philistines, the Lord delivered him. In response, he composed this psalm, which includes these verses.

*I sought the Lord and he answered me, and delivered me from all
my fears.*

Look to him, and be radiant; so your faces shall never be ashamed.

*This poor man cried, and the Lord heard him, and saved him out
of all his troubles.*

*The angel of the Lord encamps around those who fear him, and
delivers them.*

*Many are the afflictions of the righteous; but the Lord delivers him
out of them all.* Psalm 34:4-7, 19, RSV

When I came home from church one day, one of our sons, Tim,
said, "Dad, I had a God-sighting today!" He went on to tell me
that he'd had a problem getting to soccer practice that day.
Since we have four children, a daughter and three sons, all of
whom are active in school and sports, we sometimes get schedule conflicts that make us feel more like air traffic controllers
than parents. Neither Sarah nor I could drive Tim to practice, so
he rode the two miles on his bike. But when he got to the school
practice field, no one was there. Then he remembered: The practice had been rescheduled across town! He was wondering what
to do when the mother of one of the other soccer players drove
into the lot. She knew soccer practice was at a different location,
but she thought some of the boys might have forgotten. She put
Tim's bike in her van, drove him to practice, and then brought
him home after practice, since Sarah would have had no idea
about the change. Tim was smiling ear to ear as he finished his
story, "The Lord didn't leave me alone at the playground. I got a
ride across town."

What could have been just another irritation and a coinciden-
tal solution in a boy's ordinary day had become a window
through which Tim saw God working. What would our churches
be like if all of us cultivated such sensitivity and thanksgiving?
How would it change your life if you looked for God before you

157

encountered situations and then again when those situations have passed? How would this discipline affect your overall outlook on the challenges, irritations, and small victories of each day?

Guidelines for Review

Give yourself fifteen minutes at the end of the day with your Bible, journal, and calendar. The purpose of this time is to walk back through the day in quiet reflection.

Write in your journal the highlights and lowlights of the day. I have a friend who uses the term "peaks and pits" to describe the events of the day. You may only have time for one or two. Don't get bogged down in a catalog of all that happened that day—or this exercise will become a heavy burden. Answer the question "Where did I see the hand of God today?" or "Where did I have a hard time seeing the hand of God today?"

Pray and reflect over the situations or incidents you have highlighted. As you do, focus on three primary actions: thanksgiving, confession, and instruction. Take time to thank God for his care and provision. Confess and release your sin and regret. Then ask, "Lord, what were you trying to teach me?"

Prepare your materials for the next morning. Do what you can at night to make it easier to get started in the morning. Most of us have a difficult time getting up and at our morning exercises. If we cannot find our Bible, journal, or calendar, we will most likely say, "Oh, forget it!" and go back to bed or on to other matters.

As you practice the simple exercise of review, you will learn to recognize the ways God's grace, presence, and power are woven throughout each day. Special moments, too quickly forgotten, will be remembered and savored. They will become the food that nourishes stronger faith. I think this is one aspect of what David meant when he said,

> *Be angry, but sin not;*
> *commune with your own hearts on your beds and be silent.*
> *Offer right sacrifices,*
> *and put your trust in the Lord.*

> PSALM 4:6, RSV

Anxious people are three times miserable: They miss the best in life, anticipate the worst, and are especially nervous when things are just perking along. As Corrie ten Boom says, "Worry does not empty tomorrow of its sorrow; it empties today of its strength." The disciplines of this chapter help us overcome worry by learning to focus on the presence of God in the thick of things.

God is at work in everything. Preview and review teach us to anticipate with Christ. *This is more than a matter of making prayer requests and tracking the answers.* In previewing and reviewing we are heightening our awareness of God's activity in our lives—even in situations where it surprises us or appears in a different form than we had expected. And as we look for God and listen for him, we become conscious participants with him as he works in others' lives and our own.

NOTES

1. *The Medusa & the Snail,* quoted in *Bartlett's Familiar Quotations,* 15th ed., ed. Emily Morison Beck (Boston: Little, Brown, 1980), 884.
2. Dietrich Bonhoeffer, *Life Together* (New York: Harper & Row, 1954), 99.

SOUL-SEARCHING

Questions for Reflection and Discussion

1. In what area(s) are you most vulnerable to worry? What are your most frequent areas of worry? How does worry affect your spiritual life?

2. In addition to releasing our worries to God in prayer (see Philippians 4:6-7), this chapter suggests that we be proactive through the spiritual exercise of *previewing,* in which we picture Christ with us, giving us victory over specific areas of worry. How do you react to this suggestion?

    a) It strikes me as a lot of work for nothing.

    b) I don't understand the point of it; what difference could this make?

    c) I am intrigued by the possibility of turning the power of my thought life from dwelling on what could go wrong to dwelling on what God could do.

3. We are encouraged to "go through our days with a holy curiosity, looking for the signs of God's presence." Reflect on the past week. When did you see God at work? What happened?

4. God's people had a number of festivals to celebrate God's mighty works in their lives. In addition to Passover (the Feast of Unleavened Bread), the Feast of Booths, or Tabernacles, (Leviticus 23:34) commemorated God's sustaining of Israel in the wilderness; the Feast of Purim (Esther 9) commemorated their deliverance from the threat of genocide; the Feast of Weeks, later known as Pentecost (Exodus 23:16), commemorated the first fruits of the harvest; the Day of Atonement (Leviticus 23:26-31) celebrated God's mercy. If you were to develop your own personal yearly calendar of feasts, what "holy days" would you have to commemorate God's work in your life? Consider your conversion

experience, anniversaries, times of special provision by God, and times of special service to God. List these and consider how you could celebrate them over the course of a year.

5. Which exercise, *previewing* or *reviewing,* would be most helpful in your spiritual life at this time? Why? Reread the material on that exercise and practice it for a set period of time (such as three days a week for two weeks), using the guidelines. Reflect in your journal how the exercise affected your spiritual vitality over that period of time.

CHAPTER NINE

The Daring Dialogue

🌿 PRAYER

Lois Main returned to her home in her little town, following a three-day spiritual retreat. She was eager to share the new insights she'd gained, especially about prayer.

The next day was Sunday. When she awakened, she felt strangely depressed. She attributed it to the letdown after her retreat. But when she went to church, she met other women who felt the same way. One woman said, "It feels as if there are children in trouble."

The odd feeling stayed with the women throughout the day, and that night at evening services they continued to pray for whatever was causing the mysterious sense of urgency. It was after midnight when they left the church.

Lois went home. But she couldn't get to sleep. Was God trying to tell her something?

The ominous feeling grew stronger. Then, she seemed to hear God speaking insistently to her, "Pray for the people [of this town] . . . get out and pray for my children. Now."

"Yes, Lord." She dressed and went out into the starlit night. She began walking down all the streets of the town, praying, "O Lord, protect the people; watch over the children." She walked past the shopping plaza, the pharmacy, the jewelry store, the inn.

At 5:30 A.M., Lois slipped back into bed for a few moments' rest, feeling that she had done what God asked her to do.

Soon, the town was awake, beginning its Monday morning activities. Little did they realize what lay ahead for them that day. The town was Coalinga, California. At 4:42 that afternoon, May 2, 1983, an earthquake struck the area with such force that nearly every building was destroyed. A *Guideposts* article relates, "At the Coalinga Hospital, the doctors geared up for an expected onslaught of victims. Instead of an onslaught, however, only 25 people came—and most of them with minor injuries. The most severe casualty was a man with two broken legs. *Not one life was lost!*"

In the days that followed, Lois learned that two other women had also received the urgent message "Pray for my people." They, too, had left their beds to pray through the town.

Their prayers were heard.[1]

Prayer is our essential connection with God. We often approach prayer as an exercise rather than an actual conversation with a heavenly Father who loves us, waits to hear from us, and has much to say to us—if only we will apply ourselves to listening.

STAGE ONE: MONOLOGUE

Most of us move through several developmental stages of prayer. The process is not the same for everyone, but there are three general "levels" of prayer that apply to all of us.

First, as new believers, we think of prayer as "talking to God," with the emphasis on *to*. Prayer at this level is a one-sided conversation. We inform God of our needs or the needs of others. We may take a few moments to thank him, but the content of the prayer is request driven. We are also inclined to include instructions as to how God might best answer our prayers! A person at this level can have a vital prayer life. The Lord is merciful, often answering such prayers in wonderful ways. But we need to see that prayer at this stage is incomplete in terms of developing our sensitivity to God's presence.

At some point, our prayer moves beyond being request driven as we develop a more complete repertoire of communication with God. We discover that there are a number of elements to prayer in addition to petition. This broader concept of prayer is seen most clearly in the Lord's Prayer. Jesus gave us the Lord's Prayer not only as a specific text to be recited but also as a model for expanded prayer. The Lord's Prayer is the greatest prayer known to humanity. These few words span the spectrum of divine purpose and human concerns. They sweep from the majesty of God in heaven to the earthly details of daily bread. This prayer upholds the highest ideals for men, women, and children, while recognizing the realistic obstacles of human temptations and failure. It searches us, instructs us, inspires us, and empowers us to become all God intended us to be.

Jesus' Prayer Model: The Lord's Prayer (Matt. 6:9-13, NKJV)

"Our Father in heaven."   We celebrate and stand secure in our identity and relationship with the Giver of Life and all things. If your father or mother has not "measured up," you can be "reparented" by the Lord, who gave us new life in Christ. What does it mean to me today, in the midst of things, that I am a child of God? God is eager to be in fellowship with me as his own child. As Archbishop Trench says, "We must not conceive of prayer as overcoming God's reluctance, but as laying hold of his highest willingness."

Not only is God close enough to care, God is great enough to help. Before I pray, I need to remember the resources and power of God, who is above all things, unlimited by time and space and any other earthly constraints. What limits have I put on God that hinder my prayer and weaken my faith?

"Hallowed be your name."   God's honor is my highest calling. How does my lifestyle honor his name?

"Your kingdom come. Your will be done on earth as it is in heaven." God's agenda determines our agenda. What does God's kingdom look like? How would it look in my family? School? Workplace? Community? Congregation? Have I surrendered my agenda so that I can eagerly pursue his? What would Jesus do in these situations?

"Give us this day our daily bread."   God is ready to provide whatever we need this day, including our practical needs. The love that he demonstrates through providing for us in small ways gives us confidence in his provision of all our needs. What do I need today?

"And forgive us our debts, as we forgive our debtors."   The grace of God shown *to* us must show *through* us to others. One definition of forgiveness is that "I surrender my right to hurt you back."[2] If I cling to bitterness and hold grudges, my hands and heart aren't free to receive God's mercy. Whom do I need to forgive? What do I need to confess?

"And do not lead us into temptation, but deliver us from the evil one." God is the great protector and guardian of our lives. We commit ourselves to his care, arming ourselves with the full armor of God for the spiritual battle of each day. Read Ephesians 6:10-18. Where do I find opposition keeping me from the full experience of God's grace and the full implementation of God's plans? Release God's power into those areas.

"For yours is the kingdom and the power and the glory forever. Amen."
Our prayer circles around to where it began. We begin and conclude with our focus upon God. Alleluia! He has a sovereign purpose that will be established by his sovereign power for his
sublime praise.

Meditation on the specific elements of the Lord's Prayer can
lead into rich new avenues of dialogue with the Lord. It is surprising how insights come as we slow down and consider each
word and phrase.

ACTS: Another Proven Model for Prayer

Many people have found the ACTS acronym to be helpful in
reminding them of important aspects of prayer. We begin our
prayer with *adoration,* by focusing on the greatness and goodness
of God. As we express our appreciation for God, our confidence
is built for entrusting our lives to God's care. Adoration is mod-
eled for us in Psalms and in the great prayers of Scripture, as
already seen in the Lord's Prayer.

When we take the time to consider the worth of God, we can't
help but acknowledge our need for God. This leads us into *confession.* In confession we are honest with God about who we are,
what we've done and haven't done, and how much we need him.

Following our confession, we offer *thanksgiving* to God for
what he has done in our lives and in the world. Adoration
focuses on the nature and character of God, and thanksgiving
expresses our gratitude for answered prayers and for mercies we
never anticipated.

Finally, in light of our adoration, confession, and thanksgiving, we offer to God our specific needs; the formal term for this
is *supplication.* When the other three steps precede our supplication, our requests are more in line with God's character and
plans, and we are more confident that these requests will receive
God's attention.

STAGE TWO: DIALOGUE

These models guide us into a much richer prayer life, but a deeper level of prayer comes when we begin to realize that it is meant to be a dialogue, a two-way exchange of thoughts and ideas. In other words, prayer includes listening to God.

Most of us falter when it comes to listening for God's side of the prayer conversation. We hesitate because we are nervous about anything that is so subjective or that might threaten to compromise the sole authority of the Bible. We are wise to be cautious. Much damage has been done by people—even teachers—who have taken their experience as authoritative over Scripture. Yet the testimony of God's people across the centuries is that God communicates with them in prayer. We must take listening seriously when we consider God's call to Abram, Jacob's dream of a ladder, the boy Samuel hearing God call his name, and the people hearing the Father say of Jesus, "This is my Son, whom I love; with him I am well pleased." George Müller, noted for his intense prayer life in support of the Bristol orphanage, said, "The most meaningful time of prayer is the fifteen minutes *after* I say 'Amen.'"

My mother, Lillian, once told me a story that has made a deep impression on my own prayer life. She was going through a time of emotional turmoil. My father was traveling a great deal on business, and Mom felt the weight of her struggles intensified by her loneliness. Dad called every night, but it wasn't the same as his being alongside her. "I was praying in the dining room one evening while you boys were in bed," Mom said, "and I felt a hand on my shoulder. I knew it was the Lord. He said, 'I am with you, Lillian. It will be all right.' That moment changed my life. Even though things didn't get easier right away, God's presence gave me new strength."

What's interesting is that Mom was very reluctant to share that story for a number of years. She was confident of what had happened to her, but she felt that people would not accept it. They would dismiss it or devalue it—and it was too precious to her to risk that. But when she told me, I knew it was real. And when I have shared it with others, it has moved a number of people to relate similar experiences. Was it the touch of the Lord or a product of her own imagination? We have to ask ourselves, What would produce that response when she had no conscious expectation? In the final analysis, these questions are unanswerable.

The only productive questions are these:

- Did the experience bring glory and honor to the name of the Lord (truth consistent with God's Word and the experience of God's people)?
- Did the experience bear fruit in faith (belief) and faithfulness (behavior)?

Listen to the cry of your heart for the nearness of "Abba." Feel the longing of your heart for a touch. And don't be afraid to expect God's personal communication with you.

I realize that this is one of the most difficult topics in the area of spirituality. But it is precisely this difficulty that makes it so important for us to address it. As a pastor, I have found people longing to make sense of experiences such as these, for which they were never prepared, and concerning which they had never received any instruction. I hope that what I've said here will spark a holy curiosity to search the Scriptures and the thoughtful reflections of others on this subject. I believe that learning to listen will transform your prayer life from a duty to a delight.

Guidelines for Listening Prayer

Quiet yourself. This will probably be easier to do once you have said all you feel the need to say. Some people begin prayer by listening—there's no formula. What is important is your quietness before God. If there are distracting thoughts—such as errands you need to run—jot them down and forget about them (more on this subject later). You may have learned some techniques for relaxing your mind and body; use them to make yourself still.

Ask God, "Lord, if you could say anything to me right now, what would you say?" I encourage people to have their journal open, ready to write the ideas that come to mind. A word, phrase, or sentence may come. You may think immediately of a passage of Scripture. Write it down, open your Bible, and read the verses around the passage you were given.

In a moment, we will explore the objection most of us have: that what we "hear" is simply a product of our own imagination. I myself was a skeptic, but a number of experiences have convinced me that God still communicates with us in prayer. It may come as an impression, not as a direct sentence. One of my most vivid examples of this came in a time of prayer with a group led by a man I didn't know well. I had asked for prayer, and as the group was about to pray, Rich said, "Doug, this doesn't usually happen to me, but I keep thinking I am to read you Isaiah 43. To be honest, I have no idea what is in Isaiah 43, but would you mind if I read it?" Of course I didn't object—because I was absolutely stunned: I had spent that entire week memorizing Isaiah 43:1-5! How could Rich have known? Some would write this off as a coincidence. All I know is that when I take time to humble myself and listen, "coincidences" happen.

If you don't hear anything, relax and enjoy the stillness. Be assured that God *is* present. He speaks to you through Scripture and guides your life through his grace and love. Sometimes God does not speak to us; during these times we can learn to be content with his presence, with or without any message or insight.

If you don't hear anything, meditate on this question: Is there anything that keeps me from hearing God?   Maybe you haven't really stilled your own thoughts enough. Perhaps some part of you really doesn't want to hear God because you are struggling with an issue and are afraid that God will ask something of you that you don't want to do. Sometimes our enemy the devil has a high interest in "jamming the signals." Not only is prayer our way of connecting with God, it is our means of spiritual warfare (addressed in chapter 16), and Satan will try to hinder our prayers.

Make note of what God has said, and look for ways in which you can apply what you have heard.   Some people keep prayer lists, in which they write down their requests and God's answers to those requests. Others record in a journal the impressions they receive during prayer. You might write down what you have heard on an index card and carry it with you throughout the day. We really do forget most things unless we record or apply them in some way.

How to Check Your Spiritual Hearing
What does God say to us? How does he speak to us? How do we know this is not the product of an overactive imagination? We need to consider these questions carefully.[3] My simple advice is to undertake a holy experiment of asking God to speak to you. Several principles should guide you as you explore this dynamic of prayer.

1. We must not presume to ascribe to what we hear the same authority we ascribe to the Bible.   Whatever the Lord may seem to communicate with us is best considered in the light of God's Word rather than as a new revelation.

2. We must test what we hear by God's Word.   Nothing that comes from God would contradict the authoritative teaching of Scripture.

3. We must be willing to evaluate the validity of what we hear by holding it up to our experience. For example, my mother shared with my dad what she had heard, but otherwise kept it to herself. It became a word of encouragement to her as she proceeded through her situation. And it proved to be true for her.

4. If we believe we have heard some specific direction for our lives, we must seek confirmation and counsel from wise friends and spiritually mature counselors, such as pastors. One of the most unsettling problems in this area is failing to hold our experience loosely and make it available for checking and evaluation. I would encourage you to err on the side of caution, humbly asking others you know and trust what they feel about your sense of God's direction. In one case, I know of a man who felt God was leading him to make a move from business into the founding of a new ministry. He felt that faith required him to proceed in spite of the strenuous protests of his family and the loving counsel of friends. Since his move, things have never seemed "quite right." The ministry has always struggled and has borne little fruit. While we are cautious about judging this person, I think he could have proceeded far more harmoniously and, in the long run, effectively, if he had tested his sense of God's leading by opening it to the evaluation of other believers.

Sometimes God gives us a vision for a ministry, a task, or a promise, and we assume that this word is for *right now,* when, in the Lord's timing, it isn't to become manifest for some time. The counsel of wise friends, family, and counselors can prevent us from pushing the plan before its time. We do well to remember Abraham and Sarah, who ended up forcing God's promise of a son. They decided that it was time, and Abraham lay with Hagar, the handmaid, in order to bring God's plan to pass. God's plan was always true—Abraham had not heard incorrectly. But Abra-

ham and Sarah moved toward the Lord's plan in their own timing, and that brought new complications.

5. *We must be extremely careful if we think we have heard something for
someone else.*   The best approach, after careful examination of
your motives, would be to tell the person that you have been
praying for them and you wonder if these ideas make any sense
to them. It is unwise (and in some cases arrogant!) to say to
another person, "The Lord told me to tell you. . . ." Offer what is
on your mind as a loving suggestion, and then trust the person
to work through it with the Lord.

BIG THINGS HAPPEN THROUGH LITTLE PRAYERS

Some people who hear of God's answering prayers for lost
jewelry, pencils, and parking spaces find themselves wincing. It
seems like a trivialization of God's power and, more significantly,
a terrible indictment of God's priorities. They find it difficult to
understand that while tragedies are happening all around us,
God would answer a prayer for vacation reservations!

While my wife, Sarah, was at our women's conference one
year, she headed up a team of women who prayed for any
requests that the women wrote down and put in a prayer basket.
On Saturday morning, she was to give an announcement about
the prayer basket, but when the time came, she wasn't at the
meeting. The women were puzzled that Sarah was late, but they
went ahead. When Sarah came in, she was surprised that the
meeting had begun. She was late because she didn't know what
time it was; she had lost her watch. This watch was a special gift
from her parents. She had looked everywhere. It wasn't with her
jewelry; she had taken everything out of her suitcase twice,
shaken her sleeping bag—it was nowhere. She prayed about it
and decided to go ahead to the meeting.

During the message, she got a picture of a bag of cough drops next to her bed with her watch curled up at the bottom of the bag. When the meeting ended, she went back to the cabin—and found her watch in the cough drop bag—just as she had pictured!

Now some people would say, "Well, of course that happened to Sarah—she's more spiritual." Granted, she is an earnest prayer warrior, but she doesn't believe she's any different from anyone else. She's not sure how this sort of thing happens, but we are both convinced it was a "love gift" from God. It gave her great confidence as she prayed for requests large and small from the women on the retreat. Her testimony was a great encouragement to many people there.

Love is known best in the small things. I am most deeply touched *not* by Sarah's gifts on my birthday but by the little notes she slips into my suitcase. I am most encouraged by the people who take time to know and appreciate the little idiosyncrasies that make me who I am. A couple in our congregation heard that I really like apricot nectar. Periodically we will open our front door to find a can of apricot nectar sitting on our porch. What joy and affirmation comes in that gift!

God's love reveals itself in the little things. God is not too big to care; he's too big to fail. More than a few spiritual pilgrims have impeded their own progress by thinking that God really cannot be concerned about the little things.

It's most helpful to me to realize, first of all, that God's power and care are infinite; they are not diminished or distracted or diverted by a large number of requests coming from infinite petitions. We cannot conclude that a robbery wouldn't have occurred if God had been paying attention to that situation instead of to my "little request." How are we supposed to know when really important tragedies are happening? And who measures what is important to us? And what of the exhortations in

Scripture, "Have no anxiety about *anything,* but in *everything* by prayer and supplication with thanksgiving let your requests be made known to God" (Phil. 4:6, RSV, italics added) or "Cast *all* your anxieties on him, for he cares about you" (1 Peter 5:7, RSV, italics added)?

Why does God answer small prayers? To encourage us so that we can be strong for our own struggles. So that we are refreshed and can stand alongside others who are afflicted and encourage them in confidence that God cares about the important matters in their lives. Love and confidence are best cultivated in the little things, in the attention to detail that inspires the confidence to trust in "the big stuff."

STAGE THREE: UNCEASING PRAYER

A high school student walked up to me after church one day and said he needed help understanding what he called "the most discouraging passage of Scripture" he'd ever read. I silently prepared myself for a discussion on election (such as Romans 9) or the fear of losing our salvation (such as Hebrews 6) or our call to "Be perfect, therefore, as [our] heavenly Father is perfect" (Matthew 5.10). I was taken aback when he said, "Pray constantly" (1 Thessalonians 5:17, RSV).

Barry put the dilemma very succinctly: "Well, if I do what this verse says, I'll never get anything else done. And if I try to do the things I have to do, like study algebra and chemistry, I can't be praying all the time!"

Now, some people would say that this verse is merely setting a high ideal and it shouldn't be taken literally. They would paraphrase it to mean, "Do your best to pray often, any time of day." I tended to follow this interpretation myself, but I am beginning to see that there are ways to develop a habit of ongoing prayer that move us closer to the ideal.

The Jesus Prayer

My journey into more constant prayer began with learning from a fellow Protestant about "The Jesus Prayer," developed in Russian Orthodox spirituality. In his book on Calvinist spirituality, *Space for God,* Don Postema presents "mental prayer," which can be practiced not only in a monastic cell but by a layperson active in the demands of daily life.

> The constant inner prayer of Jesus is an unbroken, perpetual calling upon the divine name of Jesus with the lips, the mind and the heart, while picturing his lasting presence in my imagination and imploring his grace wherever I am, in whatever I do, even while I sleep. This prayer consists of the following words: "Lord Jesus Christ, have mercy on me."[4]

When I first read about this, I had two problems with it. First of all, the repetition of it reminded me of what Jesus said about the mindless repeating of prayers. Jesus was quite clear that we do not have to badger God with incessant chatter, saying what we want over and over again (Matt. 6:7).

But I am learning that we must not be simplistic in our understanding of repetition. There are numerous examples in the Bible of vital prayer that went over the same ground time and again. David prayed for seven days for God to spare the life of the child Bathsheba had conceived through adultery with him. He must have pleaded with God over and over again (2 Sam. 12:16-23). Paul prayed the same prayer three times to be released from his thorn in the flesh (2 Cor. 12:8). The problem is not with saying something over and over again—otherwise what do we make of our daily repetitions of the Lord's Prayer? The problem enters when the repetitions are viewed either as meritorious in earning God's attention or as magical manipulations that can coerce God's action.

I have come to see that the Jesus Prayer is not a means of stirring God to action but rather a way of stimulating my faith through a deeper awareness of God's grace. It stirs my faith as I bathe the day with a prayer for mercy—mercy shown in forgiving my sin, in providing for my needs, in guiding the small steps of my daily routine, in protecting me from unseen dangers, in sustaining me through problems, disappointments, and suffering, and in empowering me for God's service. In all things I want the mercy of God through Jesus Christ.

A second related concern I had was the mantralike quality of the prayer. A mantra is "a symbolic sound causing an internal vibration which helps to concentrate the mind and aids self-realization, e.g., the repeated syllable 'om.'"[5] Was this Jesus Prayer a subtle infiltration of Eastern religion, contaminating and detracting from biblical practice? Several considerations helped me work through this. First, the Jesus Prayer is a legitimate prayer; it is not a meaningless sound. Second, it is not repeated for the sake of "vibrations" to bring me into harmony with the universe. It is repeated in order to awaken my often distracted heart to the working of God's mercy in my life. But one additional insight moved me over the line to embrace this concept. The Jesus Prayer is a powerful way to affect the "inner dialogue" that is always running through our minds anyway! It takes advantage of the "self-talk" principle.

We usually speak aloud at the rate of 150–200 words per minute. What we may not realize is that we constantly talk privately to ourselves at the rate of approximately 1,300 words per minute![6] This self-talk shapes our thoughts, feelings, and behavior. Many spiritual teachers see the careful stewardship of our self-talk as a primary source of spiritual and mental health. People's attitudes change for the better when they exchange negative self-talk, such as "I always fail; I'm just no good," for positive affirmations such as, "I am loved by God and can do, by his strength, whatever he calls me to do." This much I know: When my mind is filled with prayer, including the simple, powerful words of the Jesus Prayer, much useless, empty, even destructive self-talk is driven from my mind. I think such a practice as this is at least one major aspect of Paul's exhortation in Philippians 4:8: "Finally, brothers [and sisters], whatever is true, whatever is noble, whatever is right, whatever is pure, whatever is lovely, what-ever is admirable—if anything is excellent or praiseworthy— think about such things."

The Way of the Pilgrim, the book from Russian Orthodox mysti-cism that presents the Jesus Prayer, instructs the seeker:

> Take a seat in solitude and silence. Bend your head, close your eyes, and breathing softly, in your imagination, look into your own heart. Let your mind, or rather, your thoughts, flow from your head down to your heart and say, while breathing: "Lord Jesus Christ, have mercy on me." Whisper these words gently, or say them in your mind. Dis-card all other thoughts. Be serene, persevering and repeat them over and over again.[7]

The pilgrim practices the prayer over and over for a period of days, increasing the frequency from three thousand times a day to twelve thousand times. "[Soon] my lips and tongue recited the words without any effort on my part. I spent the whole day experiencing great happiness. I began to feel that the Prayer had, so to speak, passed to my heart."[8]

If you feel resistance toward this practice, consider the power of songs to make their way into our mind so that we say we can't get them out of our head. This is a manifestation of the human capacity of self-talk, of an active mind that is in continual motion. The Jesus Prayer is an intentional effort to program spir-itually revitalizing material into our minds.

---

*T*he Jesus Prayer is an intentional effort to program spiritually revitalizing material into our minds.

This model of continual prayer need not be limited to the
Jesus Prayer. We can fill our hearts with any of the simple verses
of Scripture, saying them over and over as a way of filling our
hearts. It helps if they are brief and have a sense of rhythm to
them. "I can do all things through Christ who strengthens me"
(Phil. 4:13, NKJV); "Cast all your anxiety on him because he cares
for you" (1 Pet. 5:7). The Beatitudes of Matthew 5:3-10 are also
appropriate. Each person can have the joy of weaving a meaningful verse into the fabric of each day through conscious repetition. Eventually, these prayers will come to mind "on their own"
without conscious effort—even as we find other less-than-desir-
able thoughts arriving without invitation. It's all part of the process Jesus described when he said, "For out of the abundance of
the heart the mouth speaks. The good person brings good
things out of a good treasure, and the evil person brings evil
things out of an evil treasure" (Matt. 12:34-35, NRSV). Unceasing
prayer is a means of storing new treasures in our hearts.

---

*U*nceasing prayer is a means of storing new treasures in our hearts.

A Time-Honored Way of Weaving Prayer into Your Day

Another means of weaving prayer into our days is to observe specific times for it. This practice has roots in the early Christian
community. The *Didache,* an early church document, encour-

aged Christians to pray at least three times a day. By the time of Tertullian, the first major Christian author to write in Latin (living in the late 100s and early 200s), believers were rising to pray at midnight. This practice developed in response to Psalm 119:62: "At midnight I rise to give you thanks." A method of prayer seven times a day, based on Psalm 119:164, emerged in the monasteries: "Seven times a day I praise you for your righteous laws." Modern commentators take the number seven as a sign of completeness, meaning that the psalmist is devoted to prayer throughout the day. Benedict of Nursia (480–547), founder of the Benedictine monastic order, was the one who combined many of the practices of the early church with the psalmist's ideal and formalized within his order a daily schedule for prayer known as the Daily Office or the Divine Order. He believed the chief work of the monks was the *opus Dei*, the work of God. For him, this meant punctuating the monastic day and night with periods of prayer. These were periods of formal, oral, community prayer that included psalms, hymns, and Bible readings for each period of prayer, called the Hour *(hora)*.

The day began with the "vigils," or the Night Office (now called Matins), which was prayed at approximately 2:00 A.M. in the winter, though it was combined with Lauds during the shorter days from Easter through the middle of the fall. The prayers of this time focused on confession.

The second period of prayer began the Day Office and was held at daybreak. This was originally called Matins, since it came in the early morning, but it came to be called Lauds from the recitation of the praise *(Laudes)* psalms, Psalms 148–150. This prayer time often includes the *Te Deum*. This ancient prayer gives us insight into the richness and depth of our spiritual ancestors' devotional lives. It is an invigorating model for our morning prayer, beginning with strong affirmations of truth and concluding with confident supplications for help.

Te Deum

We praise Thee, O God:

We acknowledge Thee to be the Lord.

All the earth doth worship Thee, the Father everlasting.

To Thee all angels cry aloud;

The heavens and all the power therein.

To Thee cherubim and seraphim continually do cry:

Holy, Holy, Holy, Lord God of Sabaoth.

Heaven and earth are full of the majesty of Thy glory.

The glorious company of the apostles praise Thee.

The goodly fellowship of the prophets praise Thee.

The noble army of martyrs praise Thee.

The holy Church, throughout all the world, doth acknowledge Thee.

The Father of an infinite majesty;

Thine adorable, true, and only Son,

Also the Holy Spirit, the comforter.

Thou art the King of glory, O Christ.

Thou art the everlasting Son of the Father.

When Thou tookest upon Thee to deliver man,

When Thou hadst overcome the sharpness of death,

Thou didst open the kingdom of heaven to all believers.

Thou sittest at the right hand of God, in the glory of the Father.

We believe that Thou shalt come to be our Judge.

We therefore pray Thee, help Thy servants,

Whom Thou hast redeemed with Thy precious blood.

Make them to be numbered with Thy saints in glory everlasting.

O Lord, save Thy people, and bless Thy heritage.

Govern them, and lift them up forever.

Day by day we magnify Thee;

And we worship Thy name ever, world without end.

Vouchsafe, O Lord, to keep us this day without sin.

O Lord, have mercy upon us, have mercy upon us.

O Lord, let Thy mercy be upon us, as our trust is in Thee.

O Lord, in Thee have I trusted;
Let me never be confounded.

The next four periods of prayer were Prime at 6:00 A.M., Terce at 9:00 A.M., Sext at 12 noon, and None at the ninth hour of the day from sunrise, or 3:00 P.M. Benedict wrote, "In the Day Office, therefore, we ought praise our Creator for His just judgments, and at night we will rise to confess to him."9 Each of these periods included a hymn, a lectionary of psalms and readings from epistles specified for each day, reciting the *Kyrie eleison* ("Lord have mercy"), and dismissal.

Vespers (evening prayer) was timed to end at sundown, with the rising of the evening star. The last office of the day was Compline, named from the same root as our word, *complete.* It was celebrated as darkness fell, or just before bedtime. Psalms 4, 91, and 134 were to be repeated each day. These are truly appropriate psalms to conclude our days: resting "in the shadow of the Almighty" (Ps. 91:1) so that each of us can say, "I will lie down and sleep in peace, for you alone, O Lord, make me dwell in safety" (Ps. 4:8).

The Rule of St. Benedict concludes the description of counsel for these practices saying,

> If this arrangement is unsatisfactory to anyone, he may do otherwise if he has thought of a better one. *No matter what, all 150 psalms must be chanted during the week so that on Sunday Matins the series may start afresh.* Monks who chant less than the entire Psalter, with canticles, each week are slothful in their service to God. Our spiritual fathers performed with determination in one day what we now take a whole week to do.10

It is helpful for us to explore a number of models for daily prayer, but each of us must find a discipline that works for us. It may be helpful to take a retreat during which you practice the

Daily Office, just to get a sense of prayer weaving the fragments of the day together. Then, you may find a way to modify and adapt the schedule to set the pace for your day. Most likely, you can develop a morning and evening prayer discipline, with a different emphasis for each time. For instance, the morning is a time of praise and surrender to God's Spirit, seeking direction for the day. The evening is a time of confession and thanksgiving, resting in the sovereignty of God.[11]

WHAT ABOUT DISTRACTIONS AND WANDERING THOUGHTS?

When we first begin a more intentional prayer discipline, we often find that our devotional time is suddenly filled with thoughts of things we have to do, things we forgot to do, and things we know we shouldn't do! We can compare this experience to that of a person who, after years of living with open doors, suddenly decides to shut them. The visitors who used to enter her home anytime they felt like it will start pounding on the shut doors, wondering why they are not allowed to enter. Only when they realize that they are not welcome do they gradually stop coming.[12]

We are not surprised when our change of lifestyle involves a period of adaptation. As we persist, fewer and fewer distractions present themselves. In addition to persistence, keeping paper and pencil handy to write down any significant thoughts can also relieve us of the tension and fear of forgetting.

I used to think that prayer was coming to God to get what I wanted. Now, I realize prayer is coming to God to receive what he has for me.

NOTES

1. Richard H. Schneider, "Quake," *Guideposts* (Nov. 1983): 2–7. Excerpted and rewritten by Douglas J. Rumford.

2. Archibald Hart, *Feeling Free: Making Your Emotions Work for You* (Old Tappan, N.J.: Fleming H. Revell Company, 1979), 85.

3. A fine, biblically based, practically illustrated book that treats this subject in more depth is *The Joy of Listening to God* by Joyce Huggett (Downers Grove, Ill.: InterVarsity Press, 1986).

4. Don Postema, *Space for God* (Grand Rapids, Mich.: Bible Way, 1983), 44.

5. *Eerdmans' Handbook to the World's Religions* (Grand Rapids, Mich.: Eerdmans, 1982), 414.

6. David Stoop, *Self Talk: Key to Personal Growth* (Old Tappan, N.J.: Fleming H. Revell Company, 1982), 33.

7. Postema, *Space for God*, 45, quoting *A Treasury of Russian Spirituality*, edited by G. P. Fedotov, excerpted from pp. 283–345.

8. Postema, 45, noting his footnote.

9. *The Rule of St. Benedict* (New York: Image Books, 1975), 66.

10. Ibid., 68 (emphasis added).

11. For a glimpse of these practices in the present, I recommend *The Genesee Diary: Report from a Trappist Monastery* by Henri J. M. Nouwen (New York: Image Books, 1976).

12. Henri J. M. Nouwen, *Making All Things New* (San Francisco: Harper & Row, 1981), 72–73.

SOUL-SEARCHING

Questions for Reflection and Discussion

1. How would describe your prayer life at present?
   a) Monologue
   b) Dialogue
   c) Unceasing

2. What are some of the frustrations and difficulties you have experienced concerning prayer?

3. Have you ever had an experience like the one the author's mother had, when the Lord seemed to touch her in a special way? If you have, how has it affected you? Have you shared it? If you haven't had such an experience, what is your response to such stories?

4. What is your greatest difficulty in the idea of listening to God in prayer?

5. The author gave several specific guidelines to ensure that we don't presume too much concerning what we "hear" from God in prayer. What are those guidelines? Would you add any others? Have you seen these types of guidelines ignored by yourself or others?

6. Why does God answer small prayers?

7. For many people, unceasing prayer is a difficult concept to practice. How do you respond to the suggestion of using the Jesus Prayer as a model? In what way could you adapt it to your prayer life?

8. How does the Jesus Prayer differ from the "prayer" of eastern religions?

9. Is there a way you could utilize the suggestions of the Daily Office to shape the pace of your busy days? What would such a schedule look like for you?

CHAPTER TEN

Celebrating the God Who Is with Us

⚜ WORSHIP

I HAD seen his name and face in the paper, but I was truly surprised to see him in church with his family. "Mike" was a business entrepreneur in town who had come under investigation by government authorities, apparently based on allegations by disgruntled employees. I dropped a note of welcome the first week, then called them on the phone the following week.

"I can't tell you how much I need this right now," he said. "I hope you don't mind if we just come to worship and leave. That's all I can handle at this time." I could tell he was leaving the door open but didn't want to talk with me about any specifics.

Some months later, he greeted me at the door after worship.

"Do you have time to meet with my wife and me this week?"

At our meeting in my study he began with these words. "If it hadn't been for the church, I don't know how we would have made it through these last few months." As we talked it was clear that it was *the experience of worship* itself that had nourished them.

A limited amount of fellowship had encouraged them, but they had kept mostly to themselves. The sermons had provided some inspiration, but nothing out of the ordinary.

"It was just being with God's people . . . feeling that I could join my weak prayers to their prayers. . . . And somehow I began to see everything much more clearly. . . ." He couldn't say any more.

Things did *not* go well for this man's business. Over the course of the next year, a number of factors conspired to make it impossible for him to continue. He lost his house and had to relocate. But every once in a while he returns, gives me a big hug, and says, "I'm still on the road with Jesus."

Worship is a great clarifier. Mike had said, "Somehow I began to see everything much more clearly." This reminds me of a powerful insight from the psalms. Asaph, composer of Psalm 73, wrestled with his own bitterness at his misfortune. The first three verses are a classic confession of someone who knows the truth about God but feels shortchanged.

> *Surely God is good to Israel,*
> *to those who are pure in heart.*
> *But as for me, my feet had almost slipped;*
> *I had nearly lost my foothold.*
> *For I envied the arrogant*
> *when I saw the prosperity of the wicked.*

We are tempted to lose our sense of perspective, especially when we see people succeeding in life without God. It is especially distressing when we feel that we are falling far behind. Following a rather graphic description of the wicked, the psalmist nearly caves in to a sense of futility. "Surely in vain have I kept my heart pure" (Ps. 73:13). But at that point, the power of worship breaks the mesmerizing hypnosis of self-pity.

> *When I tried to understand all this,*
> *it was oppressive to me*
> **till I entered the sanctuary of God;**
> **then I understood their final destiny.**
>
> PSALM 73:16-17 (emphasis added)

This was Mike's experience. He had envied the prosperous and done everything in his power to achieve his own success—only to end up in a mess! But when he literally entered the sanctuary, things began to become clear. His childhood religion, long forsaken in his early adult years, had provided the foundation that would later direct him to the Lord's house. Life had knocked the wind out of Mike. In the worship of God, he found his breath again.

We are leading out-of-breath lives. Even if we aren't facing a specific crisis, we are in daily peril of being overwhelmed. As we scramble to make too many appointments, to decide among too many choices, to fulfill too many obligations, and to understand too many issues, we can come to the end of a day breathless. An exhaustion beyond physical fatigue weighs down the spirit, leaving us with vague feelings of regret and dissatisfaction.

We were made for a different way of life. As people created in the image of God, we were not designed to lead lives of anxious toil. The psalmist says, "It is in vain that you rise up early and go late to rest, eating the bread of anxious toil; for he gives sleep to his beloved" (Ps. 127:2 NRSV). We were created to work and to rest, to invest our gifts in God's service and then reflect on God's goodness. In the classic words of the Westminster Confession of Faith, "The chief end [or purpose] of man [and woman] is to glorify God and enjoy Him forever." This enjoyment, however, seems far out of reach, even for the most committed followers of Jesus. The daily demands of life and even our urgent sense of discipleship overwhelm the call to glorify and enjoy God. In truth, many people haven't a clue what enjoying the Lord feels like.

Until we become rested, relaxed people, the normal weariness and stress of life—not to mention the major traumas and griefs that come upon us—will prevent us from enjoying God or feeling much gratefulness toward or longing for him. We must learn how to take a life-giving breath. God saw from the beginning what we would need. This is what the Sabbath is all about.

WHAT HAVE I BEEN MISSING?

Most middle-class Americans tend to worship their work, to work at their play, and to play at their worship. As a result, their meanings and values are distorted. Their relationships disintegrate faster than they can keep them in repair, and their lifestyles resemble a cast of characters in search of a plot.[1]

Regardless of our class in society, it is clear that most of us have mixed up the values of temporary and eternal matters.

We *need* to worship. Worship is not something God needs because he has an ego problem. Worship is the means by which we meet with the living Lord. In that encounter, God gives us himself. Worship releases us from the grasp of this world. In worship, we become available to God so that he might bless us with his presence, his purposes, and his power for our daily lives.

---

*I*n worship, we become available to God so that he might bless us with his presence, his purposes, and his power for our daily lives.

What exactly happens during real worship? We have some indications from Scripture about what God had in mind.

Worship Draws Us into God's Glory and Work.

"You must observe my Sabbaths. This will be a sign between me and you for the generations to come, so *you may know that I am the Lord*" (Exod. 31:13, italics added). Without worship, we lose a living relationship with God. Our loyalty to God may continue, and many of the outward activities may continue, such as church attendance, financial support, serving on committees, advising youth groups, contacting people new to the church, or visiting the sick. But the sense of God's presence is only a memory—a dim, distant memory.

Few activities strengthen our faith more than cultivating a richer, fuller understanding of God through worship. The promise is that we will know that God is the Lord. How? By taking time to focus upon his Word and to remember his works, our spirits awaken to the hope that is ours in the "sign" of the Lord's Day. Praise invites us to consider the nature and character of God. In Revelation 7:12, the multitude worships and adores God by ascribing seven characteristics to him. "Praise and glory and wisdom and thanks and honor and power and strength be to our God for ever and ever. Amen!" The worshipers are affirming and celebrating the matchless glory of the Lord.

When we speak of God, "who created heaven and earth, who is before all things . . ." we are piling up descriptive phrases. This is far from a dry grammatical exercise, however. This is a powerful means of enriching our prayer life. As we describe God, pushing ourselves to ascribe more and more honor to him, our faith is strengthened, our vision grows, and our hearts are encouraged. We don't need to focus on in-depth descriptions of our problems; we need to describe in more vivid and comprehensive terms the Lord who is the answer to our problems. This helps us understand why the psalmist exhorts all creation, saying, "Let everything that has breath praise the Lord" (Ps. 150:6).

We don't need to focus on in-depth descriptions of our problems; we need to describe in more vivid and comprehensive terms the Lord who is the answer to our problems.

What good is praise? Does it give something to God that God lacks? Such a thought comes perilously close to devaluing and distorting the eternal nature and being of God. God is complete in and of himself. Therefore, strictly speaking, God does not need our praise. Yet he desires it. Why? Is God, to put it rather bluntly, on an ego trip?

As he wrestled with these questions, C. S. Lewis found the exhortations to praise God to be a great stumbling block. In his book *Reflections on the Psalms,* he describes how praise seemed to present an image of God craving "our worship like a vain woman who wants compliments." He then discovered that the problem lay in his failure to appreciate the nature of joy:

> But the most obvious fact about praise—whether of God or anything—strangely escaped me. I thought of it in terms of compliment, approval, or the giving of honor. I had never noticed that all enjoyment spontaneously overflows into praise. . . . The world rings with praise—lovers praising their mistresses, readers their favorite poet, walkers praising the countryside, players praising their favorite game. . . . My whole, more general, difficulty about the praise of God depended on my absurdly denying to us, as regards the

supremely Valuable, what we delight to do, what indeed we can't help doing, about everything else we value. I think we delight to praise what we enjoy because the praise not merely expresses but completes the enjoyment; it is its appointed consummation.[2]

Our own experience tells us that praise completes the joy of an experience. Have you ever been to a silent sporting event at a baseball or football stadium? The noise is almost unbearable. That's because the best part is cheering the home team's victorious accomplishments. And the most enthusiastic fans rehearse those great moments to one another over and over—and over and over!—again. Likewise, we will find energy coursing through our spiritual lives when we rehearse—over and over—the mighty acts of God in history, as well as his acts in our life stories. We celebrate and exclaim over the joy and wonder of our relationship with the Lord.

Praise becomes the pivotal point of our daily lives as we center on the Lord's greatness and his goodness toward us. Adoration completes the connection of faith. Appreciation completes the experience of grace. We can begin to live in the overflow of joy!

Worship Makes Us Available for God to Transform Us.
We are to keep the Sabbath "so you may know that I am the Lord, *who makes you holy*" (Exod. 31:13, italics added). The Lord's Day is a day of rest and grace in which we celebrate not only the creation of the world in six days but also the new creation of our lives through the resurrection of Jesus Christ on the first day of the week. In a culture that emphasizes performance, we find it very difficult to understand that the most significant aspect of our life transformation comes from our being available to God. Worship puts us in a place where God can reach us.

We are to be active participants, however, in this transforming process. There is a sense in which our worship experience depends in part on the old adage "You get out of it what you put into it." When we come with expectation, ready to encounter the living Lord, we will receive far more than if we expect God to do all the work. As we begin a worship service, it is good to remind ourselves that God is ready to meet us. The real question is this: Are we ready to meet God? Are we ready to hear from God's Word *not* simply new truth that may interest us but truth that will touch and change our lives? Are we prepared to offer honest prayers and listen for his response? Are we prepared to contribute, as appropriate, to the worship service? My experience as a worshiper and as a pastor tells me that many of us have little idea of how to worship in this way. I will give some specific principles later for helping us move forward in this area.

Worship Gives Us Rest.

Worship is a time for us to savor the satisfied rest that grows out of an eternal perspective on life. This rest is not inactivity, but an activity that defines all others. The principle that emerges from this promise is this: Worship overflows into our life work, and our life work flows into our worship. "For six days, work is to be done, but the seventh day is a Sabbath of rest, holy to the Lord" (Exod. 31:15). Our lives are rooted in the created order and plan of God, not limited or oppressed by the plans and systems of human beings. The Lord's Day is a call to reclaim our purpose and our place in creation, breaking free from the clamor of other calls. The principle of rest is broader than one day in seven. We see that the land was to have a sabbatical, lying fallow every seventh year (Lev. 25:2). And all the people were to enjoy the Jubilee after the seventh set of seven-year periods; that is, every fifty years (Lev. 25:8).

As you enter a time of worship, one way to reinforce the principle of rest is to take a deep breath and concentrate on relaxing your body. (Note: There is a specific exercise for relaxation in the material on biblical meditation. You may not be able to move physically through the motions, but if you have practiced relaxing as part of your exercises, just the reminder to relax can bring rest to your body and heart.) It may also help you to hold your open hands palm up, on your lap, as a sign to yourself that you are not here to strive, nor to cling to anything. You are ready to empty yourself and trust in God.

Worship Retunes Us to Life's Natural Pace and Rhythm.

The Hebrew word *sabbath* comes from the term "to cease." It is a far richer term than merely indicating a cessation of activity. It is the kind of rest that savors accomplishment and appreciates the truly significant things in life. God designed worship to set the pace for our lives, freeing us from the stress of worldly pressure and the distortion of worldly values.

---

*G*od designed worship to set the pace for our lives, freeing us from the stress of worldly pressure and the distortion of worldly values.

The priority of the Sabbath is clear not only from the fourth commandment but also from God's continuing direction of his people. When the Lord instructed the Israelites to build the tabernacle, he also instructed them on the priority of the Sabbath. His exhortation reveals his design for the rhythm of life. In the midst of the holy urgency to construct the place of worship, the people were commanded to remember above all else the place of the Sabbath in the pace of their lives: "You shall keep the sabbath, because it is holy for you; everyone who profanes it shall be put to death. . . . It is a sign forever between me and the people of Israel that in six days the Lord made heaven and earth, and on the seventh day he rested, and was refreshed" (Exod. 31:14, 17, NRSV).

In other words, God calls the people to pursue his work in accordance with his will. It isn't enough to "get something done." God's people are to do God's work God's way. In this case, they were to observe the Sabbath consistently in the midst of the tabernacle's construction. It would have been understandable to "cut corners" and press ahead for a seven-day workweek in order to finish the tabernacle, the priestly garments, the altar, and other furnishings. After all, this was for the Lord! From the outset, however, God warns against the logic of religious effort that contradicts the wisdom of the Spirit.

I first took this seriously as a college student employed at a large national retail store. I had been keeping my own Sabbath by not doing schoolwork on Sundays, using it as a day of worship, fellowship, and ministry with youth groups. When I got my work schedule, I was assigned to Sundays. I was upset, but I didn't have the courage to protest, so I went to the early church service and rushed to the store, which opened at noon. My conscience was very uneasy, but I tried to ignore it. Then the next work schedule came, and I was again scheduled for Sunday. This time I asked to speak to my department manager. He was a rather gruff, no-nonsense person. As we sat down in the coffee shop, my heart was pounding, and my mouth was dry.

"Dave," I said, "you know that I really want to do a good job here. But there's one thing that I'm having a hard time with. I'm a Christian, and I don't feel it's appropriate for me to work on Sunday."

"Doug, nobody wants to work Sunday, Christian or not. That's just the way it is."

"I understand that," I replied, my heart in my throat—I was surprised by the depth of my emotion. "But I am active in my church and with our youth groups. I'm not trying to give you a rough time, but I don't see how I can work Sundays." I didn't know how to explain to Dave my theology of keeping the Sabbath; I also knew that he could "show me the door"! A long pause ensued.

"Here's what I'm willing to do," Dave finally said. "I will give you Sundays off, unless I am stuck, but you will have to close most Friday and Saturday nights. That's the only way I know to make it somewhat fair for others who will have to cover Sunday."

I thanked him, agreeing to his compromise. I said I appreciated his flexibility. And that's how things were for the remaining year I worked there.

I realize many people have never even considered working Sundays to be an issue, so I don't share this as an ideal to be imitated. The point is that I had developed a discipline for Sundays. I had experienced blessing as a result of it. I didn't make a big deal about it, but when it was challenged, I had to speak up— when I finally got the courage. God honored that.

The Jewish scholar Abraham Heschel called the Sabbath "a sanctuary—a cathedral in time." In *The Sabbath: Its Meaning for Modern Man,* Heschel presents a rich treasure house of profound truth concerning the nature of the Sabbath. He writes, "Six days we wrestle with the world, wringing profit from the earth; on the Sabbath, we especially care for the need of eternity planted in the soul. The world has our hands, but our soul belongs to Someone Else."[3]

The Lord's Day is the pacesetter, reminding us that all other days find both their purpose and culmination in this day. Again, Heschel's insights unlock God's wisdom: "Six days we live under the tyranny of things of space; on the Sabbath we try to become attuned to holiness in time, a day on which we are called . . . to turn from the results to the mystery of creation; from the world of creation to the creation of the world."[4]

When we stop to worship, we start to live! Worship recalibrates the guidance systems of our lives. Worship keeps us from the disorientation that comes from misvaluing the "stuff" and activities of life in this world.

TIME TO "JUST DO IT"

Glen's worship experience had been fairly typical—not a great experience, something of a duty. But he said that the greatest change came for him when he made a policy decision that, no matter what, he would be in church on Sunday morning. "That decision changed things for me in a number of ways. First, it ended the debate I used to have every Saturday night and Sunday morning: Would I go to church, or wouldn't I? But more than that, it made me think of worship in terms of my relationship with the Lord instead of what the choir was singing or the sermon topic."

Glen was beginning to see worship as a time for refreshing his relationship with God. All that goes with true worship has the potential to renew us. Praise keeps God's grace in Jesus Christ fresh and vivid before our eyes. Praise, like a muscle, grows stronger through exercise. Through the reading of God's Word—the many accounts of how God has acted upon the lives of people—our worship challenges us to believe God for more. Through prayer we learn to test the apparent limits we've attributed to situations, daring to go forward in the confidence that arises from our sense of the presence of God in glory. Faith is fed—and freed—by worship.

We call worship a discipline or a spiritual exercise because it only happens when we choose to make it so, as Glen did. We practice our praise, our spiritual rest, and our openness to God's transforming us. We commit to practice these things because they are urgently necessary—to our wholeness as human beings and to our daily spiritual health.

When we do worship, we find that the living God comes to us in a variety of life-changing, soul-stirring, heart-challenging ways:

- embracing us in his grace,
- healing us with his touch,
- giving us a taste of glory,
- instructing us in his Word,
- connecting us with a community of faith, hope, and love,
- and empowering us with his Spirit, for all of life.

PERSONAL WORSHIP / COMMUNITY WORSHIP

Personal worship grows best in the garden of community worship. When the people of God gather together, they experience God's presence in a way they cannot experience it alone. We share our differing gifts in music, preaching, intercession, and other creative expressions of faith. We reap the benefit of the traditions of God's people.

When the early church was being shaped, the power of God flowed through the community gathered for worship. This is not to say that individuals didn't pray alone or sing praises to God in what we might call "personal devotions." But it is clear that God did great things as the people gathered together (see Acts 2:42-47 and 4:23-35).

If there is any risk about the development of spiritual maturity, it is that of isolation, withdrawing from community. People living in Western culture, especially, tend to follow the pathway of individualism rather than the roadway of community. Both dimensions are important.

Worshiping together is one of the most significant exercises for stimulating personal growth and the spiritual vitality of God's people. As we share our gifts with God and each other, we experience the body of Christ at work. As we receive the gifts of others, we see the richness of God and experience the wisdom of his giving many gifts "for the common good" (1 Cor. 12:7).

Personal worship can be greatly enhanced through music. David sang psalms, and Paul exhorts us to "sing and make music in your heart to the Lord" (Eph. 5:19). An extensive collection of worship music is available for all tastes, from classical to country, from ol' time gospel to contemporary, from ancient Gregorian chant to alternative Christian rock.

I would also encourage you to make worship an aspect of *all* your spiritual exercises. Thanksgiving and praise can weave themselves throughout your devotions and service. As you explore the character of God, praise God. As you face the reality of sin, let God's grace enfold you. Let his Word inspire a doxology. Worship is not merely a time set apart. It helps us set all time apart for God.

Guidelines for Worship

As a pastor, I am aware that family conflict is probably highest on Sunday morning, as parents and children get ready for church. I know this from personal experience and from observation. Some days you can almost see the tension as people wheel into the parking lot. Getting a number of people organized to go to the same place is always a challenge, so we need to show ourselves grace. But we also need to realize that Sundays come regularly; they're not a surprise. We are wise to take some time to prepare ourselves not only to endure them but also to reap the richest rewards from them.

In *Making Sunday Special,* Karen Mains tells of her family's goal for "Sunday to become the joyful focal point of [their] weekly lives." Achieving this goal meant intentional preparation throughout the week. This book presents the honest struggles of one family, along with numerous practical principles and models. Individuals and families differ in their scope of application, but each one can take steps to discipline themselves to overcome the obstacles that so often disrupt worship.

The discipline of preparation for worship involves few new ideas, but rather calls for the use of common sense combined with wise time management.

Prepare yourself spiritually. We can do this by reading the Scriptures that will be the basis for the sermon or the Sunday school lesson. Pray for those who will be leading and for your own participation. Take a personal inventory of the week so that you are better prepared for confessing your sin. Reflect on your schooling, work, or other primary activities, to offer them to the Lord and to seek the Lord's direction for the next week.

Prepare yourself physically. Get enough sleep to be refreshed and alert for Sunday morning. Have your clothes ready. Be sure the car has enough gas so you don't have the pressure of stopping en route to church. Have the food plans and items ready so that you won't be planning dinner when you should be mentally free to worship.

Prepare yourself relationally. Seek reconciliation where there is difference or division (Matt. 5:21-23).

Prepare yourself financially. Set aside the money or write your check for your tithe or offering.

Upon entering your time of worship, offer yourself to God. "Lord, what do you want to give me during this time? I want to receive it." This is not a selfish request but one that makes us available to the Lord. It is also a good discipline to pray specifically for those who are facilitating, leading, and preaching in the worship. This simple act gives us an immediate sense of involvement.

None of these disciplines are to become legalistic rules. Their purpose is to make room for God by removing the distractions and pressures that so often disrupt our pursuit of God's best.

SOMETIMES THE BEST COMES AFTERWARD

The conclusion of the worship event may be just the beginning of God's work in your life. It is important that we learn to reflect on our worship. The amazing promise of worship is that it is a personal meeting with God! When we meet with God, we will need to respond in a variety of ways. We will want to reflect on the meaning of his message for our lives and respond to his call to action. We need to learn how to carry the gifts gained from our worship experience into the experience of our daily lives.

I encourage note taking throughout the worship service to provide the opportunity to reflect on the worship experience throughout the week. You cannot stop the service to savor a thought that came in prayer, or the words to a hymn or chorus that touched your heart or inspired new faith, or to write a note to someone who may benefit from an insight you gained during the sermon. But a quick note jotted during the service can help you recall the experience and remind you to take action. Then you can use the discipline of review to go deeper into what God seemed to be saying. Your journaling for the week may begin with further study on a thought or experience that came through the worship experience.

The treasures of worship can be mined through formal or informal discussion following the service. Resist the temptation to critique the service or the worship leaders. That can take you far from the blessing of what God did for you. Instead, share what you found most helpful. A number of high school and college groups enjoy getting together for lunch after church and taking time to respond to the question "What did God say to me through the service today?" Families can also cultivate this habit driving home in the car or around a meal. It's important to stress, however, that this be handled with sensitivity to each person's needs and interests.

The public worship of God's people is vital to our spiritual health. It imparts meaning, direction, and energy to the other days of the week. May God touch us in our worship, freeing us from the stress of worldly pressure and the distortion of worldly values. May we truly learn what it means to glorify God and enjoy him forever.

WHEN GOD SEEMS ABSENT

We really cannot talk about God's presence without acknowledging the difficulty many people have with a sense of God's absence. Every Christian experiences one or many forms of God's "absence." Our first step in responding to this is to understand the different situations in which we feel this spiritual aloneness.

Guilt: Where Does God Go When I Go Wrong?

When we are guilty of some wrongdoing or when we are suffering from feelings of guilt, whether justified or not, we usually feel as if God has left us. God is not truly absent in such a time, though the sense of positive connection has been disrupted.

If we are, in fact, guilty of some sin, then we can deal with it through confession and repentance. But don't interpret a sense of God's displeasure with absence. David described God's hand as heavy upon him—very much present in a misery-producing way! (Ps. 32:4). He spoke of losing the joy of his salvation but not his salvation itself (Ps. 51:12). The immediate sense of fellowship may be disrupted, but we are still not alone.

I knew of a pastor who preached a series of impassioned sermons on the absence of God. It puzzled many of his parishioners until it was later revealed that he had been guilty of sexual mis-conduct—and he felt desperately alone, having betrayed his marriage and ordination vows. (Please don't suspect everyone who preaches such sermons as speaking out of the same context!) It took confession, repentance, and counseling to restore a sense of God's presence—though he says, "It will never be the same until I see his face." He has a lingering sense of remorse and regret that continues to dog his steps.

If we are plagued by guilt feelings that may have no foundation in actual sins of commission or omission, then we need to explore these feelings in God's presence. If we know that the feelings are unfounded, we need to speak the truth to ourselves and identify Satan's lies about us. Writing about it in a journal can help us rediscover God's grace and presence. I encourage people to begin simply by writing a letter to Jesus. "Dear Jesus, Where are you? The last time I remember being with you was . . . [after reflecting on this, continue by completing this statement]. Ever since _____ I have felt I lost touch with you. . . ." Those who discipline themselves to reflect on these matters often find God coming to them in the process.

Ordinary Life: Where Is God in Life's Routine?
By faith, we know that God has not deserted us, but sometimes we simply don't sense his nearness. We remain faithful, but our hearts feel wooden. There's no thrill to our devotions; there are no doves descending as we pray, no harps playing as we read God's Word. It's all ordinary, very ordinary. This seems to be part of the normal process of spiritual growth. We move through the initial "infatuation phase" of spiritual life to the maturation phase of walking by faith, not by feelings.

I once heard a counselor say, "No marriage really grows until the infatuation is knocked out of it." By that, she meant the need to move beyond the idealization of a person and relationship to the practical realities of routine, hard work, persistence, failure, disappointment, and adjustment to life-as-it-is and to the person-as-he/she-is.

God wants our faith, character, and lifestyle to mature so that we don't depend on good feelings. Often the people who sense God's presence most are those who know him least! He is merciful to new Christians who often need an extra emotional boost, that sense of God's nearness that others of us wish we could recapture! But as we grow, the Holy Spirit weans us off the security of *"feeling* close to God" so that we learn to be people of power and conviction, with or without the emotional supports. This doesn't mean that we'll never feel close to God again, only that he doesn't want us so dependent upon it.

Crisis and Suffering: Where Is God When My World Caves In?

Authors such as Philip Yancey have attempted to wrestle honestly with the goodness and love of God in the midst of life's worst. Having been so far spared some of life's toughest hits, I have been continually instructed and encouraged by the faithful people who witness to God's nearness when life steals what we value most. One man, Ted, who lost his teenage son in a freak accident, told me several years later, "The Lord is good. It still hurts when we think of Tim, but walking with Christ has made it clear." He couldn't say any more than that to describe it verbally or intellectually, but the testimony of his tears and honest conviction spoke to "the love of Christ that surpasses knowledge" (Eph. 3:19, NRSV).

At times like these, our best response is to cry out to God, clinging to the hope we forged in better days. This was the strategy of the psalmist in Psalm 42:

> As a hart longs for flowing streams,
> so longs my soul for thee, O God.
> My soul thirsts for God, for the living God.

When shall I come and behold the face of God?
My tears have been my food day and night,
while men say to me continually,
"Where is your God?"
These things I remember, as I pour out my soul:
how I went with the throng,
and led them in procession to the house of God,
with glad shouts and songs of thanksgiving,
a multitude keeping festival.
Why are you cast down, O my soul,
and why are you disquieted within me?
Hope in God; for I shall again praise him,
my help and my God.

PSALM 42:1-6, RSV

The ability to endure the sense of God's distance is based on memory, not emotion. We don't deny our feelings of being cast down, but we aren't crippled by the experience, either. Rather than discounting all that had ever happened, the psalmist cherished past experiences with God and God's people. These became the footholds that kept him from slipping into deeper despair.

"The Dark Night of the Soul"

This anguished sense of God's absence was labeled by St. John of the Cross. The "dark night" is an intense realization when "the self is stripped even of any remaining spiritual gratification and of every consoling image of itself."[5] Our self-despair arises from an inner honesty that sees our lingering sinfulness, from our inability to cling to God by our effort and by our knowledge that this world can never satisfy. The experience of desolation can be devastating. John of the Cross held out hope, however, that this experience was the prelude to the dawn of illumination and union with God. It could be called a deeper encounter with grace.

This mystical view of spiritual growth is patterned after the experience of Moses in Exodus 19 and 20. "And the people stood afar off, while Moses drew near to the thick darkness where God was." The allegorization of Moses' experience provides a model for those who are trying to make sense of their faith experiences in the light of biblical experience.

"If your Presence does not go with us, do not send us up from here" (Exod. 33:15). Moses' plea is that of every heart as we are called to go out into the wilderness of life's responsibilities. The fear of going alone can stifle our spiritual vigor. These are times when growth can be most painful—but most enduring once it has come to pass. There are no simple solutions to the dark night. It is a season in which we learn to seek after and cling to God in new ways.

NOTES

1. Gordon Dahl, *Work, Play and Worship in a Leisure-Oriented Society* (Minneapolis: Augsburg Publishing House, 1972), 12.
2. C. S. Lewis, *Reflections of the Psalms* (New York: Harcourt Brace, 1958), 93–95.
3. Abraham Heschel, *The Sabbath: Its Meaning for Modern Man* (New York: Noonday Press, 1951), 13.
4. Ibid., 10.
5. Gordon S. Wakefield, *The Westminster Dictionary of Christian Spirituality* (Philadelphia: The Westminster Press, 1983), 104.

SOUL-SEARCHING

Questions for Reflection and Discussion

1. How would you describe your current attitude toward worship?

   a) I enjoy church but don't really know what it means to "enter into worship."

   b) Worship is a central part of my daily life.

   c) As much as I love God, I really don't see what difference worship is supposed to make in my life.

2. The author describes worship as the "great clarifier." What does this mean? How could worship serve this purpose in your life?

3. Worship is said to fulfill four primary purposes in our spiritual lives. What are these? Are these purposes you can relate to and from which you could benefit? Which purpose seems most important to you at this time?

4. What is the relationship between worshiping with a congregation or group and worshiping alone?

5. Some specific guidelines for worship are offered. Which of these would be most helpful to you at this time? What steps could you take this week to implement it?

6. What are four common reasons for a sense of God's absence? Are any of these especially significant in your life?

7. What goal would you like to set for your worship discipline?

God's presence is a fact, but our experience of God's presence is a skill that we cultivate. We have explored the spiritual exercises that increase our awareness of God's intimacy and fellowship with us and that nurture our experience of God's presence. These include:

- our initial encounters with God and our response of faith
- confession and our experience of forgiveness
- preview and review
- prayer
- worship: both personal and in the family of faith

To develop a sense of God's presence, choose an area that best touches your spiritual need at this time. Don't try to give attention to all of them. One discipline woven into your life will accomplish more than the sporadic exercise of many.

The sense of God's presence is firmly rooted, not in our emotions, but in his Word. The next area of caring for your soul involves learning to encounter God's Word so that it is life changing.

THREE

Making Sense out of Life: The Eternal Perspective

SOULSHAPING AT A GLANCE

Exercises That Increase Our Awareness of God's Presence

- Repentance
- Confession
- Preview
- Review
- Prayer
- Worship

Exercises That Help Us See Life with an Eternal Perspective

- **Bible study**
- **Meditation**
- **Spiritual reading**

Exercises That Free Us from Evil's Power and Connect Us to God's Resources

- Fasting
- Silence
- Solitude
- Battling temptation
- Prayer for spiritual battle

Exercises That Direct Our Lives toward Kingdom Purposes

- Building character
- Building relationships
- Spiritual direction
- Spiritual friendship
- Stewardship
- Spiritual service through spiritual gifts

A dear friend of mine is nearly always happy. Her cheerfulness and good humor refresh all those who come into contact with her. After knowing her for a while, I asked, "So are you always this cheery?"

"Not always," she said, and told me she had been through a painful divorce and had lived with intense financial pressure to care for her four children, in addition to dealing with the emotional pain of her husband's betrayal.

"But there's no trace of bitterness," I said.

"One morning, soon after the divorce became final, I was praying, and the thought came to me that God is watching out for me. He will never betray me. So I decided I just wasn't going to let the pain of the past steal my joy!" A wonderful smile crossed her face, and I saw the power of faith.

Our outlook on life depends very much on our "inlook." Carolyn's outlook on life changed when she took time to pray and to affirm the truth about God. She is one of countless testimonies to the fact that "as [a man] thinketh in his heart, so is he" (Prov. 23:7, KJV). More than any other factors, our attitude and mindset shape how we respond and interact with all of life. If our hearts are parched, we will often see only the dryness in life. If our minds are captive to the assumptions of this world, we will see little to inspire hope and joy in the midst of hardship. How do we change?

Spiritual vitality springs from the artesian well of a renewed mind. "Do not conform any longer to the pattern of this world, but *be transformed by the renewing of your mind*" (Rom. 12:2, italics added). We are not powerless in the face of life's difficulties and challenges because we have both the resources of God and the transforming power he releases through a renewed mind. The second primary aspect of soulshaping is making sense out of life by learning to look at life from God's perspective.

Why are we alive? Why is there suffering? What is God's will for our lives? In the course of living apart from God, we have turned to a variety of sources, patching together a hodgepodge of explanations and principles for life and conduct. When we receive new life through Christ, however, we also receive the "mind of Christ" (1 Cor. 2:16). As we seek to follow Christ, we begin to challenge old assumptions and look at everything with new eyes. Over the course of our lifetime (if we participate with the Holy Spirit), this new mind corrects our view of the world and every aspect of life.

Perhaps you've heard of "McArthur's Universal Corrective Map of the World." Produced in Australia, the map is arranged with the south at the top and the north at the bottom! People who are accustomed to traditional maps that picture northern countries at the top of the map and southern countries at the bottom are initially disoriented when they see Australia in the upper left hand corner, with the tips of South America, India, and Africa pointing up![1] McArthur reminds us that our outlook on life is based on certain assumptions that may be subject to alteration.

Spiritual maturity comes as God replaces worldly assumptions with biblical truth, a truth that directs our steps daily. This truth must not only permeate our thinking, but it must percolate through our hearts and behavior. The spiritual exercises presented in this section enable us to move beyond a sterile, intellectual study of God's Word into a dynamic encounter with the Living Word, Jesus Christ, through the written Word. In the process, we learn to approach life from the divine perspective.

Harry Blamires challenges us to think Christianly:

To think secularly is to think with a frame of reference bounded by the limits of our life on earth: it is to keep one's calculations rooted in this-worldly criteria. To think Christianly is to accept all things with the mind as related, directly or indirectly, to man's eternal destiny as the redeemed and chosen child of God.2

NOTES

1. Charles H. Kraft, *Christianity with Power* (Ann Arbor, Mich.: Servant Books, 1989), 23–24.
2. Henry Blamires, *The Christian Mind* (London: SPCK, 1966), 44.

CHAPTER ELEVEN

Restored Living through Renewed Thinking

❧ BIBLE STUDY

DURING an American Bible Society distribution campaign in Zimbabwe years ago, one of the recipients gave a rather antagonistic response.

"If you give me that New Testament, I will roll the pages and use them to make cigarettes!" the man told Gaylord Kambarami, the General Secretary of the Bible Society of Zimbabwe.

"I understand that," Gaylord replied. "But at least promise to read the page of the New Testament before you smoke it." When the man agreed, Gaylord gave him the New Testament, and that was the last he saw of him. That is, until last year.

While Gaylord was attending a Methodist convention in Zimbabwe, the speaker on the platform suddenly spotted him, pointed him out to the audience, and said, "This man doesn't remember me, but fifteen years ago he tried to sell me a New Testament. When I refused to buy it, he gave it to me, even though I told him I would use the pages to roll cigarettes. I smoked Matthew and I smoked Mark and I smoked Luke. But when I got to John 3, verse 16, I couldn't smoke anymore. My life was changed from that moment!"

The cigarette-smoking antagonist had become a full-time church evangelist, devoting his entire life to showing others the way of salvation he found in God's Word.[1]

Unfortunately, we often enjoy amazing conversion stories like this one and still miss the point. This person, uninterested in religion, found himself transformed as he encountered the Word of God. While we rejoice at his conversion, we forget that God's Word has the power to change us *after* conversion. In fact, the Bible should be changing us still, years and years after we have become spiritually born again. It is the nature of the Bible to change us. But it can only do so when we allow ourselves to be encountered by its truth.

WHAT WE CALL "ETERNAL PERSPECTIVE"

Some of the classic spiritual writers referred to *sub specie aeternitatis,* Latin for "from the aspect of eternity." In other words, we are to learn to see life in the view of things both seen and unseen, and of things eternal as well as those past and present. An eternal perspective not only develops knowledge about God and the things of faith, but it views all of life as if we were "seated with [Christ] in the heavenly places" (see Eph. 2:6 and Col. 3:1).

God's Word is the foundation for this renewal. And we can use the Bible in many ways in order to develop mental maturity. Study of God's Word, meditation, and spiritual reading are three primary ways in which we can participate with God in transforming the way we view the world and go about our lives.

God has endowed us with a marvelous mind, with thinking power that is largely untapped. But our spiritual alienation has affected the way we think. We need to allow God to shape our thinking. This will involve as much unlearning of old ideas as it will learning new, biblical ones.

For instance, one idea that dies hard is that *performance is the basis of acceptance*. I have struggled with this on my own spiritual journey. When I look at my life from a worldly perspective, I am caught in the traps of comparison and competition. I am reduced to being driven by ambition or devastated by failure. Then a corrective word comes from the Lord, "Come to Me, all you who labor and are heavy laden, and I will give you rest. . . . For My yoke is easy and My burden is light" (Matt. 11:28-30, NKJV). As we learn to rethink our assumptions, we find freedom from oppressive burdens and freedom for enjoying life as well as meeting its demands.

Another worldly idea is that *circumstances dictate our feelings and limit our future possibilities*. A friend of mine asked me how I was doing. "OK, under the circumstances," I replied.

"What are you doing *under* them?" Gary asked. That simple quip gave me quite a jolt. Fortunately, he didn't just walk away to leave me feeling guilty for getting *under* the circumstances. He took time to listen and pray with me about the particular pressures I was feeling. The sense of burden definitely lifted. And a sense of anticipation rose as we prayed for God to show his grace and power in the circumstances.

These are just two assumptions that set the course of our lives and, unfortunately, shape our souls for the worst. Only as we turn to God's truth, and a perspective that takes us beyond what we know, can we be restored to spiritual—and mental—wholeness.

> But God, who is rich in mercy, out of the great love with which he loved us even when we were dead through our trespasses, made us alive together with Christ (by grace you have been saved), and *raised us up with him and made us sit*

> *with him in the heavenly places in Christ Jesus.* (Ephesians 2:4-6,
> RSV, emphasis added)

Read these verses again and phrase them in your own words.
They are truly astounding! In his classic *True Spirituality,* Francis
Schaeffer comments on the same concept expressed by Paul in
Romans 6: "In our thoughts and lives now we are to live as
though we had already died, been to heaven, and come back
again as risen."[2]

We could line up statement after statement that reframes the
way we see life to the way it actually is in God's eternity. Here are
just a few:

- God has spoken and still speaks to us in the Bible.
- God created all things and continues to work in the world today.
- God is willing to reveal his will for us as we abide in him.
- God hears and answers prayer, providing the spiritual and material resources we need for all situations.

How would your life change if you truly believed these statements and then applied them to specific situations? Could we be
cynical and pessimistic if we really believed that God is at work in
the world and that he is willing to let us in on what he's doing?
Would problems overwhelm us so easily if we really were convinced that God answers prayer?

Think about your general approach to life and try to write out
the statements that you are *actually* living by. How are they different from the statements above?

If we are living for today alone, we will behave far differently
than if we see our actions in the light of eternity. If we rely only on
the resources we can perceive with our senses, we will respond far
differently than if we looked confidently to God's provision.

THINKING OUR WAY INTO A NEW WAY OF LIFE

Behavior that isn't rooted in renewed thinking will not endure. We all know the truth of this. We know how many times we've received new information that excited us. A week or two later, though, it's as if we had never heard it. We took in the information, but what should have become a catalyst for change merely remained stored data.

Our spiritual struggles are fought first on the battlefield of the mind. Dark thoughts lead to dark days. God's thoughts lead to bright days. Our hope for change comes from the principle stated most clearly in Romans 12:2: "Do not conform any longer to the pattern of this world, but *be transformed by the renewing of your mind*" (italics added). We examine our human logic and limitations in light of revealed principles and the infinite reality of God Almighty. "We take every thought captive to obey Christ," wrote Paul (2 Cor. 10:5, NRSV).

"A mind that is stretched by a new experience can never go back to its old dimensions," said Oliver Wendell Holmes. Spirituality is truly a stretching process. But God wants to do more than stretch our mind; he wants to change us from the inside out, moving beyond "Do this" and "Don't do that" to literally "make new" our mind.3

No Longer Victims

Have you noticed lately how everybody is a victim? We "can't help" the way we act. We are at the mercy of multiple forces, all of them out of our control. No wonder we are so spiritually powerless!

A victim surrenders his power to someone else or to some external force or circumstance. Consider the difference between two of Jesus' disciples, Judas and Peter. Judas was overwhelmed by his traitorous actions and his circumstances. He could not recover and, in his despair, took his own life. Peter also turned his back on his Lord, in spite of earlier vehement protests to the contrary. He allowed himself to be victimized by the pressure of circumstances, but he was later willing to be helped up and out by the grace of the Lord. Even in his own death, I suggest that Jesus was not a victim in the sense that we use the term today. He suffered at the hands of others—but they never touched his soul! Being a victim is a matter of the soul. As Jesus went to the cross, he said, "No one takes [my life] from me" (John 10:18). He refused to be a victim—even though he was victimized!

When you see yourself as a victim, you give away your power. Through the spiritual exercises of renewing the mind, we learn how to challenge the victim mentality. We learn of our rights in Christ and prayerfully explore why a person or circumstance has so much power to control our lives. "Victim thinking" robs us of responsibility and dignity, the two primary pillars of human hope and value.

Yet, we have not been created to act like victims. God has given us the ability to decide what we will believe and to choose the course of our thinking. And we are made in such a way that our emotions and actions grow out of our beliefs and our mode of thinking. So, although there are many forces and events in life over which we really have no control, we can still control the way we respond.

One of the most vivid examples of this comes from Viktor Frankl. In *Man's Search for Meaning*, he tells of his experience as a Jew in a Nazi concentration camp. He relates how the Nazis stripped the Jews of *everything*: their clothes, their books and papers, their jewelry—every valuable possession and memento that gave meaning to life. "But there was one thing the Nazis could never take away—our freedom to choose our attitude."[4]

Our belief system is the key to emotional and spiritual health. As we study God's Word, replacing our worldly beliefs with God's truth, we affect our emotions, as well as every other aspect of our life and conduct. Because we can choose a new way of believing and thinking, we have hope for breaking free from dark emotions and deep wounds of the past.

---

*B*ecause we can choose a new way of believing and thinking, we have hope for breaking free from dark emotions and deep wounds of the past.

We see an example of this in Paul's reflection on his own sin. His past persecution of Christians, including his part in the stoning of Stephen, could have generated an unbearable burden of guilt. But his biblical, grace-based belief system enabled him to process his guilt in a fascinating way.

> *I thank Christ Jesus our Lord, who has given me strength, that he considered me faithful, appointing me to his service. Even though I was once a blasphemer and a persecutor and a violent man, I was shown mercy because I acted in ignorance and unbelief. The grace of our Lord was poured out on me abundantly, along with the faith and love that are in Christ Jesus.*
>
> *Here is a trustworthy saying that deserves full acceptance: Christ Jesus came into the world to save sinners—of whom I am the worst. But for that very reason I was shown mercy so that in me, the worst of sinners, Christ Jesus might display his unlimited patience as an example for those who would believe on him and receive eternal life. Now to the King eternal, immortal, invisible, the only God, be honor and glory for ever and ever. Amen. (1 Tim. 1:12-17)*

God's grace and mercy in Christ transform Paul's sin into fuel for praise. Instead of falling into despair, he breaks into his own doxology. This is far different from Judas, whose guilt was so overwhelming and whose understanding of grace was so minimal that he was crushed by despair (Matt. 27:1-5).

The Bible clearly teaches that the hope of personal change is rooted in two basic resources: the power of the Spirit within us,[5] and the renewal of our minds by allowing God's Word to instruct us. Jesus' emphasis on teaching is a clear testimony to the fact that right thinking is central to spiritual vitality and a life that pleases God. With this in mind, we turn eagerly to God's Word so that our thinking can be shaped by the truth of God.

SHAPED BY THE LIVING WORD

"The Word of God is living and active." These words from Hebrews have been demonstrated in dramatic fashion time and again in the course of history. Augustine (A.D. 354–430), bishop of Hippo in North Africa, was one of the most profound thinkers and articulate theologians of the early church. He attributes his conversion directly to reading the Bible. In the following passage he describes his misery in sin and his response to a suggestion for action.

> I probed the hidden depths of my soul and wrung its pitiful secrets from it, and when I gathered them all before the eyes of my heart, a great storm broke within me, bringing with it a great deluge of tears. . . . For I felt that I was still enslaved by my sins, and in my misery I kept crying, "How long shall I go on saying 'Tomorrow, tomorrow'? Why not now? Why not make an end of my ugly sins at this moment?"
>
> I was asking myself these questions, weeping all the while with the most bitter sorrow in my heart, when all at once I heard the sing-song voice of a child in a nearby house. Whether it was the voice of a boy or a girl I cannot say, but

again and again it repeated the chorus, "Take it and read, take it and read." At this I looked up, thinking hard whether there was any kind of game in which children used to chant words like these, but I could not remember ever hearing them before. I stemmed my flood of tears and stood up, telling myself that this could only be God's command to open my book of Scripture and read the first passage on which my eyes should fall. For I had heard the story of Antony, and I remembered how he had happened to go into a church while the Gospel was being read and had taken it as an instruction addressed to himself when he heard the words, "Go home and sell all that belongs to you. Give it to the poor, and so the treasure you have shall be in heaven; then come back and follow me." By this message from God he had at once been converted.

So I hurried back to the place where Alypius was sitting, for when I stood up to move away I had put down the book containing Paul's Letters. I seized it and opened it, and in silence I read the first passage on which my eyes fell: "No orgies or drunkenness, no immorality or indecency, no fighting or jealousy. Take up the weapons of the Lord Jesus Christ; and stop giving attention to your sinful nature, to satisfy its desires." I had no wish to read more and no need to do so. For in an instant, as I came to the end of the sentence, it was as though the light of faith flooded into my heart and all the darkness of doubt was dispelled.[6]

Christianity is not a code of ethics determined by people but a way of life absolutely dependent upon the existence of God, who sent his own divine Son to die for us. This God also sent the Holy Spirit to empower us to begin the process of transformation from people controlled by the world and the "old self" to people who are living in the freedom of obedience to God. With this as our foundation, we must conform our lives to the revelation/authority on which our faith rests. Those who discover this truth directly from God's Word are transformed—and become transforming forces in the world. Martin Luther had been deeply troubled spiritually. In the course of an intensive study of Scripture, God opened his eyes, touched his heart, and struck the spark that ignited the Protestant Reformation.

> I greatly longed to understand Paul's Epistle to the Romans, and nothing stood in the way but that one expression, "the righteousness of God," because I took it to mean that righteousness whereby God is righteous and deals righteously in punishing the unrighteous. . . . Night and day I pondered until . . . I grasped the truth that the righteousness of God is that righteousness whereby, through grace and sheer mercy, he justifies us by faith. Thereupon I felt myself to be reborn and to have gone through open doors into paradise. The whole of Scripture took on a new meaning, and whereas before "the righteousness of God" had filled me with hate, now it became to me inexpressibly sweet in greater love. This passage of Paul became to me a gateway to heaven.[7]

God's Word is living and powerful! It is the means by which God has given us a firm place to stand together in the midst of confusing and conflicting voices. God's words are a reference point for all Christians everywhere—a common language and a set of standards that can sufficiently guide our decisions.

Inspired by the Holy Spirit, the Bible continues to impart the breath of new life and thought to us. When we apply God's Word to our lives, our faith is reawakened, our thinking is corrected, our character is shaped, our obedience is inspired, and we are sustained through trials and suffering. This process is no secret;

the spiritual exercises of study and meditation are basic require-
ments of spiritual restoration and vitality. Combined with prayer,
they are the aerobics of the spiritual life. They are essential to
our spiritual stamina. Without the disciplines that make God's
Word reality in our living, all other activities will fall short of
their intended results.

Guidelines for Bible Study That Is Life Changing

Although the Bible is a complex book, worthy of the highest
scholarly effort, it is also a blessing to the most simple, sincere
study. While some people are intimidated by the Scriptures, trusting only the experts to tell them what it means, the Bible itself
claims to be available to all who read it. As Paul writes, "Let the
word of Christ dwell in you [plural] richly as you teach and
admonish one another with all wisdom" (Col. 3:16). Since the
time of the Reformation, the Bible has once again become available to the people. This does not deny the place of scholarship,
but it affirms the fact that God's Word is for everybody.

There are numerous Bible study methods and systems. My purpose here is not to add one more "better" or "perfect" method
to follow. Most of us know more about Bible study than we have
time to apply! The real question is: How should Bible study be
changing me? Why is it good for my soul? How does it restore a
blah spiritual life? What would I consider the "active ingredient"
in Bible study? In order to talk about Bible study in this way, I
will describe the "Basic Believer 101" method, which is *inductive*
Bible study. It consists of four steps, and these steps, applied to
any type of study, will make the difference between mere study
and study that does a real work on your soul.

Prayer. Sometimes we leave out this step, but the Bible is
inspired by the Holy Spirit (2 Tim. 3:16), and it relies upon the

Holy Spirit to give us understanding. The psalmist prayed, "Open my eyes, that I may behold wondrous things out of thy law" (Ps. 119:18, RSV). This is called "a prayer for illumination"; we pray, "Lord speak to me through your Word. If there is anything special you have to say to me today, speak through this passage and give me eyes to recognize it." We are asking God to shed his light on our pathway. This is not merely a formality. It is a genuine acknowledgment that we are ready for God to address us. It is like putting the phone on the hook and expecting it to ring. This prayer reminds us that the Bible is no ordinary book and that, through it, we have the privilege of interacting with the living Lord.

Observation. During the summer between my sophomore and junior years in high school, a youth leader, Keith Brown, challenged me to read the New Testament and memorize the subject matter of each chapter. I took him up on it and read nearly every day, observing the contents and topic of each chapter, writing them in a notebook. The next summer, I saw Keith at camp. "Hey, Keith," I said, "sit down and get comfortable. Matthew 1: the genealogy of Jesus; Matthew 2: the wise men; Matthew 3: John the Baptist. . . ." Throughout that week I took Keith through the New Testament, chapter by chapter. I tell this not as a boast but because that challenge to study laid the foundation of Bible knowledge for a lifetime of study and discipling others. Though I confess to forgetting some of the chapter titles (Don't ask me to keep the synoptic Gospels straight!), that study was the most important step I took in hiding God's Word in my heart.

In addition to overview reading (such as I did, or such as reading through the Bible in a year), you may want to read a specific section of the Bible over and over again for a month. Many people do this with Psalms and Proverbs or the Epistles. Or you may read in conjunction with a Bible study you're in. The only caution in that case is to discipline yourself to read for your soul, not for completing a study guide. Any of these methods is different from "Bible roulette," in which we simply open the Bible and expect God to speak to us. I hasten to add that God has mercifully worked in this way, as Augustine testified! Such a habit of reading, however, makes as much sense as blindfolding yourself and reaching into the kitchen pantry, promising yourself you'll eat for dinner the first thing you grab. A balanced diet consists of intentional nourishment from a number of food sources. Spiritual health means disciplining ourselves to read and study the entire Bible— even if some parts seem like our least favorite foods.

One of the best tools to motivate us to Bible study is a clean desk and a simple chart with the date and the passage already scheduled. This gets us over the hump of decision making that can be just enough to discourage or distract us. If you decide to study in the early morning, have your Bible open on your desk, your journal and pen ready, and—if it's your custom—the coffeemaker already set on a timer to be ready when you awaken. Do what you can the night before to make it easier in the morning.

As you read, go over the passage once to become familiar with the context and the content. Then read it a second time, reading for something that speaks to your heart. Focus your attention on a particular verse, phrase, or word in the passage. I encourage people in their rereading to watch for a verse that "jumps out at them." Write it down at the top of a piece of paper or in your journal. You'll be surprised at what you *don't* notice until you physically copy the verse onto paper.

Having selected a passage, observe some of the basic characteristics of the passage. The questions of observation are the familiar journalism questions:

- *Who* are the main characters?
- *What* is happening?

- *What* is the purpose of the passage?
- *When* is this happening in history and in the lives of the characters?
- *Where* is the action taking place?
- *How* is the action or teaching conducted?
- *Why* is this passage in the Bible?

The why question will usually move you into interpretation, but you may make an initial note at this point. You should try to answer these questions from the reading itself. Do not turn to commentaries or study Bibles *until* you have given the Holy Spirit and your own thinking a chance! One of the great joys of the inductive method is discovery. There's no greater satisfaction than when you find something yourself. Once you have taken a few moments to make these observations, you will feel more at home with the verse, ready for the next step.

Meditation. Determining the meaning of a verse or passage can be a huge task, especially if the passage is complex or controversial. Since we are not dealing with interpretation for academic, teaching, or preaching purposes, however, we are able to be less rigorous, though not careless. For devotional purposes, give yourself freedom to muse on the verse. *Lord, what are you saying to me? Why has this verse captured my attention?* As you listen, write down your thoughts, questions, and impressions. The interpretation builds on determining what the verse meant to the first hearers/readers. Then we translate it to our day and our specific life situation. A useful discipline is to rephrase the verse in your own words. Eugene Peterson's *The Message* is a powerful example of rephrasing Scripture to capture not only the actual words in translation but the contemporary meaning in a way that brings the Word alive.

Develop confidence in your own insights. When I was in an

upper-level English class at the university, my professor encouraged us to write our own insights on whatever we were reading. We were reading Melville's *Moby Dick* at the time, and I wrote an insight on the comparisons of the biblical character Ishmael with Melville's Ishmael. The process was invigorating. I felt a new "authority" in my study and class discussion. This was one of the first times I realized that there was more to knowledge than just quoting others. Dr. Dykstra encouraged us to develop our own thoughts, test them out, and see if others would concur—or if they had missed it altogether. Many of us are too timid to trust that God could actually speak to us, giving us wisdom and insight into his Word. Trust him! God is not restricted to speaking to Bible school or seminary graduates!

Application.　The purpose of Bible study is a changed life. Application is easiest to develop if the passage lends itself to measurable goals. For example, if you read 1 Corinthians 16:1-4, you may be convicted to apply the principle of weekly proportional giving of your income, starting with a small percentage and moving higher over a set period of time. Other passages, however, are difficult to frame in terms of measurable goals. For instance, let's say you read about God's call to Moses in Exodus 3 and studied verse 14, where the Lord says he is to be called "I AM WHO I AM." How do you develop a measurable application from a statement so profound and all-encompassing? One of the best ways is to ask yourself: Has there been a time when this fact about God would have helped me? What misconception about God does this correct for me? How would I have responded differently in my attitude or behavior, based on this new understanding of God? Looking back on specific situations in our lives in this way provides both a means of redeeming past mistakes and of helping us visualize concrete changes in our lives.

I have always appreciated this series of questions that can also help us in making specific applications:

- Is there an attitude to be changed?
- a sin to be confessed?
- an action to be taken or avoided?
- an example to follow?
- a promise to claim?[8]

And I add:

- a characteristic of God I need to appreciate and affirm for my life?
- a truth (doctrine) to be understood and applied?

In order to carry the fruit of study into our days, I suggest keeping a list of verses and insights in a journal or personal planner (schedule book). I have developed a set of pages where I list Bible verses, sayings, and personal insights. I call these my "activators" because they awaken energy and reorient my thinking.

John Stott tells of the time Billy Graham addressed some six hundred ministers in November 1970. Dr. Graham said that if he had his ministry to do all over again he would study three times as much as he had: "I've preached too much and studied too little." He later told Dr. Stott of Dr. Donald Barnhouse's statement: "If I only had three years to serve the Lord, I would spend two of them studying and preparing."[9]

STUDY UNLOCKS THE MYSTERIES OF GOD

"For my thoughts are not your thoughts,
neither are your ways my ways,"
declares the Lord.
"As the heavens are higher than the earth,

> *so are my ways higher than your ways*
> *and my thoughts than your thoughts."*

ISAIAH 55:8-9

These verses present a bleak picture as we set about the task of
understanding God's will for our lives. We cannot trust our natural reasoning. How are we to know what God wants us to do? As
if anticipating our question, the Lord proceeds to speak about
his Word.

> *As the rain and the snow come down from heaven,*
> *and do not return to it without watering the earth*
> *and making it bud and flourish,*
> *so that it yields seed for the sower and bread for the eater,*
> *so is my word that goes out from my mouth:*
> *It will not return to me empty,*
> *but will accomplish what I desire*
> *and achieve the purpose for which I sent it.*

ISAIAH 55:10-11

We do not despair because there is one hope for our thoughts to
become more like God's thoughts and our ways more like God's
ways. The refreshing image that communicates this hope is rain
in a parched land. God's thoughts are like the rain, coming
down through his Word. His truth is sown in our minds so that it
will bear the fruit of a new way of thinking, an eternal perspective on life.

Distorted concepts of God arise from the limitations of human
thinking and the pain of human experience. People who have
suffered at the hands of abusive parents find it difficult to pray,
"Our Father." Their love and trust have been violated by those
who carried the name of Father or Mother. As we study the
Bible, however, we learn that God parents us in a way that

respects our dignity and values our fragile lives. He doesn't exploit us, nor does he manipulate us. As we ponder the truth of Scripture, the Holy Spirit can soothe our grief, heal our wounds, and reshape our ideals of love and intimacy.[10]

As we grow in our study, we are also given countless insights into the awesome majesty of the Lord God Almighty. Our puny images of God are continually revised as we study the names and acts of God revealed in Scripture: the Lord of Creation, the Judge of the Flood, the Compassionate Deliverer of the Exodus, the Patient Sustainer of the Wilderness Wanderers, the Founder of David's Royal Line, the Inspirer of Prophets, the God Incarnate, the Holy Spirit empowering the early church, the Coming King, to highlight a few of the major themes.[11] Study enables us to develop a biblical concept of God. We break free from our ignorant prejudices, and we correct our misconceptions.

STUDY EXPOSES THE DECEPTIONS AND DISTORTIONS OF WORLDLY THINKING

I was talking with a man who came to know Christ recently, as I led him through a one-on-one Bible study. "I really don't understand what is happening," he said. "I am starting to see things I never saw before and think about things I never even cared about before." That, in its simplest form, is evidence of the mind of Christ in this new believer. He was honestly recognizing new aspects of life emerging; he was discovering a different way to see and approach life; he was revising his priorities; and he was finding a significant measure of freedom from some troubling thought habits.

Study is not merely the accumulation of information but the pursuit of wisdom, which is knowledge applied to life. In 1 Corinthians 2, Paul is exploring the wisdom God gives us—wisdom communicated by God's Spirit. "We have not received the spirit of the world but the Spirit who is from God, that we may understand what God has freely given us" (verse 12). What has God given us? "For who has known the mind of the Lord that he may instruct him? But we have the mind of Christ" (verse 16). This assertion causes us to stop short. Have I been thinking as Jesus would think?

It's important to note, however, that being endowed with the mind of Christ does not guarantee the effortless manifestation of Christian thinking in our daily lives. This was the problem Paul was addressing in Corinth. This is a problem we experience today: mentally stunted believers! Harry Blamires's book *The Christian Mind* sounds a significant call to the Christian community to enter into the rigorous discipline of learning to "think Christian" in the midst of the secular culture.

> The Christian mind has succumbed to the secular drift with a degree of weakness and nervelessness unmatched in Christian history. It is difficult to do justice in words to the complete loss of intellectual morale in the twentieth-century Church. One cannot characterize it without having recourse to language which will sound hysterical and melodramatic. There is no longer a Christian mind. There is still, of course, a Christian ethic, a Christian practice and a Christian spirituality. . . . But as a *thinking being*, the modern Christian has succumbed to secularization.[12]

How do we learn to think more clearly with the mind of Christ? We develop the mind of Christ by studying the mind of God revealed in his Word. We learn God's perspective, purposes, priorities, and principles very clearly from the apostles and the prophets. *While there will always be mystery concerning God, that which we must know for faith and life is presented fully in the teaching and experience of God's people in the Bible.* As we train ourselves to perceive the thinking of the world, we learn to test it against the counsel of God. Wisdom and power for living come as we break free from distorted values, subtle lures to temptation, and claims to truth that have no basis from a biblical perspective.

STUDY RELEASES SPIRITUAL ENERGY FOR DYNAMIC DISCIPLESHIP

A woman called me in the midst of a severe marital conflict. Her husband, an executive officer in a multinational corporation, was away from home frequently, but he criticized her for the decisions she often had to make in his absence. This time he had "gone too far," and she was desperate for some type of change, even divorce. I listened to her extensively, and we decided together that they might benefit from a referral to an excellent counselor. As we were concluding our conversation, I said, "Before I pray, I encourage you to get your Bible and read 1 Corinthians 13 slowly, several times a day. Study each verse, each phrase, asking God to speak to you." We closed in prayer.

Several weeks later she called again. Here's her story in her own words:

> Doug, things got *worse* after my phone call to you! We went to counseling several times, but after one session I was so angry that I told Henry I would not sleep in the same room with him. He went to bed furious and embarrassed that our children would see this "humiliating behavior," as he called it. He woke up angry. As he was getting dressed, he noticed my Bible on the dresser with a piece of paper marking 1 Corinthians 13. He opened the Bible and began to read. He read it several times (he told me later). It hit him like a ton of bricks. He came to me that morning with tears in his eyes and said that he was going to try to change and love me the way the Lord wanted him to love me.

Through reading, considering, studying, and meditating upon God's word to us, we discover the truth we need in order to become whole people. We learn about God, ourselves, and this world in which we live. We cultivate our values, our priorities, our understanding of kingdom life, and the principles for kingdom living. The goals of our study are to know God, to develop a biblical outlook on life, and to develop biblical principles for living and challenging the sinful systems of this present world.

How do I stay fresh in my spiritual life? One of the secrets is understanding what David McKenna calls the Law of Syntropy. He describes the Law of Entropy from physics, which asserts that whenever physical resources such as wood, metal, or oil are recycled, the product quality drops in each successive cycle. But the Law of Syntropy describes an opposite principle at work in the spiritual/mental realm. "The spiritual and intellectual resources improve and expand with use and reuse. . . . Physical resources are to be conserved; spiritual and intellectual resources are to be exploited."[13]

A similar understanding is presented by Mortimer Adler. He writes: "The worst mistake we can make is to regard mental fatigue as if it were physical fatigue. We can recuperate from the latter by giving our bodies a rest. But mental fatigue that results from failure cannot be removed by giving in to it and taking a rest. That just makes matters worse. Whatever the specific stumbling block is, it must be cleared up, and fast, before the fatigue of failure swamps us."[14]

I have found this to be true in my own experience time and again. I can be feeling tired and unmotivated, and then an idea comes to mind that ignites a spark of energy, restarting my mental engine. I have sat down at my desk at home for my early morning Bible study, gritting my teeth in obedience, feeling that my heart was so unresponsive that God wouldn't even want to bless me. Then as I read, an insight comes that brings me fully awake and alive. What a joy!

One such insight came when I was reading Revelation 4 one morning. I was not feeling very inspired until I read John's amazing description of the reality that is ours in worship: "After this I looked, and there before me was a door standing open in heaven." These words jumped out at me, as if for the first time. Worship is the open door to God's presence! We meet God in worship, and this meeting is more than we can ever imagine. But what I noticed for the first time was that John was ushered "in the Spirit" right to the throne! There was no waiting room or foyer for preparation. Why? Because the way is completely open through Jesus Christ! The writer of Hebrews expressed it this way: "Let us therefore approach the throne of grace with fullest confidence, that we may receive mercy for our failures and grace to help in the hour of need" (Heb. 4:16, PHILLIPS). We have direct and immediate access to the throne of grace.

Thoughts like these tap the inner reservoir of spiritual power that God has placed within us. Our hearts recognize the truth and rejoice to receive it—even if it's truth that is difficult to take.

As we consider the role of God's Word in the cultivation of spiritual vitality, we need to be open to the power of the Word in ways we may not have previously considered. We—especially those of us in Western culture—are accustomed to logic, argument, and the literary-cognitive aspects of Bible study, such as those we have just considered in the principles of inductive Bible study. But the Word of God has more to offer us as we dare to take deeper steps into its power and meaning.

NOTES

1. *American Bible Society Record,* March 1990.
2. Francis A. Schaeffer, *True Spirituality* (Wheaton, Ill.: Tyndale House, 1971), 41.

3. The power of the mind has been studied and taught by people across a widely diverse theological and nontheological spectrum. This teaching ranges from Norman Vincent Peale's *The Power of Positive Thinking*, through Robert Schuller's concept of possibility thinking, into the prosperity principles of Napoleon Hill's *Think and Grow Rich* (Hill has a Christian Science background) and on into the human-potential movement and psychological principles of people who clearly do not advocate the Christian faith and ethic, such as Albert Ellis, founder of the rational-emotive school of psychology. While this broad spectrum makes many faithful followers of Christ nervous, it is, in fact, evidence that the human mind that God has created is very powerful and this power can be used (or abused) in any number of ways.

4. Viktor Frankl, *Man's Search for Meaning* (New York: Simon & Schuster, 1984).

5. John 14:12-17; 1 John 4:4; Ephesians 3:20.

6. Augustine, *Confessions*, Book VIII (New York: New American Library), chap. 12, 182–183.

7. *Eerdmans' Handbook to the History of Christianity* (Grand Rapids, Mich.: Eerdmans, 1977), 366.

8. "The Christian Adventure, Step One," *Ten Basic Steps toward Christian Maturity* (Arrowhead Springs San Bernardino, Calif.: Campus Crusade for Christ, 1968), 29.

9. John R. W. Stott, *Your Mind Matters* (Downers Grove, Ill.: InterVarsity Press, 1972), 55.

10. Helpful passages on the nature of God's love and care for us are Psalm 23, Psalm 103, and Ezekiel 34. The Ezekiel passage is especially pertinent because, although it doesn't mention parents, it addresses the

abuses of leaders and presents a vivid picture of the healing, affirming love of God for each person.

11. A number of lists provide the names of God for meditation. One of the most complete I've come across is that of Henry T. Blackaby and Claude V. King, *Experiencing God: Knowing and Doing the Will of God* (Nashville: Lifeway Press, 1990), 220–221.

12. Harry Blamires, *The Christian Mind* (London: SPCK, 1966), 3.

13. David McKenna, "Recycling Pastors," *Leadership* 1, no. 4 (fall 1980), 25.

14. Mortimer Adler, "Success Means Never Feeling Tired" [no further reference available].

SOUL-SEARCHING

Questions for Reflection and Discussion

1. What has been your experience with Bible study?

   a) I read the Bible when the mood strikes.

   b) I have started and stopped too many times to count.

   c) I have been discouraged by too many difficult passages I don't understand.

   d) I have found a method that works well for me.

2. The author describes at least three primary benefits of Bible study. What are they? What benefit most interests you at this time? Why?

3. There are a number of principles that enable us to shape our thinking under the eternal perspective. The most significant are:

   a) God has spoken and still speaks to us in the Bible.

   b) God created all things and continues to work in the world today.

   c) God is willing to reveal his will for us as we abide in him.

   d) God hears and answers prayer, providing the spiritual and material resources we need for all situations.

   How do these principles bring a new angle to the opportunities and problems you are facing? What response do they invite from you as you seek to work with God? What worldly assumptions do they correct? What other elements would you add?

4. What are the four steps in inductive Bible study? Summarize them.

5. Choose one (or any number) of the following passages and apply the four steps, writing your study in your journal.

a) 2 Timothy 3:10-17

b) Hebrews 4:12-16

c) Psalm 119:1-8 or 9-16 or 17-24

d) Deuteronomy 8:1-10

e) Joshua 1:1-9

f) John 14:15-26

CHAPTER TWELVE

Encounter with the Living Word

❧ MEDITATION

ONE Sunday evening, as we gathered for prayer at the conclusion of the service in which I had been teaching on spirituality, Nicole asked if she could speak. Here's her story from that night:

> Several weeks ago, God began to do something in my life when Doug led us through a meditation on Jesus' healing of the paralytic in Mark 2. You remember how we were asked to picture ourselves in Capernaum, with the crowds coming to Jesus and the paralytic being carried by his friends. Well, I saw myself as the paralytic on the stretcher. When we got up on the roof, however, a whirlwind came along, like a tornado, and swept me up, out of reach of my friends. I was terrified and wanted to get back to earth, but I couldn't. I kept reaching down, trying to grab Julie's hand—she was one of the friends who was carrying me—but we couldn't touch.

When the meditation time ended, I was still in the air! I was deeply troubled by this experience. I must tell you that I've only been coming to church for several months now, and I really don't know much about Christianity. I decided I needed to talk to one of the pastors, so I met with Dr. Ernie Bradley, on staff here. He took time to answer my questions and explained the way of salvation through Jesus Christ. I wanted time to think about this, so I didn't make any decision at that time.

Tonight, when we began to sing, I immediately saw myself back in Capernaum, hovering in the air above the roof with my friends! Then, as we sang "Amazing Grace," it all made sense. My friends grabbed my hand and lowered me to the roof, then into the presence of Jesus. He told me I'm forgiven and free!

What a joy! The whole group burst into tearful applause at the power of God. I was delightfully amazed that God had used a meditation, which I had reserved for "more mature Christians" as the means of bringing a new birth!

GUARDRAILS FOR THE MEDITATION TRAIL

Some people feel quite uneasy about meditation. There is some foundation for that. Meditation, a spiritual discipline dating back to the psalms of the Old Testament and before, has turned up in some modes of spirituality that are not Christian. Unorthodox sects and organizations have tainted practices, including meditation, that formerly served the highest Christian purposes.

The New Age movement and many of its authors and leaders have robbed Christians of some of their basic spiritual vocabulary. And, out of fear of sounding like them, we have become more and more silent in those areas in which we most clearly need to speak. We are giving away words that have fed and directed the souls of many generations before us. Words like *imagination, meditation, spiritual direction*—classic terms of orthodox Christian teachers and pastors—now have the aura of suspicion wafting from them. Suspicion isn't the only smell we detect; this spiritual dilemma reeks of the devil's presence and works. Satan knows that spiritual activity transforms us; he knows that if we meditate very much, we will begin to see the way things really are—and we'll be onto him!

Satan, remember, is in the business of counterfeits. This, combined with the natural tendency to "all or nothing" thinking has led many people to draw solid lines where they can't be drawn, dismissing as heresy some of the central means of God's grace in Jesus Christ. Consider the subject of angels. If the deceiver can appear as an angel of light, does that mean we are to dismiss every angel or angelic encounter as counterfeit? What about Mary's dialogue with Gabriel? What do we make of the angel who liberated Paul from jail, or the statement of Hebrews 1:14—"Are not all angels ministering spirits sent to serve those who will inherit salvation"? Obviously, the New Age preoccupation with angels does not make the Word of God false any more than the extraction of opium from poppies means that we should destroy all poppies! Such simplistic thinking robs us of the fullest experience of life as God intended.

One of the most volatile areas of discussion in the current debate of spirituality focuses on the concepts of imagination and creativity. These are at the heart of what it means to be human, created in the image of God. As image bearers, we have the joy of partnership with God in what we might call secondary creation: taking the "stuff" of life and rearranging it into new forms for the glory of God and for a better life in his service. This is plainly accepted in the physical world of raw materials, manufacturing, and labor. It is also clear in the spiritual world. From the

Exodus songs of Miriam to the visions of Ezekiel and the parables of Jesus, and beyond Scripture to the imaginative writing of John Bunyan's *The Pilgrim's Progress* and C. S. Lewis's fantasies and science fiction, people have encountered God through the gift of imaginative thought.

Yet impostors have arisen who use God-given traits, such as imagination, to supplant and deny the true God. What, then, do we do with the concept of imagination? It seems to me that dismissing it because others have misused it is like banning all cars because someone had a fatal accident. I would rather reexamine such gifts in the light of Scripture so that they can be redeemed for the glory of God and for the growth of God's people.

The big question will arise as to how we keep our meditations in check. How do we keep from heresy, from false and deceptive guidance, from clever rationalizations that we may love more than the Lord, from concepts that draw us into unfruitful lives? In dealing with touchy subjects such as meditation and imagination, four principles have always helped and protected me:

We Affirm the Authority of God's Word over All Human Experience.
Our techniques must not contradict the Word of God, nor must our conclusions. This explains why meditation is placed second in sequence to the study of God's Word. Meditation builds upon our mental understanding of God's Word; it does not replace it. Our conversational prayer and meditation are not substitutes for the Word; they are the fruit of our study. We are to become more earnest students of the Word. Initially, there may be a fascination with imaginative encounters with God's Word, but these must be balanced with the careful exegesis of the texts upon which we meditate.

We Consult the Witness of History.
How have God's people dealt with these issues in the past? As Ecclesiastes says, "There is nothing new under the sun." In the

*M*editation builds upon our mental understanding of God's Word; it does not replace it.

area of meditation, for example, we find a continuous thread of
spiritual vitality affirming and developing this discipline across the
centuries. The community of faith has left us rich resources, such
as the Spiritual Exercises of Ignatius of Loyola, as well as wise cautions, such as the counsels of Jonathan Edwards concerning spiritual excesses.[1] Referring to Loyola's Exercises, Puritan scholar J. I.
Packer writes, "They remain a potent aid to self-knowledge and
devotion to the Lord Jesus, even for those outside the Catholicism
in which they are so strongly rooted."[2] Maturing believers appreciate the diverse gifts of God's people and avoid making simplistic
judgments.

*We Consider the Character of the Presenter and the Effects in His/Her
Life and the Lives of Those Associated with Them.*
This is much more difficult, because our judgments of a person's
character are subjective, affected by our emotional reactions to
him or her, whatever gossip we've heard or read, or even our
reaction to what the person is saying (and sometimes we react
negatively to something that is true, yet painful to face). Yet
Jesus gave us this standard: "You shall know them by their fruit."
As we consider a practice, we look for signs that Christ is honored, the Word of God is upheld, and lives are changed in accordance with godliness. Nicole's experience has borne fruit.
Nearly three years later, she is helping to lead worship in our congregation and has said to me, "I am changing. I no longer hold
many of the same views I held before accepting Christ. I still
don't always agree with you, Doug, but I really am changing."

We Dwell in a Faithful Community That Nurtures Us and Holds Us Accountable in Our Pilgrimage of Discipleship.
A disconnected disciple is a contradiction in terms. Christ has called us not only to himself but to his people. Even as we wouldn't scuba dive without a buddy or climb a rock face without a belayer to hold the safety ropes, so we don't venture into the deeper areas of spiritual life without the support, guidance, accountability, and cautionary influence of peers and mentors. The greatest security is found in honest friendships that are submitted to Christ.

This all sounds risky—and it is. But growth takes place at the edge of risk. Mysticism scares people, even as it shook Moses at the burning bush, Ezekiel in the desert with the wheels within the wheels, and Paul with his vision of the third heaven. *But the greater risk is to cut ourselves off from the Lord who wants to reach us, to transform us, to equip us, and to mobilize us for God's kingdom.*

Growth takes place at the edge of risk.

Why do I bring these matters up right from the start? Because I am committed to walking "in the light, as he is in the light" (1 John 1:7). It reminds me of my first rock climbing and rappelling experience in the Sierra Nevada Mountains. As my family, friends, and I prepared for a 150-foot descent over a cliff, we wanted to know what the problems were from the start. Once we knew the problems and how to handle them, and having come to fully trust our guides, the risk of a lifetime became the thrill of a lifetime. The frank acknowledgment of tension and difficulty helps us trust each other. These concerns about meditation must be addressed, or you may be discouraged from reading further.

God has a practice of calling us into unfamiliar territory—but for the purposes of deepening our lives and adding to our adventures in grace.

BIBLICAL WAYS TO MEDITATE

The exhortation to meditate is found throughout the Scriptures. "This book of the law shall not depart out of your mouth; you shall meditate on it day and night" (Josh. 1:8, NRSV). Likewise, Psalm 1 says, "but his delight is in the law of the Lord and on his law he meditates day and night." The Hebrew term for "meditate," *haggah,* is the word for "muttering," as in reading something to yourself aloud. We say the words over and over, as when struck by a new idea.

Meditation means stopping long enough to turn a single thought or idea over and over in your mind—viewing it from as many angles as possible. The goal is not the quantity of facts but the depth of understanding. The following story, often told in leadership studies, applies to the exercise of meditation.

THE FISH, PROFESSOR AGASSIZ, SAMUEL SCUDDER, AND HARVARD UNIVERSITY

Scudder relates that when he first started with Professor Agassiz, the professor placed the specimen of a fish in front of him with this instruction:

"'Take this fish,' said he, 'and look at it; we call it a haemulon; by and by I will ask what you have seen.'

"With that he left me but in a moment returned with explicit instructions as to the care of the object entrusted to me.

"'No man is fit to be a naturalist,' said he, 'who does not know how to take care of specimens.'

"I was to keep the fish before me in a tiny tray, and occasionally moisten the surface with alcohol from the jar, always taking care to replace the stopper tightly. . . .

"In ten minutes I had seen all that could be seen in that fish, and started in search of the professor—who had, however, left the museum; and when I returned, after lingering over some of the odd animals stored in the upper apartment, my specimen was dry all over. I dashed fluid over the fish as if to resuscitate the beast from a fainting fit, and looked with anxiety for a return of the normal sloppy appearance. This little excitement over, nothing was to be done but to return to a steadfast gaze at my mute companion. . . ."

Agassiz did not return for several hours. Scudder, distasteful though his task was but unable to leave it, got pencil and paper and began to draw the fish. To his surprise he discovered some new features he had not previously observed.

Eventually Agassiz returned. First he commended Scudder on undertaking to draw the specimen, saying, "That is right; a pencil is one of the best of eyes." Then he asked, "Well, what is it like?" and listened attentively to Scudder's brief recitation on what he had observed. When Scudder finished, Agassiz waited as if he were expecting more and then, as though disappointed, said, "You have not looked very carefully; why you haven't even seen one of the most conspicuous features of the animal, which is as plainly before your eyes as the fish itself; look again, look again!" And Scudder was left to spend the rest of the afternoon with the haemulon!

At the end of the day Agassiz instructed Scudder to return and continue his study on the following day. The next morning he was cordially (and reassuringly) greeted by the professor, who appeared to be quite anxious for Scudder to see all there was to be observed about the fish:

"'Do you perhaps mean,' I asked, 'that the fish has symmetrical sides with paired organs?'

"His thoroughly pleased 'Of course! Of course!' repaid the wakeful hours of the previous night. After he had discoursed most happily and enthusiastically—as he always did—upon the importance of this point, I ventured to ask what I should do next.

"'Oh, look at your fish!' he said, and left me again to my own devices. In a little more than an hour he returned, and heard my new catalogue.

"'That is good, that is good!' he repeated; 'but that is not all; go on.' And so for three long days he placed that fish before my eyes, forbidding me to look at anything else, or to use any artificial aid. 'Look, look, look,' was his repeated injunction.

"This was the best entomological lesson I ever had—a lesson whose influence has extended to the details of every subsequent study, a legacy the professor has left to me, as he has left it to many others, of inestimable value, which we could not buy, with which we cannot part. . . .

"The fourth day, a second fish of the same group was placed beside the first, and I was bidden to point out the resemblances and differences between the two; another and another followed, until the entire family lay before me, and a whole legion of jars covered the table and surrounding shelves; the odor had become a pleasant perfume; and even now, the sight of an old, six-inch, worm-eaten cork brings fragrant memories.

"The whole group of haemulons was thus brought in review; and, whether engaged upon the dissection of the internal organs, the preparation and examination of the bony framework, or the description of the various parts, Agassiz's training in the method of observing facts and their orderly arrangement was ever accompanied by the urgent exhortation not to be content with them.

"'Facts are stupid things,' he would say, 'until brought into connection with some general law.'"[3]

In meditation, we are looking at the fish. We are taking the time to ponder the Word of God, allowing the Holy Spirit to reveal the riches of wisdom. This is far more than simply surveying the material for content purposes.

There are two primary approaches to meditation in orthodox Christian tradition: cognitive and discursive. These both have biblical roots and have been practiced throughout church history.

COGNITIVE MEDITATION

This is the first level of meditation. At this level, we are actively thinking in the analytical part of our brain and consciousness. We're also concentrating on words and their meanings rather than on images. We are developing a logical sequence of thought, putting our ideas in orderly fashion.

This is the most common mode of meditation and where I recommend most people begin. It builds on our study of the Word but takes us beyond observation to in-depth pondering.

An Example of Cognitive Meditation

Begin with the sentence, "I will meditate on God's Word day and night." Explore those words. Day and night. Daytime: I will take his Word into my work to guide my behavior, to influence the way I make decisions and treat others. The Lord is with me all day and night. Night: I will take comfort in his Word, to cover the disappointments of the day, to assure me of forgiveness as I confess the sins of the day. I will meditate on his Word day and night. . . .

Guidelines for Cognitive Meditation

1. Select a brief verse or passage that attracts your attention.   This may interest you because of a particular problem you are having at this time or because you feel it promises rich insight. You may want to do some basic study of the verse, such as defining a term using a Bible dictionary or checking a confusing concept in a commentary. The less of this, however, the better, since you want to come to the passage as "fresh" as possible so that the Holy Spirit, not the latest commentary, guides your meditation.

2. Say or write it several times until you "have it" without having to look at it.   This helps it take root in your mind. You aren't distracted by the other verses around it and can focus on this single thought.

3. Begin to ponder the verse.   One way to do this is to look at it in as many ways as possible. In the above example, I simply took the routine activities of the day and tried to picture as many ways as possible that God's Word could enter into my day. In the same way, I thought about the activities of evening and night. Someone may ask, "What is the purpose of trying to think of many different applications?" The value of this is to see one or two specific insights emerge that are especially helpful. But you need not be preoccupied with quantity. You may simply consider the verse in light of one situation.

4. Write what comes from your meditation in your journal.   You may be the type who does the meditation through writing—that is my personal preference. Or, you may be the type who finds writing disruptive. In that case, leave a few moments at the end to summarize your experience and the insight you received.

Some people find this a very satisfying exercise and never

desire anything different. There are others, however, who find themselves nourished with a second type of meditation, usually known as discursive meditation.

DISCURSIVE MEDITATION

Research on the functioning of the brain has helped us understand that there are two primary aspects to the brain.[4] The analytic functions, rooted in the left hemisphere of the brain, are balanced by the intuitive functions of the right hemisphere. In the intuitive mode, we view things in terms of their completeness instead of in separate parts. We see how things link together, how they make sense as a whole. This type of thinking is visual and symbolic, connected to stories, art, the physical body, and movement.

Which mode—analytical or intuitive—is the most spiritual? Neither one! But most people, according to the personality traits they were born with, develop one mode more than the other. This means that they will automatically be more comfortable with some forms of meditation than with others. It also means that in meditation we can stretch ourselves and try to strengthen our weaker part. Those of us who are more comfortable with thinking analytically will be enriched by giving the intuitive dimension of our brain the opportunity to grow and aid us in our spiritual growth. Those of us who function easily in the intuitive mode would do well to learn how to approach all of life with more careful and logical analysis. Spiritual growth involves experiencing God in light of our whole being.

In discursive meditation we clear our minds of other distractions and consciously focus on a portion from Scripture, either a word, phrase, or passage. My own definition of discursive meditation is "encountering the living Lord through the written Word by the power of the God-given faculty of imagination." The role of imagination is central to a vital experience in meditation. "Our lives are dyed the color of our imaginations,"[5] said an ancient philosopher. In imagination we find energy to solve problems in creative ways, to uncover new possibilities, to experience aspects of life as vividly as if they were actually occurring at the time. Scripture comes alive as we sanctify this God-given ability, opening ourselves to experience God at a different level.

One of the keys to using our imagination is to involve all our senses as we approach a biblical passage. If you are with Jesus at the feeding of the five thousand, see the crowds and the setting, hear the noise, smell the fragrances and odors, feel the grass as he invites you to sit, taste the bread and the fish. Such an exercise of concentration puts us more fully in touch with things we never considered before. The impact of the supernatural miracle becomes more impressive—where *did* all this bread come from? The boy's gift is more touching—he did what he could. Great preachers, communicators, and storytellers have often cultivated this skill without conscious awareness—and we have grown through their ministry. Now we are encouraged to step out in new ways, to discover the riches of Scripture for ourselves.

In a discursive meditation, we move through a rational series of steps "in dialogue" with the verse (thus the designation "discursive" meditation, or dialogical meditation). The left brain is still engaged, but it is not dominating.

Guidelines for Discursive Meditation

The experience of Nicole that I related at the beginning of the chapter happened in response to a guided discursive meditation I led on Mark 2. It followed this outline, which I use personally and in leading groups. This meditation is based on a story in Scripture. Stories are good to start with because storytelling automatically engages your imagination. This is probably why Jesus used storytelling so much in his ministry.

Selection of the Material

Ask for the Holy Spirit's guidance as you select the material for your meditation. Selections from the Gospels, especially encounters with Jesus, and the parables, are often the most fruitful starting places. Pick a passage that seems to address an issue you want to bring to the Lord.

Preparation—Physical and Mental

1. Physical relaxation. The condition of our body affects the way we take in information and how much good it does us. Have you ever tried to concentrate on an important conversation while you were extremely nervous about an entirely separate issue? Our lives are filled with tension, and at any given hour of the day it becomes necessary to release that tension in preparation for doing a task or learning something new.

One relaxation method many people have found effective is to sit upright on a firm chair and relax your body from the feet up, tensing and relaxing a few muscles at a time. Begin by extending your right leg and pointing your toes up so that your foot is perpendicular to your leg. Hold them tense for five to ten seconds, then relax and return to a normal position. Breathe deeply as you tense the muscles and breathe out slowly as you relax them. Do this with the other leg, then with each arm, then clench and release each hand. Finally, hunch your shoulders and relax them, then do neck rolls. Breathing is one of the most important facets of relaxation. Take deep breaths from the diaphragm (without lifting your shoulders) and expel them easily, counting to ten. This oxygenates the blood, refreshing the body.

2. Focus. Someone has called this "the recollection of the scattered self." The object is to turn your full attention to the Lord and his Word. This is a good time to offer simple prayers or to repeat short Scriptures such as, "The Lord is near to all who call upon him, to all who call upon him in truth" (Ps. 145:18, RSV), or "Open my eyes, that I may behold wondrous things out of thy law" (Ps. 119:18, RSV).

Initial Reflection

1. Develop a vivid scene in your mind.   Get the sense of the physical aspects of the passage; the air, the temperature, time of day, smells, textures, tastes, appearances of people, objects around, landscape . . . involve all your senses—be there!

2. Reflect on the material.   What is happening in this situation? Why? What are the feelings in the environment? What are people saying?

Conversation

1. Select one person in the situation with whom to dialogue.   It may be an open invitation to the crowd, or you may want to talk to a bystander or a main character or to Jesus. Often you will feel an attraction to one character.

2. Write a short paragraph in the first person, as if this character were speaking.   For example, on Mark 2, "I, the paralytic, wondered if life would ever interest me again. . . ."

3. Move toward the person and enter into dialogue.   Ask questions and listen; express fears, concerns, gratitude, love.

Conclusion

1. Gradually return to your present situation.   For example, you may picture yourself walking from the dusty streets of Jerusalem onto a back road near your home and then arrive back at your present location.

2. Debrief.   Consider the insights gained from the meditation. Evaluate images and symbols and the messages they may be communicating. Remember Nicole calling a pastor to help her sort out the whirlwind and her inability to "make the connection" with her friends. You may write, draw a picture, or write a poem or song to summarize the meditation.[6]

An Example of Discursive Meditation

The best way I know to give you a clear concept of what I mean is to present one of my own meditations. The following is a meditation on the story of Naaman with Elisha from 2 Kings 5. Naaman, a Syrian commander and political enemy of Israel, was suffering from leprosy. His wife's maid was a young Israelite girl. This maid told Naaman's wife about Elisha, the prophet, who could cure Naaman. So Naaman went to Israel to seek healing from leprosy. He was told by Elisha's servant, "Go and wash in the Jordan seven times, and your flesh shall be restored, and you shall be clean" (2 Kings 5:10, RSV). Naaman was angry, first of all, because the prophet didn't see him but merely sent a servant. Second, Naaman thought this was a ridiculous prescription for healing.

In my meditation, following a time of relaxation, I prayed, "Lord, let me enter the river with Naaman. Show me what he might have been experiencing." Here's the actual text of my meditation. It has been edited slightly, to shorten it. I use initials for myself and Naaman.

> N: I, Naaman, great among men but horrible to look at, was caught in the profound dilemma of great achievement in the world and living death in my heart and body. I was an angry, bitter man. My great accomplishments in war were but the manifestation of the wretched battle waging within me. God—the ache. . . ! Always ". . . but he is a leper." To be admired and detested . . .

D: Naaman, when did your quest begin?

N: My body was broken, but my spirit—No. That dear Jewish girl offered me an additional hope. I had tried many things before that. Nothing worked. This girl, seeing the ache of my wife—bless my wife—and fearing to approach me, spoke of a prophet in Israel. This time I could hear.

D: I know the history; is there more you have to tell me?

N: You've heard it before, but be patient to receive.
I wanted a show; God wanted to be glorified.
I gathered the greatest resources I had;
God demanded my brokenness.
I wanted to earn; God wanted to give freely.
I wanted to boast; God wanted silence.

D: I am eager to hear of your experience as you went through each of the seven dippings into the Jordan River.

N: Have you ever played blindman's bluff? You feel so silly as people watch you stumble. . . .

Have you ever been soaking wet when all around you are dry, comfortable, and handsome? You want to hide.

Have you ever feared beginning a task and having no concrete assurance of success?—chill, fear.

Has your heart fluttered with hope?

Have your eyes burned as the fire of imagination ignites a dream of wholeness?

Have you laughed at taking yourself too seriously?

These are some of the things I felt as I stood at the river's edge.

I stepped into the water with resignation. Somehow hope and fear were on the bank.

The first dip—overwhelmed by the physical sensation of the water. The miry bottom, the flow of my robes with the current.

259

The coldness and smell. The muted noises in my ears. I felt as if I would never get through six more. Why couldn't it stop now? *Up*—A breath of air. I dare not open my eyes. Warm sun. Dripping. A different silence on the bank. *Down.*

The second dip—will this never end? Home—wife—the maid—the king—silly. *Up. Breath.* Dare not open eyes. *Down.*

The third dip—why did Elisha tell me to do this? How did he know that to ask me to do this was hardest of all? I'm a *man*—a *man!*—a *warrior!!* Can I receive? Be passive? Allow the water to flow over me?

Up. Breath. Dare not open eyes. Aware of water swirling around waist, legs in current. I am still. *Silent.* The water is moving. I have no control except whether to go under or come up.

A stirring on the bank comes to my ears. I have been up a long time. They probably think I've given up. They fear my wrath. My back is to them. If they could see my . . . smile.

The fourth dip—awareness of the flow of the stream and its subtle, gentle, continued power. It is the master. It could carry me away, but I could never carry it.

Carry away that rage and fear, fear. Flotsam—eyes shut. *Up. Breath.* Three times to go. Awareness fills me. I am drawing life from the water. *Down.*

The fifth dip—carry away pride. Pride, Pride, Pride. I dare to open my eyes under water. I can see nothing but a murky brown. Then I note the diffusion of warm, bright light.

Up. Breath. Two more times. Anxiety is silenced, but excitement remains. "Be not afraid. You will be clean."

The sixth dip—I am at home in the river. Its current is like a familiar caress. It washes me. It washes me. Again I open my eyes, under water. I feel as if my whole body were eyes opening to see life again. They've been shut too long. *Up. Breath.* Deep, delightful breath. Thank God. God? God?? God! God.

One more dip—I thought I would never come to this point. Time and transformation.

The seventh dip—the embrace of life. The embrace of God. His presence cleansed the leprosy of my heart. It was *joy* to be submerged in *him*. To die and be buried in the waters. Only in this way does new life come. My skin tingled as if menthol had been rubbed all over me.

Up very slowly. Eyes open to behold, first, the land of *God*. Then I looked at my hands. A laugh of joy escaped, breaking open the silence like an alabaster flask of perfume. I was clean!! Tears. Tears. Holy joy.

I stood for a long time. Precious communion with Elisha's God—my God? Yes, my God.

The stirring on the bank claimed my attention. I turned, and love swept over me.

"Look! *I am clean!*"

Oh, that they had each been healed. . . .

Blessed be the Lord God Almighty because he has washed me and made me clean.

D: Thank you. Praise God.
N: This cleansing is yours. Remember it. Share it with others. Celebrate it. Yield to the purifying water and fire of the loving Spirit.
D: Gratefully. Thanks be to God.

When I completed this meditation, I felt as if I had truly witnessed God at work. My mind was alive to his presence. My heart was awake with new hope for my own healing and growth and for specific individuals I felt were too proud, like Naaman, to humble themselves for healing and reconciliation with God. As I encountered the living Word through prayerful imagination, I saw the process of transformation that all human beings go through. I saw

Naaman pass through the powerful image of God's baptism. I thought of how many people pass through such baptismal experiences. I don't mean the literal ritual of baptism but the immersions of suffering and trials in life that strip away the leprosy of their souls. I saw more clearly the process of conversion, as a person moves through fear and resistance (often hidden behind pride) to confusion, to awareness, to openness and acceptance, and to celebration in the new life that only God can give.

I was also in awe of the power and clarity of the dialogue. Those who are creative artists know the sense of receiving something they didn't create. I had a sense that God had given me a legitimate insight into the transformation of Naaman. Of course, I knew this was not literally Naaman speaking from the grave—that would be heresy and folly of the most serious order! (Deut. 18:9-13). Still, I had a clear sense that the Spirit was teaching me by bringing added dimensions to the written Word.

That's the fruit of this meditation. God gives us the ability to project ourselves into a different setting in order to experience his truth in a fresh way. The thought of such an exercise might make us nervous, at least at first. But by neglecting this ability, we are failing to cultivate the very seeds of vitality that God has planted inside us.

Why does God create art? Why does he create imagination and beauty? He has provided these things to give greater depth and breadth to our lives. When we neglect or disparage them, we limit ourselves to a partial taste of the banquet that is ours in Christ. Our Lord is waiting for us to acknowledge and practice the gift of meditation so that its holy power can awaken our worship, increase our joy, and motivate us to greater obedience.

God has also provided us with the resource of others' imagination and insight, which is the subject of the next chapter.

NOTES

1. See Jonathan Edwards, "A Treatise Concerning Religious Affections" in *The Works of Jonathan Edwards,* Vol I (Carlisle, Penn.: The Banner of Truth Trust, 1974), 234-343.
2. J. I. Packer, "Ignatius of Loyola," *Eerdmans' Handbook to the History of Christianity* (Grand Rapids, Mich.: Eerdmans, 1977), 411.
3. Adapted from case study #376-240 by E. Raymond Corey. Harvard Business School (Cambridge: Harvard University Press, 1976, revised 1995).
4. Two interesting books on this are written by Tony Buzan. *Make the Most of Your Mind* (New York: Simon & Schuster, 1984) and *Use Both Sides of Your Brain* (New York: E. P. Dutton, 1983).
5. Marcus Aurelius, quoted by Douglas V. Steere, "A New Set of Devotional Exercises," in *An Anthology of Devotional Literature,* ed. Thomas S. Kepler (Grand Rapids, Mich.: Baker Book House, 1947), 769.
6. I developed this particular model using a variety of resources, including Carolyn Stahl, *Opening to God* (Nashville: The Upper Room, 1977), and Elizabeth O'Connor, *Search For Silence* (Waco, Texas: Word Books, 1972), 141–142.

SOUL-SEARCHING

Questions for Reflection and Discussion

1. What is your initial reaction to the idea of meditation?

2. The author suggests four principles that serve as "guardrails" to the practice of meditation. What are they? Do you agree? Are there others you would add?

3. What principles of meditation can you draw from the example of "The Fish, Professor Agassiz, Samuel Scudder, and Harvard University"?

4. What is cognitive meditation? Are there ways in which you have practiced this type of meditation, perhaps without thinking of it as a form of meditation?

5. What is discursive meditation? What do you find most intriguing about this type of meditation? What concerns do you have about it?

6. Choose one type of meditation, review the guidelines for it, and practice it. You may want to begin with one (or more) of the following passages:

    a) Matthew 14:13-21 What do you do with a hungry crowd?

    b) Matthew 14:22-33 Stepping out on faith

    c) Mark 9:2-13 A glimpse of glory

    d) Luke 8:22-25 Facing the storm

    e) Luke 24:13-35 What do you do when God lets you down?

    f) John 2:1-11 The difference Jesus makes

CHAPTER THIRTEEN

Learning from Others' Testimonies

❧ SPIRITUAL READING

I N a fascinating book that explores the process of becoming a Christian, Emilie Griffin describes an important aspect of her own journey toward Christ:

> For me, conversion—this turning over of one's life and energies to God—came about first through a slow and hesitant pilgrimage, both intuitive and intellectual. In my journey I was helped by reading first-person accounts by other converts, especially those who were contemporaries or near contemporaries of mine. In their experience I could see my own. . . . The resemblance between their struggles and my own gave me the courage to trust my own experience more.
>
> The converts who influenced me most at that time were C. S. Lewis, Bede Griffiths, and Thomas Merton. . . . I think I must explain that it was the inner lives of these people

with which I identified so strongly, for their outer lives were very different from my own. . . .

Also it was clear to me from the beginning that their stories were not stories of "how I became a practicing churchman" or "how I became a Roman Catholic" but stories of a personal encounter with God. This was just what was beginning to happen to me. In the ways their paths led them, I saw many parallels to my own experience.[1]

Spiritual reading is not merely the reading of Christian books. Spiritual reading takes the insight and writing talent that God has given to a number of his children and allows their words and their journeys to enrich us in the here and now. One of the most exciting aspects of spiritual writings is that, through them, we can commune with fellow believers and spiritual teachers of centuries past. You might think of spiritual reading as a sort of fellowship with believers of all times and places.

You don't race through spiritual reading. Although you may analyze it, that's not the primary goal. And you don't study spiritual readings—no matter how ancient and well respected—as you would the Bible, any more than you would study the magazine articles and books and letters of contemporary writers as though they were Scripture. The most powerful spiritual writings, of course, develop out of the writers' interactions with the Bible itself, such as Martin Luther's reaction to the book of Romans, which became the starting point for the Protestant Reformation.

Think of the difference between reading the newspaper and reading a love letter. The newspaper is given a quick scan and discarded. A brief love note, however, is read over and over again, not for the content, but for the sense of presence and emotional connection it inspires. This is how we must read God's Word. And this is how we derive the most benefit from the writings of other believers.

When we read in this way, we are savoring the message, prayerfully letting the words soak into our minds. The goal of the reading is to put us in touch with the Lord. The classic expression of this discipline comes from Baron von Hügel (1852–1925), a Roman Catholic layman who served as a spiritual director to many people.

> That daily quarter of an hour, for now forty years or more, I am sure has been one of the greatest sustenances and sources of calm for my life. Of course, *such "reading" is hardly reading in the ordinary sense of the word at all.* As well could you call the letting a very slowly dissolving lozenge melt imperceptibly in your mouth "eating". Such reading is, of course, meant as directly as possible to feed the heart, to fortify the will—to put these into contact with God—thus, by the book, to get away from the book to the realities it suggests. . . . And above all, perhaps it excludes, by its very object, all criticism, all going off on one's own thoughts as, in any way, antagonistic to the book's thoughts, and this, not by any unreal (and *most dangerous*) forcing of oneself to swallow, or to "like", what does not attract one's simply humble self, but (on the contrary) by a gentle passing by, by an instinctive ignoring of what does not suit one's soul. This passing by *should be without a trace of would-be objective judging;* during such reading we are out simply and solely to feed our own poor soul, such as it is here and now. What repels or confuses us now may be the very food of angels; it may even still become the light to our own poor souls in this world's dimness. We must exclude none of such possibilities, the 'infant crying for the light' has nothing to do with more than just humbly finding, and then using, the little light that *it* requires.
>
> I need not say that I would not restrict you to only one

quarter of an hour a day. You might find two such helpful. But I would not exceed the fifteen minutes *at any one time;* you would sink to ordinary reading, if you did.[2]

BRIEF IS BETTER

Many of the spiritual classics can be read in brief portions in a way consistent with von Hügel's admonition to limit the time to fifteen minutes. Baron von Hügel's other advice is wise and helpful, especially considering the wide theological spectrum covered by many classics of spiritual devotion.

Evangelical Protestants, for example, may feel the urge to screen their reading of Roman Catholic spirituality out of concern for theological compromise. When we follow von Hügel's counsel to treat such subjects "by a gentle passing by, by an instinctive ignoring of what does not suit one's soul," we discover insights we can value that we never considered before. It has been said that you may need to read these books as one eats fish: Enjoy the meal, but watch for bones. In spite of the bones, these writers go to the heart of the spiritual journey we all travel. You will find them saying things you have thought but never put into words. Their honesty will cause you to search your own heart.

When we read spiritually, our goal isn't to consume so many books in a year or to gain intellectual mastery over the content. Spiritual reading is more like taking a vitamin tablet. The size of the tablet is small compared to a normal meal, but it gives essential nutrients to our bodies. A small portion of material written by gifted, spiritual pilgrims can nourish the soul for the day. The point is to read a little, then stop when you have come to one thought that stirs your spirit. That is a morsel of grace for you to savor. Sit still and meditate on it. Journal it, by writing the thought at the top of a fresh page of paper and writing your heart response and prayer. Then, return to it at the end of the day, reflecting on what it means.

---

*T*he point is to read a little, then stop when you have come to one thought that stirs your spirit. That is a morsel of grace for you to savor.

READING THAT CHANGES US

One benefit of this discipline has been the cultivation of what I would call interactive reading. Often I read simply to understand what the author is saying, allowing my own responses and insights to pop like fireworks and fade away. But interactive reading helps me take the spark of an author and allow it to light a fire that gives sustained light for my own journey. I'm usually pleasantly surprised to see how I develop a thought more completely.

As with the discipline of meditation, I think it may be most helpful to show you what spiritual reading is like by sharing from my own experience. The first book I read in this way was Augustine's *Confessions*. Don't let the title put you off. In our day, the title *Reflections* would better describe the content of the book. Let me share two journal entries I recorded after reading brief sections from Augustine. First, I was reading Augustine's reaction to sin:

> My God and my mercy, how good you were to me in sprinkling so much bitterness over that sweetness [of physical desires and lust]. . . . I was fettered happily in bonds of misery so that I might be beaten with rods of red-hot iron—the rods of jealousy and suspicion, and fears and anger and quarrels (Book III, Chapter 1).

In response, I wrote:

> Augustine continually penetrates the paradoxes of sin and
> of God's judgment and mercy. Sin is bittersweet bitterness
> and grace begins as bittersweet sweetness. The miseries
> attendant to sin are gracious spurs meant to turn us from
> sin; like thorns at the edge of a briar patch, to keep us from
> entering further into that dangerous wood.

At another point, Augustine writes, "I was both confounded and
converted" (book 6, chapter 4). The combination of those
simple words arrested my attention. I have always endeavored to
"assist the process" of people's conversion by trying to answer all
the questions. Here Augustine speaks of conversion coming in
the midst of uncertainties. I wrote:

> I get a sense of assurance from Augustine: that I do not
> have to possess all the answers in order to experience the
> reality that God answers all. In other words, our minds and
> spirits do not necessarily require detailed answers; they
> need to be assured that there is an answer in keeping with
> love, human worth, and rationality. It's a mistake to wait
> until all questions are answered. Life with God is not cut
> and dried. We may encounter God in such a way that all
> doubts vanish. We then apprehend reality in a way the
> mind cannot comprehend.

Spiritual reading is a fascinating way to be instructed and encouraged by profound spiritual leaders from the past. Their writings
may sound a bit stilted, and their expressions may at first sound
foreign. But a little effort soon reveals that they have passed on
the same roads that we travel. God has revealed insights to them
that can illumine our way. They will become trusted friends who

challenge and comfort us, and who encourage us by their own honesty. Whether or not we choose to walk as they walked, we will be greatly enriched by their accounts.

CHOOSE WHAT IS BEST FOR YOU AT THIS POINT IN YOUR JOURNEY

Not every Christian will be drawn to the weighty works of John Calvin or Martin Luther or even Francis Schaeffer. The point is to consider an author's work in such a way that it leads us to meditation and prayer. There are other levels of reading, however, that nourish and encourage us. There's something out there in the world of words that stirs your heart.

There's an abundance of inspirational/devotional reading, spanning the spectrum from very light in content to quite intense. There are books of poetry and collections of quotations. Even fiction that develops along biblical themes can nourish us, because we are designed to be inspired by storytelling in a way that's different from the benefit we receive from lectures or other teaching-oriented writing (Jesus often taught through telling stories). Some people are spiritually fed by reading journals or biographies and autobiographies of Christians whose stories they admire.

Some people are touched more deeply by images or sounds. Music of many styles, some instrumental and some with lyrics, has ministered to the souls of God's people for centuries. Paintings and sculptures can give us much to reflect upon. We are especially blessed by the existence of many works of art that were inspired by Scripture, by stories and characters from the Bible. All of these are communications of God's wisdom, love, and wonder, offered to us through the eyes, ears, and skills of people he has gifted for just this purpose.

A LIST OF SOUL-STIRRING BOOKS

The following is a selective list of books, from the many fine resources that are available. I have chosen these because they have stood the test of time and have had a significant impact on my own spiritual vitality.

- E. M. Bounds *Power through Prayer*
- John Bunyan *The Pilgrim's Progress*
- François Fénelon *Christian Perfection*
- Thomas R. Kelly *A Testament of Devotion*
- William Law *A Serious Call to a Devout and Holy Life*
- Brother Lawrence *The Practice of the Presence of God*
- Andrew Murray *With Christ in the School of Prayer*
- Henri J. M. Nouwen *Making All Things New*
- J. I. Packer *Knowing God*
- J. B. Phillips *Your God Is Too Small*
- Arthur T. Pierson *George Müller of Bristol*
- Don Postema *Space for God*
- Dr. & Mrs. Howard Taylor *Hudson Taylor's Spiritual Secret*
- A. W. Tozer *The Knowledge of the Holy*
- A. W. Tozer *The Pursuit of God*
- *The Confessions of Saint Augustine*

Spiritual reading will nourish your soul, help you commune with the saints, and open your vision to see much more of God than you could ever see with your eyes only.

NOTES

1. Emilie Griffin, *Turning: Reflections on the Experience of Conversion* (New York: Doubleday, 1980), 16–17.
2. Baron Friedreich von Hügel, *Selected Letters* (1927), p. 229. Quoted in John Baillie, *A Diary of Readings* (New York: Scribner's, 1955), Day 1.

SOUL-SEARCHING

Questions for Reflection and Discussion

1. What books and authors have played a role in your spiritual growth? List them and describe at least one or two specific lessons you gained from them.

2. How do you respond to the suggestion that we may need to read some books in the same way a person eats fish: "Enjoy the meal, but watch out for the bones"?

   a) This sort of thinking makes me nervous.

   b) A book worth reading should be "theologically correct" in every aspect, or it will most likely harm the reader.

   c) I trust myself and my understanding of God and Scripture enough to risk reading some things with which I may not fully agree.

3. Look again at the list of "Soul-Stirring Books." Have you read any of these? Do you have any of them in your own library? Which one would you like to read? One of the best ways to maintain spiritual momentum is to have "the next book" ready so that you don't stall after completing a book.

PART **FOUR**

Making the Break: From Evil's Power to God's Resources

SOULSHAPING AT A GLANCE

Exercises That Increase Our Awareness of God's Presence

- Repentance
- Confession
- Preview
- Review
- Prayer
- Worship

Exercises That Help Us See Life with an Eternal Perspective

- Bible study
- Meditation
- Spiritual reading

Exercises That Free Us from Evil's Power and Connect Us to God's Resources

- **Fasting**
- **Silence**
- **Solitude**
- **Battling temptation**
- **Prayer for spiritual battle**

Exercises That Direct Our Lives toward Kingdom Purposes

- Building character
- Building relationships
- Spiritual direction
- Spiritual friendship
- Stewardship
- Spiritual service through spiritual gifts

Steve and his wife, Jenny, had prayed with me in their living room to commit their lives to Christ about a year earlier. I had baptized their first child and another was on the way. Steve was not making dramatic progress in his faith, but I felt he was standing firmly and moving forward. One evening he lingered after a church committee meeting. He was usually one of the first out the door, but this time he hung around until everyone else was gone. He asked if I had some time to talk to him privately. As a leading businessman in finance, he was normally even tempered. But he was obviously rattled.

"There's a woman at my office . . ." and he began to shake so much that he halted in his speech, his eyes filling with tears. "There's a beautiful woman at my office who seems to be after me."

If you knew Steve, you'd know that this was probably not the product of an overactive imagination or ego. He was a young, fit, handsome, Ivy League graduate with a vibrant personality who was extremely successful in the Wall Street world of finance. As he told me the story, it sounded like a modern-day version of Joseph and Potiphar's wife (see Genesis 39).

"We've done some business deals together, traveling in and out of the city on the train. We've had lunch together a few times. I knew she was recently divorced, but nothing romantic ever happened or came up. But she's started leaving little cards and notes on my desk. She's followed me in the car. Today she left an envelope on my desk with the map to her place and a key! I'm trying to resist this—I know it's wrong. But—" and here he choked, unable to speak for a few moments. "Before coming here tonight, I drove past her house! I would never want to do anything to hurt my wife or our children. . . . What am I going to do?"

That began a long, long time of sharing, searching the Scriptures, and praying, going late into the night. By the time he left, he seemed to have come through fire and was ready to stand firm. I promised to pray for him daily for the next thirty days.

We saw each other in church but didn't have an opportunity to talk for several weeks. Then we had another committee meeting. Again, I noticed Steve lingering. When everyone else had gone, he said, "Doug, I think you saved my life. The morning after we talked, I gave the woman back her map and key and told her exactly where I stood. I told her I was totally committed to my marriage and that I didn't want there to be any confusion about our relationship. I feel so great! It's like I closed the biggest deal of my life. No—it's even better! I feel clean. If I hadn't been safe telling you, I honestly don't know if I could have lasted."

THE PATHWAY TO FREEDOM

When we begin on the pathway of faith, we will find many obstacles set before us. Some are of our own making, some are put in the road by others, and most of them are simply facts of life in this fallen world. Whatever their source, they threaten to take us captive. God has given us spiritual resources not only to nurture our relationship with him but also to protect us from the destructive forces in this world.

The exercises that seem to have the most impact on our spiritual power over evil are fasting, solitude, and silence. As we approach these disciplines, it is essential that we have a clear understanding of their spiritual, physical, and theological purposes. These particular disciplines are often seen in a negative light because they "deprive" us of something. Solitude deprives us (temporarily) of relationships; silence deprives us of speech; fasting deprives us of food. But we *enjoy* people, conversation, and food. Why give them up?

Our key in this struggle is *freedom*. Often, we mistake freedom as the ability to do whatever we want, whenever we want. That, however, is the most seductive distortion of freedom. Think of a young man who embezzles from a family business. Initially, he enjoys the freedom that the extra income gives him. But after a while, some uncomfortable questions are raised about his purchases. Soon he has to do more and more juggling of the books to cover his tracks. In his enthusiasm, he overextends his credit and needs more money than he anticipated to pay his bills. He has gotten involved with a certain group of people, but keeping up with them involves expensive activities, requiring still more money. Keeping up appearances becomes more of a challenge. He becomes a slave to his cover-up, feeling more and more nervous each day. What started as a free choice has left him trapped, his only choices being a life of deepening deception, with the likelihood of eventually getting caught, or coming clean, and all the humiliation that involves.

Freedom is not eating all the food you want but restraining your appetite, so that you can do with or without food. Freedom is not experiencing any pleasure you want but controlling yourself so that appropriate pleasures are enjoyed and savored but not required. "I know how to be abased, and I know how to abound; in any and all circumstances I have learned the secret of facing plenty and hunger, abundance and want. I can do all things in him who strengthens me" (Phil. 4:12-13, RSV). That's freedom!

Douglas V. Steere gives wise counsel concerning the spiritual disciplines that operate out of depriving us of something:

> In all asceticism the principle of abstaining from things that are precious and good (from food, from speech, from physical comforts, from marriage) for the sake of accentuating

something more good in itself is a sound principle and is sound practice, so long as it is done voluntarily and joyously and not grimly, and so long as it can be regarded as a matter of private vocation and is not universally pressed on others.[1]

Far from robbing us of joy and pleasures, these disciplines help us to pursue and maintain our spiritual maturity, our personal energy, and our joy as God's people. Far from restricting our freedom, they are pathways to freedom.

What Is Your Power Base?

As these disciplines teach us to deprive ourselves in a healthy way, they cause us to deal very directly with issues of *power.* One of the greatest distractions to spiritual growth is our tendency to draw power from our human assets instead of relying on the Lord. Like Lot, we look at the lay of the land and choose the fertile places the world presents us, not realizing that they harbor Sodom and Gomorrah (Gen. 13:10). Spiritual power is more readily found when, like Abram, we freely accept a "lesser land" that is abundant with the promises of God (Gen. 13:14-18).

Our approach to power is central to our spiritual health. If we don't settle with ourselves, and with God, where our power comes from and how we are to use it, we are likely to become victims or abusers of it. Let me begin with my own definition of power:

If we don't settle with ourselves, and with God, where our power comes from and how we are to use it, we are likely to become victims or abusers of it.

Personal power means having the resources and personal ability to pursue and achieve godly goals, to maintain our convictions and standards in the face of subtle challenge or direct opposition, and to influence individuals, groups, and relational networks (systems) for godly purposes.

What is your power base? What assets do you rely on for security and advancement in life? Your ability with words? Your influence with others? Your comforts and pleasures? Your material resources? Your athletic prowess? Your artistic talent? Your business savvy? We all have power reserves that we have cultivated carefully. *The goal in spirituality is to detach ourselves from our power resources and rely on God's.* This doesn't mean that we eliminate the natural powers we possess but that we make them subservient to the Lord.

The disciplines of fasting, solitude, and silence are commonly called disciplines of detachment, meaning that they detach us from the world. But this definition has not been fully appreciated unless we see that we detach from the world *in order to attach to the Lord.* We detach from the world in order to receive from God the power that we were allowing the world to supply us. We deny our natural appetites in order to reorient ourselves to the rich resources we find in God. Detachment not only helps us deny our "fleshly nature," but it helps us tap into the power of God, which is intended to supply our lives with spiritual energy.

The wilderness episodes of both Israel and Jesus are the classic models for detachment from the world in order to be attached to the Lord. In both situations, the first step of success was stripping away worldly illusions. As the people of Israel escaped Egyptian oppression, they didn't venture immediately into the Promised Land. As Jesus was baptized and commissioned, he didn't proceed immediately to preaching, teaching, and healing huge crowds. Instead, there was a time of training. In both cases, food and the lack of food played a central role.

HOW FASTING, SILENCE, AND SOLITUDE TEACH US TO BE HOLY

The root of *holy* indicates, "separate, distinct from." This is a central aspect of freedom. God is separate from creation. God is holy in that he is free from the physical limitations and from the sinful compulsions of the physical world. Holiness, then, is more than a moral category of sinless perfection. To be holy means that we lead a life that is separated from the toxic influences of the world, distinct from the value system and motivations of the world. Holiness means that we lead a life based on God's agenda, breaking free from the force field of worldly desires and drives. This holiness includes the pursuit of moral purity, but it goes beyond purity to develop in us a genuine motivation to seek God and God's kingdom.

To be holy means that we lead a life that is separated from the toxic influences of the world, distinct from the value system and motivations of the world.

Seen in this light, fasting, solitude, and silence take on an entirely new meaning in our battle with sin. In willingly giving up food, company, or conversation for a set time, we are weakening the power that these things have over us in daily life. We are free to choose above and beyond our natural inclinations. And we will be even better prepared to choose above and beyond the natural inclinations that are harmful to us—such as overeating, sexual promiscuity, or gossip.

I am free when I can live in this world without becoming a prisoner to it. This detachment is a positive expression of my commitment to God and my freedom in Christ. In the opening story, Steve was a free man because he resisted the exercise of his "freedom" to get sexually involved with a woman other than his wife. He was free to look his wife in the eye, with no need to hide. He was free to answer his children's questions honestly if they ever were to ask him when they got older, "Dad, were you ever tempted? What did you do?" He was free at his workplace because his integrity could not be challenged. He found a new strength in the freedom to say no.

This freedom is hard won. In the chapters of this section, we will consider the role of spiritual exercise in ensuring our freedom in Christ in the midst of a world that would take and hold us captive.

NOTES

1. Douglas V. Steere, "A New Set of Devotional Exercises," in *An Anthology of Devotional Literature,* ed. Thomas S. Kepler (Grand Rapids, Mich.: Baker, 1947), 766.

CHAPTER FOURTEEN

Working Our Appetites to New Advantage

🔥 FASTING

T HE loss of control is one of the most debilitating experiences for the soul. When we lose control over our use of time or money, or over purity of thought, speech, or actions, we lose our sense of well-being and confidence. The discipline of fasting is about control or, more properly, about what controls us. My experience in discipling people in spiritual formation is that fasting has an immediate impact on a person, revealing what controls him or her.

Nicole, whose experience with meditation I shared earlier, wrote me the following note in response to her first fasting experience.

> After leaving your office last Thursday afternoon and picking up my daughter, Erin, from the First Pres. Library, we headed to my office. On the way, I thought "I can fast tomorrow . . . *yes!*" My lunch for Friday had canceled earlier in the day, nothing special was going on . . . a perfect day.

Around 10:00 P.M. I was in the shower and all of a sudden I was so excited that I started singing (believe me, my voice is *not* for close hearing). I wasn't anxious in the least, but looking forward to Friday so very much.

The next day, Steve, Erin, and I gathered round for a short prayer before leaving our home for the day. Erin chose not to pray, but gave me a big hug and said she hoped I wouldn't get hungry.

The amazing thing was . . . I DID get hungry and immediately turned my thoughts to God and my thoughts immediately turned to my daughter . . . weird? By the fourth time this had happened, I just was about ready to give up turning my thoughts towards God as obviously Erin was getting in the way (Oh, this is rich!). I spoke to my sister, Darcelle, in mid-afternoon about this problem and she said, "Well, keep it up, and I'll drop by at 5:00 for our aerobics."

We did our aerobics (helped take the edge off my hunger) and then I asked if she would do something with me that I had always wanted to try . . . just open the Bible at random and see where it led us. I first prayed; then the Bible fell open at Psalm 78. I read the first section *about passing on the Word of God to the next generation, etc.* I looked at Darcelle and said, "God *was* turning my thoughts to Erin for a specific reason . . . *wow!*" Then Darcelle read the next several passages and they kept mentioning different kinds of food. We finally just cracked up and burst out laughing. She looked at me and said, "Well, I think you can break your fast now."

At 7:30 P.M., I had a cup of noodle soup, crackers and peanut butter, and an apple. So ended my first "prayer-fast."[1]

LESSONS FROM ABOVE AND LESSONS FROM WITHIN

In *Spiritual Disciplines for the Christian Life,* Donald S. Whitney gives a helpful survey of fasting in Scripture, condensing the purposes for fasting into ten major categories:

- to strengthen prayer
- to seek God's guidance
- to express grief
- to seek deliverance and protection
- to express repentance and a return to God
- to humble ourselves before the Lord
- to express concern for the work of God
- to minister to the needs of others
- to overcome temptation and dedicate ourselves to God
- to express love and worship to God[2]

We see from such a survey that fasting is a multifaceted exercise. Fasting could be called the italics of the spiritual life; it adds emphasis to other activities we may already be pursuing, such as prayer or repentance or discerning God's purpose for us. It brings a sense of urgency and earnestness to anything else we are undertaking. The importance of fasting is primarily in its impact on *us.* As Whitney notes, "The Bible does not teach that fasting is a kind of spiritual hunger strike that compels God to do our bidding. . . . Fasting does not change God's hearing so much as it changes our praying."[3]

In addition to the biblical lessons on fasting, each of us will draw our own insights from our practice of it. My experience in fasting has made me aware of a number of forces besides food that control my daily life.

The clock. When I began fasting, I noticed that I tended to base my activities on the time of day, and especially the amount of time before coffee break or a meal. I became aware of how much I would look forward to break, lunch, and dinner. I saw how often I thought about food throughout the day. It was quite a revelation!

But in fasting, I noticed that the food-thoughts became triggers to God-thoughts. This was a great encouragement to me, as I saw the practical power of this discipline to bring God into the midst of my routine. Feeling hungry reminds me how hungry I am for God. As Deuteronomy says, "One does not live by bread alone, but by every word that comes from the mouth of the Lord" (Deut. 8:3, NRSV). When I feel the hunger pangs, I remind myself of my reasons for fasting. When I am in prayer and fasting for my family, the hunger reminds me of our need to be nourished by God's Word together. When I am in prayer and fasting for direction, my discomfort reminds me of the discomfort of trying to go my own way. When I am in prayer and fasting for a person's healing, I am reminded of their pain, which is so much greater and more significant than mine. In nearly all situations, I am reminded how frail I am apart from God's gracious provisions.

The desire for instant gratification.   Fasting has helped me see how much I allow impulse to control my time and the use of my other resources. I'm likely to stop what I'm doing to get a cup of coffee or a snack whenever I want it. This carries over into daily activities and relationships that have nothing to do with food. A general impatience can easily control our days, fueled by the basic desire to have what we want when we want it. What is most unnerving is that we may be on the brink of a special touch of the Lord and we break in order to eat!

C. S. Lewis captures this concept in describing the demonic tempter Screwtape's "close call" at losing an atheist he had cultivated for twenty years. He was warning Wormwood to guard against encouraging in his human victim (called a "patient") "the fatal habit of attending to universal issues and withdrawing his attention from the stream of immediate sense experience." The tempter's goal is "to fix [the patient's] attention on the stream." When Screwtape's atheist-patient was reading and thinking about things that might lead him back to God (whom

Screwtape calls the Enemy), he struck in the area where the
patient was most vulnerable.

> If I had lost my head and begun to attempt a defense by
> argument, I should have been undone. But I was not such a
> fool. I struck instantly at the part of the man which I had
> best under my control, and suggested that it was just about
> time he had some lunch. The Enemy presumably made the
> counter-suggestion (you know how one can never *quite* over-
> hear what He says to them?) that this was more important
> than lunch. At least I think that must have been His line,
> for when I said, "Quite. In fact much *too* important to tackle
> at the end of a morning," the patient brightened up consid-
> erably. . . . Once he was in the street, the battle was won.[4]

The power of choice.   Fasting has made me aware of the abundant choices I enjoy in life. Within reasonable limits, I can do or
have just about anything, anytime I want. I don't mean that I can
just fly my family to Hawaii on a whim! But most of us have relative freedom to make basic choices without intense constraints.
Fasting is a new window on this freedom. When we choose to
deny ourselves, even temporarily during our limited fast, we see
how much of our freedom we take for granted.

What I eat.   As I have practiced the spiritual disciplines, I have
paid more attention to physical exercise and nutrition. Fasting
made me aware of my snacking and of my cravings for salty
snacks and sweets. It helped me reduce the unthinking consump-
tion of junk food.

BREAKING THE PULL OF FORCES INSIDE AND OUTSIDE US

As you can see, there are multiple advantages that go with
the practice of fasting. But the primary purpose of fasting is to

detach us from the magnetic pull of our appetites in order for us to align our lives with God's purposes and values.

Physical hunger is one of the most powerful and basic drives of life. As such, it represents one of the world's strongest attractions. Food has many spiritual connotations beyond mere nutrition. We use food for comfort—as when I come home from a long church meeting and head straight to the consolation of the refrigerator. Food can be an expression of pride—as we insist on name brands and prime cuts and great restaurants. Food is a reward—as we give ourselves a special treat for a job well done—or at least, done! Food is also a distraction—as we see our children open the refrigerator for the second or third time in half an hour, as if something new were going to appear. Food is an indulgence—as we spoil ourselves, taking a little extra piece (or two or three) of chocolate. When we begin to see the many messages conveyed through food alone, we see that we can gain a lot of insight into our souls merely by paying attention to what our physical appetites say about us.

Fasting breaks our appetites, the powerful drives that reside in our physical bodies, which control so much of our motivation and dictate so much of our activity. In 1 Corinthians 6:12-13, Paul puts our freedom to do things in the context of our freedom *from* having to do them. "'All things are lawful for me,' but not all things are helpful. 'All things are lawful for me,' but I will not be enslaved by anything" (RSV). When you fast, I would suggest you memorize these verses as a reminder that you are not merely giving up food when you fast. *You are taking back control over your life.*

Guidelines for Fasting

1. Determine the purpose of your fast.   There's a difference between dieting and fasting. Simply going without food will not

290

bring spiritual energy or restoration. Review Whitney's ten categories to see if any apply to your particular need or desire at this time. Complete this sentence in your journal: "Lord, I am fasting at this time because . . ." Someone has said that fasting is praying with the body. Then what are you praying for? This purpose will guide and sustain you through your fast.

2. *Determine how long you will fast.* In a normal fast, you abstain from food for a set period of time but permit yourself to drink water. A partial fast is a limitation of food and liquid but not a complete abstention. A first step in developing this discipline is to begin with a partial fast from lunch one day to lunch the next (skipping dinner and breakfast). Allow yourself only fruit juices and water for the twenty-four hours.[5] After several weeks, try a normal fast, drinking healthy quantities of water. For variety, you may want to flavor your water with a slice of lemon or lime or drops of lemon or lime juice.

3. *Determine the extent of your fast.* What foods and liquids will you allow yourself? Some people, especially in the beginning, undertake a partial fast, while others commit to a complete fast except for water. Begin slowly and your body will adjust with experience.

4. *Observe the physical and spiritual dynamics of your fast.* Initially, you will likely be preoccupied with the discomfort and strangeness of the whole experience. Don't be hard on yourself. A few "warm-up" fasts will soon remove the distraction of the discipline. Then you are ready to undertake some specific disciplines, such as prayer and Bible reading, to support and direct your fast. When I fast, I often use my lunch hour for personal worship and prayer. I may remain in my study, go for a walk, or visit the church sanctuary. I also keep a journal handy throughout the day, since food-thoughts trigger God-thoughts and those God-thoughts are often helpful insights.

5. Set aside your regular mealtimes, and other times, for focused prayer and meditation concerning the purpose of your fast. The fast also frees up time normally devoted to food preparation and eating. Use this time for specific disciplines of prayer, Bible reading, spiritual reading, or journaling. These are also profitable times for silence and solitude, since being with people who are eating can make your fast more difficult.

6. Consider your interaction with others and how your fasting may affect them. Jesus makes it clear in Matthew 6 that our fasting is not to be paraded in front of others. But it may not be practical to keep it a total secret, especially in a family setting. If you are in a family, it's a personal choice to sit with them while they eat or to ask to be excused. Simply explain that you are showing your love for God or seeking his help in a special way. If you are married, it is wise to tell your spouse in advance of your fasting, so that meal and family plans can be adjusted accordingly.

7. Break your fast intentionally and nutritiously. How we conclude a fast can either carry its impact forward in our lives or disrupt and dilute the fasting experience. The most important principle is to break your fast with a light meal—with small amounts of fruits, vegetables, and juice. The length of the fast will influence how you should eat. The point to remember is that your body adjusts to less. Some people are tempted to indulge themselves in a large meal as a reward, or they simply start snacking on whatever is available. This robs us of the power of the moment of gratefully receiving the nourishment our bodies need, as we celebrate the spiritual nourishment of the fast.

During special personal seasons, you may want to try extended fasts of two or more days. I would suggest reading Richard Foster's advice in *Celebration of Discipline* on the spiritual and physical dynamics of such a fast.

One last comment is that the exercise of fasting has been

applied to many other aspects of life, as noted by Douglas Steere. The same principle applies: We give up something—for the sake of something better. A fast is considered a spiritual discipline only when there is an intentional effort to fill that space with spiritual activity. Throughout the ages, God's people have celebrated events and seasons through harvests and feasts. They have also placed themselves before the Lord in an intense and vulnerable way through fasts. This spiritual resource is as effective today as ever.

NOTES

1. Letter from Nichole Wichert (reprinted by permission).
2. Donald S. Whitney, *Spiritual Disciplines for the Christian Life* (Colorado Springs: Navpress, 1991), 156–170.
3. Ibid., 157–158.
4. C. S. Lewis, *The Screwtape Letters* (New York: Macmillan, 1961), 8–9.
5. Richard Foster, *Celebration of Discipline* (San Francisco: Harper & Row, 1978), 49–53, provides some helpful, practical tips on the mechanics of fasting.

SOUL-SEARCHING

Questions for Reflection and Discussion

1. If you were asked to paint a picture of freedom, what would you paint? If you were asked to tell a parable or story about freedom, what would you say?

2. What definition of freedom was given in this chapter? Do you agree? What would you add or change in this definition?

3. What is one of the greatest dangers in ascetic practices? How can we avoid this?

4. What does power have to do with fasting? What is a primary purpose of fasting?

5. This chapter has described various "power bases" that people have. What is meant by "power base"? What are your power bases? How do these pose a challenge to your spiritual vitality?

6. What does "holy" mean? What does our concept of holiness have to do with spiritual vitality?

7. If you desire to experiment with fasting, review the guidelines and review your calendar. When would a twenty-four-hour fast be least disruptive to your schedule? Make plans for your fast. Then record your experience in your journal.

CHAPTER FIFTEEN

Taking Time to Hear from Your Heart

🌿 SILENCE
🌿 SOLITUDE

A GROUP retreat in which I frequently participate begins with a brief time of worship, introductions, and orientation. Then we move into a period of silence through the evening and the start of the next morning. I remember my first experience and have seen it repeated over and over with others. The first reaction is awkward embarrassment. You leave the chapel, feeling as if your lips are glued together. You look at others, smile, and shrug your shoulders, as if saying, "This is weird—but I'll give it a try."

Soon you begin to think about all the words that fill a day—the constant chatter. How many of those words are really necessary? You begin to think about the fact that words have been your primary method of communication, and that there are so many other ways to communicate: touch, writing, the eyes, kind gestures. You may even begin to experience a sense of relief that you can be with a person without being obligated to speak to him or her. There is a sense of appreciation for one another and an intentional effort to communicate through courtesy instead of conversation. When you awaken, the silence is humbling. You cannot use words to communicate or to distract. You move into the day with a sense of alertness, watching for cues, enjoying the countless other sounds that you often miss in the barrage of words.

When given permission to break the silence, many do so reluctantly. "I wish we have could been silent the whole weekend," one man on the retreat told me after the morning chapel. "I was just beginning to get my mind to stop chattering away when you invited us to pray the Lord's Prayer aloud together. I'll be honest; I didn't pray aloud—but I can't remember when that prayer ever felt more meaningful."

THE POWER OF WORDS—AND HOW TO BREAK FREE FROM THEM

Proverbs 10:19 says, "When words are many, transgression is not lacking, but he who restrains his lips is prudent" (RSV). I am continually amazed and sobered by the power of words for good and evil. As a preacher, I must be especially careful—which I have learned to my dismay. On one occasion, I was speaking about the danger of impulsive decisions. I spoke about a time when I was a young teenager at a large youth retreat and met a girl for the first time around the campfire. She seemed really great, so we agreed to meet for breakfast. When I saw her in the daylight, she didn't look as pretty as she had the night before. "In fact," I said, "she was a real dog." I told how I did my best to avoid her the rest of the weekend. Well, the congregation laughed with me at my youthful impulsiveness and immaturity. But one woman didn't laugh. I had never met her, but she wrote a note to me:

We have never met, but I have worshiped with you for nearly six months. I have been greatly helped by your sermons—until this Sunday. Your comment about the girl who was "a dog" cut me like a knife. I am not attractive—a fact my father made sure I understood. I have struggled years with loneliness, because "beautiful people" get most of the friends. But I am learning that God loves me and is real in my life. I know you are a sensitive person. I can't imagine you would want to hurt anyone on purpose, but your words hurt deeply. Please think more carefully before you make a joke at another's expense.

I put down the letter. My initial feelings of defensiveness, mixed with deep shame and regret, melted as I sensed the Lord's gentle chastisement in her words. She was gracious enough to sign the letter and give her address, so I immediately wrote a letter of apology, expressing my appreciation for her bringing the issue to light.

"But I tell you that men [and women] will have to give account on the day of judgment for every careless word they have spoken" (Matt. 12:36). I have given talks on this verse, asking people to imagine a new invention called the "Sound Extraction Machine." This wonder of technology has the ability to extract the sound vibrations that inanimate objects have absorbed. The theory is that the vibrations of whatever an object has "heard" still reside in the object. So, let's put your steering wheel in there—what will we hear? What about your phone?

You may be thinking, *Aren't we going a little too far with this idea? Can't we have any fun? What about joking and teasing? What are we supposed to do, say as little as possible so that we don't offend anybody?* Of course, that's not the point. But with a new knowledge of the impact words make, we are free in Jesus Christ to use our words differently.

Silence breaks the power of words—words that we use to excuse, rationalize, lie, deceive, persuade, manipulate; words that we speak quickly in anger, slowly in apology, quickly in accusation, and slowly in admission of our guilt; words that fill our world with such noise and confusion that we cannot hear the still, small voice of the Lord.

Silence breaks the power of words so that we can receive *the Word*. Studies of the lives of those who've endured and gone on to achieve great things in the world reveal that they have often spent time in intentional silence.

> You will either be disciplined by events or you will make your own discipline. Therefore make your own discipline and so contribute to great events. Be emotionally strong and firm, spiritually strong as steel, but controlled so that you can bend to shocks and not be uprooted by panics.[1]

All that matters is your response to challenging events. If you are left alone to the inflowing and outflowing of human emotional relationships and the onslaughts of their passing moods you will find that your responses are immediate, you are undefended and emotionally exposed, quick to take fire. The value of these communions and of your silences is that in them you are strengthened and given poise; you are lifted high above the flood, and you are given something strong, serene, and healing. This is what is meant by the great words, "of myself I do nothing;" you discipline yourselves so that you may receive, and you turn to complete acceptance of the outpouring gift of the spirit.

SILENCE: LISTENING TO OUR SOUL

Far from being an impractical escape from the world, silence (and its twin discipline of solitude) enables us to function much more effectively in the world. An advocate of this practice was Dag Hammarskjöld, General Secretary of the United Nations from 1953 until his death in 1961. Throughout his life he was active in government service both nationally and internationally. From his writings we learn that his intensive public life in the world of politics was sustained by an intentional cultivation of silence, listening to his inner world.

> The more faithfully you listen to the voice within you, the better you will hear what is sounding outside. And only he who listens can speak. Is this the starting of the road towards the union of your two dreams—to be allowed in clarity of mind to mirror life and in purity of heart to mold it?[2]

Hammerskjöld captures two dynamics that are often at work in silence:

We gain a clearer perception of the world outside us "in clarity of mind to mirror life."
When we are silent, we take time to consider our intuitions. We test our perceptions. We are quiet enough to process, in a deliberate way, our experiences in light of our eternal perspective. We can also take a long, uncluttered look at the present world systems, as well as God's activity in the world.

This kind of meditation—possible when we have silenced all the clatter inside—is a powerful antidote to jumping to conclusions based on our reflexes, which often gets us into awkward situations.

We have the power to operate with the energy of integrity and clear thinking, as "in purity of heart" we seek to mold the world according to our values.
Silence and reflection can break the cycle of assuming that fatalism and determinism will control the course of lives and events.

When we stop talking and withdraw, we hear again the voice of faith, "For nothing is impossible with God" (Luke 1:37).

Guidelines for Practicing Silence

As with many of the disciplines, the initial attempts at silence are filled with distraction. People are often anxious to "do it right," with expectations that dramatic things should happen.

"What am I supposed to think about?" one woman asked anxiously.

"Just be still and don't worry about what you're thinking," I replied.

"Well, can I read a Bible verse or something?" she asked.

"No, just be quiet."

"How about some music?" she persisted.

"Silence is silence," I said.

She came back from the hour of silence with a puzzled look. *Uh-oh*, I thought, *I pushed too hard.*

"That was interesting," she said rather flatly. "As I sat still, my mind was like a tape on fast-forward. But after a while—I don't know how long because I put my watch away—it began to slow down. I felt relaxed and calm. That was all. How did I do?"

"How do you think you did?" I asked.

"If I was supposed to hear something from God, I didn't do all that great. But if I was supposed to trust God a little more . . . that's what happened!" she said, with a sudden start in her voice. "I didn't feel I had to *do* anything. . . . I just felt peaceful and *so* calm. I can't remember *ever* feeling that way!" The meaning of her silence broke on her as she shared with me. It was one of the most delightful "dawnings" I've ever seen. Silence had shown Ann that she could just *be* and that was all right.

Apart from the group-retreat setting I described earlier, the discipline of silence is most often combined with that of solitude, which we will consider next. What many people fail to recognize is that there are times throughout the day when we can practice this exercise. For example, when you drive the car, turn off the radio, tape, or compact disc player (and the car phone!) and be still. Leave your workplace to have lunch alone. Take half an hour or more for a walk. I have read of some people who rise in the middle of the night to have a time of silence and then return to bed.[3] Be still. Silence is silence. You will find your own treasures in the stillness. Following are some simple guidelines.

1. Find a silent place.   If you have access to a park, a quiet room, a corner in a public library, or a church sanctuary, this can greatly aid your exercise. If no quiet place is available, some have found it helpful to get a tape or compact disc with environmental sounds such as ocean waves or a rainstorm.

2. Quiet your heart and mind with a passage of Scripture.   There are a number of passages such as, "[The Lord] leads me beside quiet waters, he restores my soul" (Ps. 23:2-3) or, "Be still, and know that I am God" (Ps. 46:10) or, "In quietness and trust is your strength" (Isa. 30:15). God's Word calms you, giving you the promise of his presence in the silence.

3. Be still.   Rest. Relax. Trust God to keep you.

4. Do not strain for thoughts.   In this spiritual exercise, the stillness is the gift. We have already devoted much effort to the exercises that renew our minds and fill our thoughts with the truth of God. Silence enables these thoughts to percolate throughout our hearts and souls. They put down deep roots in ways that are beyond our understanding.

5. Be content at each phase of your journey.   At first, a sense of restfulness may come for a minute or two only. With consistent practice, however, you will be able to be still for longer periods. You will find the silence a comforting experience rather than the threat it may have presented initially.

6. *Learn to bring the stillness into the midst of daily living.* With practice, you will be able to bring the calm strength of silence into the midst of your busy, talking day. Simply pausing for a moment before responding to a difficult question or criticism may allow you to draw from the reservoir of "quiet waters" instead of tapping the broken cisterns of human weakness or defensiveness.

Usually, silence is practiced in the context of solitude; these two exercises have always complemented each other. However, each of them possesses distinct characteristics, and it is helpful to look at them separately at first. Now that we have explored silence, let's consider what it means to practice solitude.

SOLITUDE: FINDING GOD AND OURSELVES THROUGH TIMES ALONE

Alzheimer's disease makes intense demands on the family of the patient. Robertson McQuilkin, who stepped down as president of Columbia Bible College and Seminary (now Columbia International University), tells of the importance of solitude in sustaining him in caring for his wife, Muriel. Speaking of the stress he was suffering, he writes:

Then I remembered the secret I had learned in younger days—going to a mountain hideaway to be alone with God. There, though it was slow in coming, I was able to break free from preoccupation with my troubles and concentrate on Jesus. When it happened, I learned what God had taught me more than once before: The heavy heart lifts on the wings of praise.[4]

Solitude is a journey of discovery. We discover a deeper fellow-ship with God as we learn what is really inside us—both good and bad. And once we have truly searched our soul and come through that experience, we find that we've developed a new strength.

What else do we bring back from times of solitude and silence? Quiet confidence, stronger convictions, wiser discernment, and deeper compassion. Being alone is a disarming experience on the one hand, but as we discover that we are *not* alone and that God is with us in ways we never perceived before, solitude becomes a place where spiritual treasures are found.

JUST ANOTHER FORM OF INTROSPECTIVE "NAVEL GAZING"?

Can we get too caught up in introspection, wasting our time and energy on self-concerns when we need to "be about the Lord's business in the world"? Is solitude just another excuse to block out the world and obsess over our own problems?

As with any spiritual exercise, we can misuse solitude. But the spiritual practice of spending time alone not only has historical precedent in the church, but it was also encouraged by the teach-ings and example of Jesus himself: "The kingdom of God does not come with your careful observation, nor will people say, 'Here it is,' or 'There it is,' because the kingdom of God is within you" (Luke 17:20-21). The Pharisees continued to ply Jesus with questions concerning the coming kingdom.[5] His response was that the essence (though not the complete expres-sion) of the kingdom is spiritual and internal—*a matter of the heart.* Outward signs and legalistic systems, such as those of the Pharisees, miss the mark.

Jesus cultivated the kingdom within through the exercise of solitude. In his life there was a clear rhythm of involvement with the outer world and withdrawal into his own soul and communion with the Father. As we study Jesus' life, we see that he sought the solitude of the wilderness before he entered into the active ministries of preaching, teaching, and healing. Solitude allowed him to develop not only the message he presented but also his very character. Solitude also provided for the ongoing refreshment and reorientation that are necessary following extensive, demanding ministry (Mark 1:19-39; John 6:14-15).

The "kingdom within us" is a vivid image for describing the inner life of the soul. We perceive this inner life most clearly in silence and solitude. Other people, even those not professing to be Christians, have caught a glimpse of how important this inner world is. Solitude is the antidote to superficial living. Henry David Thoréau understood this from his own experiment with solitude[6]:

> When our life ceases to be inward and private, conversation degenerates into mere gossip. We rarely meet a man who can tell us any news which he has not read in a newspaper, or been told by his neighbor. . . . In proportion as our inward life fails, we go more constantly and desperately to the post office. You may depend on it, that the poor fellow who walks away with the greatest number of letters proud of his extensive correspondence has not heard from himself this long while.[7]

In solitude we finally hear "news" from ourselves. We cease to rely on outward symbols of success, such as Thoreau's "mail from the post office." In my experience, credentials have a shelf life of two minutes. We all know the experience of meeting a person with a number of impressive credentials—and finding ourselves disappointed. We expected more from a person who has such a resumé. But the resumé that matters most is that which is written on the heart by the Spirit of God in our times of commu-

nion with God. Remember our talk at the beginning of the
book, about the inner, spiritual reservoir? Rather than drawing
from the "broken cisterns" of the world, we can dig deep wells
that tap the reservoir of the Holy Spirit. The waters we draw
from wells dug in silence and solitude are the living waters that
sparkle with purity and refresh us with the cool, uncompromis-
ing taste of things beyond our present, physical world.

In solitude, we take the time to explore the landscape of the
soul. We walk through the valleys of fear, the arid places of
doubt, the lush pastures of conviction, the peaks of insight and
communion, and the streams of creativity. Because the Holy
Spirit walks with us, we can take this journey, and the journey
can change us—into purer, stronger, more joyful people.

In solitude we are able to pay attention to ourselves, to pay
attention to our motives and our desires, good and ill. Then we
can truly give ourselves to other people. The only truly unique
gift I have to give is myself. And I will have more to offer others
if I take time alone to recognize all that God has placed within
me and to develop the insights and gifts he has given me.

HELP IN FACING THE SILENCE

Physical silence and stillness are not in themselves creative.
Silence can be a destructive and disturbing force. The negative
silence of solitary imprisonment can crush the human spirit.
There is a silence of hatred, a silence filled with fear and terror,
and a silence of the unknown.[8]

It is not necessarily true that if you get quiet, everything will be
all right. Even secular psychotherapists have recognized that some
people, in order to face the truth inside themselves, need outside
support and need to be prepared emotionally ahead of time.
What does this mean to us spiritually? It simply means that we
need to enter silence with the equipment of the other disciplines.

The discipline that is probably most helpful to us when we are listening to what is inside us is the discipline of a renewed mind. What if you are wracked with horrible guilt and shame over some past event? You need the assurance of God's forgiveness and power to cleanse you from sin. What if you have learned to believe things about yourself that are false? You can only know what is false by putting it beside the truth of God's Word.

Sometimes it is also helpful to have some resource of spiritual friendship or direction to help us understand and deal with the matters that emerge from our silence. Sometimes what we find in that silence and solitude is not too comfortable. When the Holy Spirit reveals to you an attitude of sin that's been hiding in your soul, you may need another person to pray with you about it. When, in the quiet, you are finally able to hear the cries of pain from some past event, you can benefit by going to a spiritual partner who can listen, cry with you, review with you the truth of Scripture, and pray with you.

Silence is empty unless it is filled with the grace and presence of God.

I recall an experience that was quite unsettling on my first five-day retreat. By our third day, we had been in extended periods of silence and solitude. And I began to sense a darkness and mild depression, which surprised me. I wrote in my journal:

> I feel like I've had . . . 39 lashes—and I can barely stand them; I know I couldn't take one more. I sense the deep waters of entering into God's presence. It's the mystery of Moses' experience, "The people remained at a distance,

while Moses approached the thick darkness where God was" (Exod. 20:21). I think of Jesus' words, "If I have told you about earthly things and you do not believe, how can you believe if I tell you heavenly things?" (John 3:12, NRSV). Later Jesus says, "I still have many things to say to you, *but you cannot bear them now*" (John 16:12, NRSV, italics added). Oh, the merciful restraint of God. Calm my fears, Lord, that drawing closer to you could consume me, as though I were a low voltage electrical wire that tries to carry too much current. Now, lest I become smug, you have revealed one step beyond what I can handle. No boasting—my boast is in the Lord.

Silence is empty unless it is filled with the grace and presence of God. In fact, even with the grace of God, silence can be extremely unsettling. Kenneth Leech notes:

> Through inner silence, one comes to see the inner face, the focal point of spirituality. In the Bible the heart is the seat of intelligence and of life. But it is also from the heart that the depths of wickedness issue forth. The heart of man is desperately wicked according to Jeremiah (17:9), and Jesus tells his disciples that it is from the heart that murder, adultery, and other evils proceed (Mark 7:21-22). The heart therefore is in need of purification, and this is an important part of effective prayer. The purpose of silence is to allow the heart to be still and to listen to God.[9]

The issues that frighten us away from silence and solitude are the very reasons we must enter them. If we refuse to enter into solitude and silence, we will continue to be controlled by forces we haven't faced, by wounds we have kept from our Lord, and by ignorance we have refused to admit and correct.

You see, we shield ourselves with activity; we actually seek to escape God's work in our souls through *religious* activity.

---

*I*f we refuse to enter into solitude and silence, we will continue to be controlled by forces we haven't faced, by wounds we have kept from our Lord, and by ignorance we have refused to admit and correct.

Psalm 139 is a psalm to take us into our solitude and silence. The psalmist moves through a process of opening to God, first with resistance, then with a deeper understanding of God's care, and finally with a surrender to that care and the searching of God that will reveal what is necessary to take the next steps in spiritual maturity. We sense the sweeping affirmation of the presence of God, noting that there is no escape from it. At first we experience what I would call "cosmic claustrophobia"—there is nowhere to flee from God! But when David reflects on the nature of that all-encompassing presence, he is overcome. God does not pursue us as if he were a bounty hunter. Rather, God embraces us like a holy, loving, tender-but-strong parent.

BREAKING THE HOLD OF WORLDLY EXPECTATIONS AND AMBITIONS

Solitude breaks the pressure of worldly expectations, enabling us to recover the pace and perspective of spiritual vitality. Peterson's phrasing of Matthew 11:28-30 from *The Message* helps us appreciate the invitation of solitude:

Are you tired? Worn out? Burned out on religion? Come to me. Get away with me and you'll recover your life. I'll show you how to take a real rest. Walk with me and work with me—watch how I do it. Learn the unforced rhythms of grace. I won't lay anything heavy or ill-fitting on you. Keep company with me and you'll learn to live freely and lightly.[10]

It's tough to learn "the unforced rhythms of grace" when you're being rushed to and fro by the currents of daily activity. The lack of solitude affects us in ways we are not able to realize until we get away. There are strong indications that solitude can bring strength, while constantly being part of a crowd may make us extremely vulnerable. In a fascinating study, scientists found that it takes twenty times more the amount of amphetamine to kill individual mice than it takes to kill them in groups. Experimenters also found that a mouse given no amphetamine at all will be dead within ten minutes of being placed in the midst of a group on the drug.[11] We know that we need community—and God has designed us to live as members of a larger body. But we have all seen how the pressure of the crowd has distorted our vision and threatened to compromise—or, in fact, has compromised—our highest ideals and values.

Solitude breaks the power of peer pressure and influence by which we define ourselves and which influences so many of our choices and our behavior. Someone has said, "A man is what he is when he's alone." Solitude loosens the hold of this world because we see what we are without the props of life, the applause—or condemnation—of others.

MAKING ROOM FOR LOVE

Solitude replenishes our inner reservoirs. Pastor William Lohe said, "Whoever must always give, must always have; and since he cannot draw out of himself what he must give, he must ever keep near the living fountain in order to draw. . . . Solitude is the fountain of all living streams, and nothing glorious is born in public."12

> Without the solitude of heart, the intimacy of friendship, marriage, and community life cannot be creative. Without the solitude of heart, our relationships with others easily become needy and greedy, sticky and clinging, dependent and sentimental, exploitive and parasitic, because without the solitude of heart we cannot experience the others as different from ourselves but only as people who can be used for the fulfillment of our own, often hidden, needs.
>
> The mystery of love is that it protects and respects the aloneness of the other and creates the free space where he can convert his loneliness into a solitude that can be shared. In this solitude we can strengthen each other by mutual respect, by careful consideration of each other's individuality, by an obedient distance from each other's privacy and by a reverent understanding of the sacredness of the human heart. In this solitude we encourage each other to enter into the silence of our innermost being and discover there the voice that calls us beyond the limits of human togetherness to a new communion. In this solitude we can slowly become aware of a presence of him who embraces friends and lovers and offers us the freedom to love each other, because he loved us first (see 1 John 4:19).13

This is the spiritual basis for "Absence makes the heart grow fonder." It is not that absence creates a deprivation that must be satisfied. Instead, absence generates a love that is rooted in God.

*W*ithout the solitude of heart, our relationships with others easily become needy and greedy, because we cannot experience the others as different from ourselves but only as people who can be used for the fulfillment of our own, often hidden, needs.

Being away from people can enable us to engage them more fully when we rejoin them. We give others that which God gives us. We cannot receive from God if we are always with people. But when we receive from the Lord, we will be eager to share it with others. Solitude breaks loneliness, enabling us to find our affirmation in God. It reminds us that our value is secured in Christ and shared with others.

Guidelines for Times of Solitude

Solitude can be practiced in two primary ways: in the midst of life and in special times away from your normal schedule and location. Solitude in the thick of things means withdrawing for a brief time to a quiet place away from people. It can be as simple as turning off the TV or putting down the paper for fifteen to thirty minutes. This simple practice *in the midst of things* provides a vivid reminder of the central priorities in life.

The second primary means of practicing solitude is over an extended period of time. This is usually referred to as an individual retreat. The standard retreat is guided by a retreat conductor. This is for "a period spent in silence and occupied by meditation and spiritual exercises, under a conductor who leads the worship, gives the addresses, and makes appointments with any retreatants who desire confession, counsel, and discussion."[14] This more formal approach to a retreat is intimidating to some people. Keep in mind that staff members at retreats understand the hesitations that all of us feel. Spiritual "directors," or "conductors," have been trained to be sensitive to the needs—and nervousness—of others. For instance, many retreat centers are owned and facilitated by the Catholic church, yet staff members don't assume that you are Catholic when you walk in the door; they are prepared to assist you in the way you desire to be assisted. And most retreat centers offer variations on the format of the individual or group retreat.[15]

We can also take our own unguided retreats during which we set our own agenda and move at our own pace. I once heard a counselor say that we all need a day away for personal spiritual renewal at least once every three months. These are days we can give ourselves to prayer, journaling, reading, and reflecting. I've found that other churches or Christian camps are often willing to make a simple room available for such a day. Some people make overnight plans so that they arrive in the evening after dinner and have the night to quiet themselves. Then, they arise in the morning for the discipline they have set. To do this a minimum of once a year will kindle renewal—and will feed you the salt that will make you thirst for more such times.

Your own Bible study group or other small group or ministry team from church can design a retreat that incorporates silence and solitude.

Silence and solitude are not calls to permanent withdrawal. We are not making tabernacles on the mountain, as Jesus' disciples longed to do on their retreat at Jesus' transfiguration. Like them, we must go back down to the valley, where we often find people caught in the throes of spiritual crisis. It is these crises that remind us that we live in a world where evil threatens our welfare, spiritual and otherwise.

NOTES

1. Mary Strong, ed., *Letters to the Scattered Brotherhood* (New York: Harper and Brothers, 1948), 32. Cited in Ronald V. Wells, *Spiritual Disciplines for Everyday Living* (New York: Character Research Press, 1982), 64.
2. Dag Hammarskjöld, *Markings* (New York: Alfred A. Knopf, 1964), 13.
3. Dallas Willard, *The Spirit of the Disciplines* (San Francisco: HarperSanFrancisco, 1988), 163–164.
4. Robertson McQuilkin, "Muriel's Blessing," *Christianity Today* (5 February 1996), 34.
5. Another interpretation, which most consider secondary, takes the preposition to mean "among" instead of "within," with the implication that Jesus himself was a manifestation of the kingdom. Since Jesus himself was standing in their midst and they couldn't perceive it, how then would other signs help?
6. I concur with Douglas Steere's comment on Thoreau: "I like to read Thoreau's *Walden Pond* from time to time and I find that it cleanses me from some of the fevers of modern complexity. But it is of little help to me for that deeper level of the fever known as the multiplicity of the heart. For that disease more penetrating remedies must be sought than those the Cosmic Yankee could provide." Douglas V. Steere, "A New Set of Devotional Exercises," in *An Anthology of Devotional Literature,* ed. Thomas S. Kepler (Grand Rapids, Mich.: Baker Book House, 1947), 768.
7. *Walden and Other Writings* (New York: Modern Library, 1950), 723–724. Quoted in Henri J. M. Nouwen, *Reaching Out* (New York: Doubleday, 1966), 18.
8. Kenneth Leech, *Soul Friend* (San Francisco: Harper & Row, 1977), 179.

9. Ibid., 180.

10. Eugene H. Peterson, *The Message: The New Testament in Contemporary Language* (Colorado Springs: Navpress, 1993), 31.

11. Willard, *Disciplines,* 160.

12. William Lohe, quoted in *Minister's Prayer Book,* ed. John W. Doberstein (Philadelphia: Fortress Press, 1986), 279–280.

13. Henri J. M. Nouwen, *Reaching Out* (New York: Doubleday, 1966), 30.

14. N. W. Goodacre, "Retreats," in *The Westminster Dictionary of Christian Spirituality,* ed. Gordon S. Wakefield (Phildelphia: The Westminster Press, 1983), 335–336.

15. For information, you could contact your pastor. Retreat houses are strongest in the liturgical traditions, such as Episcopalian, Anglican, and Roman Catholic. Other centers, representing a wide theological spectrum (so research this as carefully), are developing across the United States and Canada.

SOUL-SEARCHING

Questions for Reflection and Discussion

1. How have you experienced the power of words in positive and negative ways?

2. How do you react to the thought of silence? Does it sound inviting, threatening, or just plain uninteresting? Why?

3. What does it mean to hear "news from ourselves"? Have you ever had such an experience? If so, explain. If not, why do think that is so?

4. How can solitude affect our relationships?

5. If you want to practice silence and solitude, review the guidelines and your calendar. When would it be least disruptive to your schedule? Where would you go? Make your plans and record your experience in your journal.

CHAPTER SIXTEEN

Spiritual Power and Freedom from Evil

🌿 BATTLING TEMPTATION
🌿 PRAYER FOR SPIRITUAL BATTLE

I N her book *On Iniquity,* Pamela Hansford Johnson tells of a young Englishman who was living in Germany when the first persecution of the Jews began during the Second World War. The first time he saw Nazis beating Jews in the streets, he was sick at the sight and rushed down a side street in disgust. The second time, he felt he ought to at least look, so he stopped and watched the cruelty for a full minute. The third time, he stayed longer. The fourth time, as he watched the jeering crowd and the terrified Jews, the sight seemed less revolting. He told himself he was becoming objective, but then he realized what was happening to him. It was not objectivity he was achieving; it was hardness. It was cold cynicism. This that he was witnessing was not a social phenomenon for academic observation. It was the icy breath of hell that was turning him into something less than human. He packed his bags and returned to England before the process could go any further.[1]

This world is a seductive place. Some people live under the mistaken notion that walking with Christ automatically reduces the likelihood of temptation and trials. That's like expecting a sailor to experience smoother sailing by leaving a lake to sail on the ocean. When we commit our lives to Christ, we enter the arena of spiritual warfare, and the battlefield is often our own souls. We are thrust into the ocean of life with all its storms. We must learn to navigate the rough waters that *will come.*

We need to understand the setting in which we live. First of all, we live "behind enemy lines." Though we sing "This Is My Father's World," in the sense of creation and the ultimate victory of redemption, the prince of the air is still at large. His defeat is certain, but his armies have not recognized any cease-fire and continue to fight with infernal persistence. The second aspect of life on earth is that this world is a place of temptation, a place of antagonism toward God and the spiritual life. How do we resist temptation and stay true to God?

Spiritual strength and energy develop as we learn to resist the dark spiritual forces of the world through the power of the Holy Spirit. The fires of trial and temptation are the greatest tests of our progress in soulshaping. Yet, they are primary tools in the Master's workshop. They drive us to the depths of our being. When a young husband and father is ambushed by temptation, as Steve was, it strips away presumptions and forces a person to do a ruthless spiritual inventory of personal principles and character strength. As we learn to master temptation, we find a new level of freedom *from* the world. The disciplines of detachment that we just discussed are conditioning exercises that help get us into shape. In this section we will look at some of the specific disciplines God provides for fighting the enemy of our souls.

There are two central factors to victory in any conflict. These were stated most clearly by the military strategist Sun Tzu around 400 B.C.:

Know the enemy and know yourself; and in one hundred battles you will never be in peril. When you are ignorant of the enemy but know yourself, your chances of winning or losing are equal. If ignorant both of your enemy and of yourself, you are certain in every battle to be in peril.[2]

Our progress and success depend on knowing the nature of the opposition we face. Our enemy is a threefold combination: the world in rebellion to God; the "flesh," or sinful nature of us, as human beings; and the devil and demonic hosts of heaven, who have rebelled against the Lord (see Rev. 12:1-17). These form what I call the "counterfeit trinity."

THE COUNTERFEIT TRINITY

From the outset, the Bible clearly prepares us to expect opposition from three sources. These three branches of opposition fight against the corresponding three parts of the Holy Trinity of God the Father, God the Son, and God the Holy Spirit.

"The World": Counterfeit of God the Father

> *Do not love the world or the things in the world. If any one loves the world, love for the Father is not in him. For all that is in the world, the lust of the flesh and the lust of the eyes and the pride of life, is not of the Father but is of the world. And the world passes away, and the lust of it; but he who does the will of God abides for ever. (1 John 2:15-17, RSV)*

The created order has fallen into disorder under the curse. The fallen world threatens our spiritual progress through distraction, disorder, and confusion. Again, this does not mean that creation is intrinsically evil—God created the world, and it is therefore good. But the world systems—political, social, civil, business, and even religious—as well as the "natural course of events," conspire to turn us from recognizing God or relying upon him. They conspire to keep us from worshiping God, and they certainly work together to prevent us from being obedient to God. Since the Fall, this is the way things have been and continue to be. Life in this fallen world threatens to seduce us to materialism or to cynicism and pessimism. Life in the world tempts us to be angry and hopeless. The mere daily round of responsibilities and trials can wear us down and defeat us.

The world is set against the Father, who created the world. It is the substitute or competitor for our worship. As we give our affection and devotion to this world, it becomes the rival of God the Creator. The world also competes as the source of our security, tempting us to rely on money, positions of power, personality, and prestige, instead of putting our full confidence in God and the resources he provides for us. Where God the Father is the first part of the Holy Trinity, the world becomes the counterfeit of God the Father and threatens to steal away our worship and reliance.

"The Flesh": Counterfeit of God the Holy Spirit
"The flesh" refers not so much to our physical bodies as to the self-centered human heart that is set against God. The desires of our human nature battle the nudgings of God's Spirit within us. Richard Lovelace presents a comprehensive image of sin and the flesh:

> [T]he structure of sin in the human personality is something far more complicated than the isolated acts and thoughts of deliberate disobedience commonly designated by the word. In its biblical definition, sin cannot be limited to isolated instances or patterns of wrongdoing; it is some-

thing much more akin to the psychological term "complex": an organic network of compulsive attitudes, beliefs and behavior deeply rooted in our alienation from God. Sin originated in the darkening of the human mind and heart as man turned from the truth about God to embrace a lie about him and consequently a whole universe of lies about his creation. Sinful thoughts, words and deeds flow forth from this darkened heart automatically and compulsively, as water from a polluted fountain.[3]

The primary tension in the Christian life is the ongoing battle between the new nature in Christ and the old nature of the flesh. Countless passages acknowledge this tension, calling for us to resist the flesh and cultivate the spirit. Romans 6–8, Galatians 5, and Colossians 3 speak clearly to this. This reality of our inner warfare is one of the most persuasive arguments for our practicing spiritual exercises. By their very nature, they displace the flesh and energize the new, Christlike person God is shaping within us.

The flesh, our sinful nature, is the counterfeit to the Spirit living within us. The old nature is the most frequent tempter to sin (James 1:13-15). As the Spirit seeks to gain control of our lives, to bring us under the dominion of God, the old nature resists and refuses to cooperate. Its appetites wail loudly, drowning out the call of holiness. Its desires push incessantly, draining our energy and attention from godly pursuits.

"The Devil": Counterfeit of God the Son

The third aspect of the counterfeit trinity is the devil and his demonic hosts. Even as Jesus encountered the devil, so we are subject to the harassment and wiles of the fallen angelic powers, who have waged their rebellion against God on the stage of human history. Spiritual warfare is aimed at our destruction, with the main goal of hurting the God who created us. We need to be armed in mind and spirit, equipped with practical strategies for victory.

I was speaking with a married couple who are active as missionaries in a nation emerging from former communist domination. They are seeing tremendous response to the gospel, especially among the youth. One of the ironies of their ministry, however, is the conflict with other Christian organizations. I asked them why they thought it was happening and how they were handling it. In the course of our conversation, they said they were in earnest prayer about it and were continually working for unity. They see elements of spiritual warfare in the conflict. The man said to me, "The enemy often hides in the weakness of the flesh of others who hurt and hassle us. Satan accentuates our weaknesses." He understood the words of Ephesians 6:12: "For our struggle is not against flesh and blood, but against the rulers, against the authorities, against the powers of this dark world and against the spiritual forces of evil in the heavenly realms."

This understanding of evil cautions us against the immature reactions of anger and bitterness toward those who oppose or trouble us. To use an analogy from shortwave radio, we must always be aware that the static in the air may come from the demonic "jamming" of the enemy. "The higher the hill of holy exalted life, the more and the stronger will be the devil's blasts and the winds of temptation."[4]

The devil is a created being who exists in direct opposition to Jesus Christ, the incarnate Son of God. He was jealous of the Lord and wanted the place of favor that belongs to Jesus Christ alone. So he rebelled against God and became the leader of others who have rebelled. Various terms are used to describe the heavenly hosts who joined in the rebellion: *principalities, powers, demons.*

Do not be overcome with anxious dread if the evil one comes (as he will) with sudden fierceness, knocking and hammering on the walls of your house; or if he should stir some of his mighty agents to rise suddenly and attack you without warning. Let us be clear about this: The fiend must be taken into account. Anyone beginning this work (I do not care who he is) is liable to feel, smell, taste or hear some surprising effects concocted by the enemy in one or other of his senses. So do not be astonished if it happens. There is nothing he will not try to drag you down from the heights of such valuable work.⁵

Our spiritual vitality seems to stir all the forces of evil into action, as it did at the time of Jesus. He was frequently challenged by the world (storms, hunger), the flesh (quarrels), and the devil (demonic disturbances). He dealt with each in a direct, confident manner. In the Scripture accounts there is no hint of silly superstition. In fact, the lack of fanfare about the spiritual deliverances Jesus performed is one of the most powerful testimonies to their credibility.

As we enter into spiritual conflict, we must keep all three sources of temptation in mind. Too often a problem is attributed directly to the devil that could easily arise from the world and the flesh. My own sense is that we are not to underestimate the devil, but neither should we give the evil ones undue attention. The best strategy is to move through an inventory of the world and the flesh before we conclude that spiritual warfare is the primary problem.

Testing and Temptation: Pathways to Growth

When we begin to doubt that temptation and spiritual conflict have any purpose or necessity, we should remember Jesus' example. At his baptism he was commissioned for his work on earth. We would expect him to begin immediately, capturing the momentum of his first manifestation to John the Baptist and the crowds—what a dramatic moment! So we are puzzled as we read in Luke's Gospel the genealogy of Jesus and then, "Jesus, full of the Holy Spirit, returned from the Jordan *and was led by the Spirit in the desert,* where for forty days he was tempted by the devil" (Luke 3:23–4:2, italics added).

I have come to think that the genealogy is a vivid insert, not to interrupt the narrative, but to illustrate Jesus' identification with all humanity—every generation—in his mission. It illustrates the promise and power of God over human events. This sets the stage for Jesus' temptation in Luke 4:1-13, in which Jesus was tested as to his identity as the Son of God, his unwavering allegiance to God, and his strategy for fulfilling the will of God in his mission.[6]

We may think of Jesus as already being totally prepared and perfect in every way, but this episode in Luke 4 gives us reason to pause. This period of temptation was clearly part of a process that readied our Lord for the ministry ahead of him. The wilderness experience was the fire that forged the metal of his character and commission into the tempered steel of faithfulness. Our spirits soar in his triumph over the evil one, as we read the stirring words: "When the devil had finished all this tempting, he left him until an opportune time. Jesus returned to Galilee *in the power of the Spirit,* and news about him spread through the whole countryside" (Luke 4:13-14, italics added). After testing, Jesus ministered in the power of the Spirit.

The Spiritual Battles of Jesus

If we study the temptations of Jesus, we find that the direct assaults by the evil one came when Jesus was intentionally concentrating on his mission of the Cross. First, Jesus was assaulted by the evil one in the wilderness following his baptism, which commissioned him for ministry. The second time the evil one is mentioned as tempting Christ is when Peter first confesses that Jesus is the Christ. As Jesus begins to teach that this means death and resurrection, Peter protests such atrocities. Jesus says, "Get behind me, Satan." (This reference demonstrates clearly Paul's assertion that our conflicts are not with flesh and blood but with the evil one, who can manipulate human sentiment and weakness). The third primary temptation comes from his flesh as he prays in the Garden of Gethsemane. His persistence in prayer, along with the intercession of the disciples (meager though it was), sustains him.

Hebrews 4:15 tells us he was "tempted in every way, just as we are—yet was without sin." His power to stand was rooted in the disciplines of the Word, prayer, and the discernment of seeing temptation from the eternal perspective.

Temptation—or Testing?

Although we often use the words *testing* and *temptation* interchangeably, there is a fundamental difference between them. A test is given with the goal of success; a temptation is given with the goal of failure. The Lord never tempts, and the devil never tests. Think of the schoolteacher giving a test to the class. His goal is to encourage the students to master the material because it will equip them for success in life. He wants them to be encouraged by their success. This is far different from temptation that is aimed at exposing our weaknesses and exploiting our vulnerabilities.

We must always assume that the spiritual life—especially its seasons of greatest growth—is cultivated in the midst of opposition. We are deceived if we expect ease and lack of conflict to be signs of God's blessing and support. Dark forces are dead set against us. In fact, the more earnest we are, the more likely we are to face seasons of intense struggle, like the wilderness, as well as the "gnats and ants" of daily irritation. And our "easy" seasons, more than indicators of our spiritual success, may be proof that we are little threat to the enemy. Why should Satan waste energy on someone who is already an asset to evil simply by being passive and ineffective?

James 1:14 says that "each person is tempted when he is lured and enticed by his own desire" (RSV). We usually want to place the blame outside ourselves: on society, on our situation, on another person. While these may be factors, the key is the corruption of the human heart. Compare the heart with a radio and temptation with radio waves. Radio waves do not affect the radio in the least unless it is turned on. Likewise, temptations wouldn't affect us at all if they didn't find a receiver in our hearts. We are too often tuned in and turned on to temptation's channel.

In times of temptation, God comes to us with all the resources we need, not only to overcome it, but also to learn from it. While God is not the source of temptation, he is quick to use it for shaping our souls.

A man was sorely tempted to embezzle funds from his company. In fact, he began plotting several surefire ways to achieve his goals. He was getting close to implementing one of his plans when one of his colleagues was caught.

"It was incredible!" he exclaimed. "The armed security descended on his office and made him pack his personal things in their presence. Then they escorted him out of the office and into a waiting detective's car that whisked him away. The entire office was aghast. We had no idea what he was up to. I was in a cold sweat—that could have been me. . . . But the hardest thing was seeing his wife in the store several weeks later. She was humiliated. I ducked down a side aisle so I didn't have to talk with her."

The scare was enough to shake him loose from the seduction of temptation. He woke up to the reality that he was truly playing with fire. He began to see that his greed had blinded him to some of the most valuable things in life, like freedom from jail and the reputation of his family. He actually could say that God taught him more through that experience than through years of Sunday school.

THE ENEMY'S STRATEGY

Many forces conspire to turn our attention from God. These include:

- distraction from spiritual priorities
- deception about the true nature of ourselves and the world around us
- discouragement over our failures
- nagging feelings of guilt over not being perfect
- exhausting attempts to live up to a legalistic, religious system
- ordinary activities that leave us weary
- amusements and "ordinary" earthly pleasures: TV, phone conversations, magazines
- personal ambitions that consume our energy
- pride that seals us off from others
- hurt feelings that pull us inward in self-pity and resentment
- depression over our lot in life
- and others

Often we fail to recognize these problems because they don't stand out as serious offenses against God, others, or ourselves. The spiritual exercises we have explored thus far take us a long way toward confronting and correcting these problems. As we increase in our spiritual awareness, and exercise new spiritual muscles, we will develop a lifestyle in which these kinds of distractions will not fit so easily. Eventually, our eternal perspective and our growing sense of God's presence will equip us to deal more and more effectively with the sin patterns that are so subtle and prevalent in our world.

But our spiritual warfare involves much more than these kinds of sins. Sometimes we receive direct assaults of temptation that not only turn our attention from God, but also often turn us against God.

Augustine's *Confessions* gives graphic accounts of his battles with temptation and impurity. Book III begins, "I came to Carthage, and all around me in my ears were the *sizzling and frying of unholy loves.*"7 He vividly describes being overwhelmed as "the brambles of lust grew up right over my head, and there was no hand to tear them up by the roots."8 Augustine articulates what we all learn by experience. It is the mystery of sin's power that the slightest yielding empowers evil beyond measure. One of the evil one's lies is that "a little bit won't hurt" or that "just this one time will release us from the pressure and distraction of temptation." Wrong! One step into temptation is like putting a raft on the rapids; you only meant to test the water, but you find yourself swept away.

The enemy's strategy in temptation is not to get us to break a law but to break a heart—God's heart. The nature of specific temptations is not as important as the fact that falling into any of them sets in motion a series of disturbances within ourselves, between us and others, and with God. Whether the counterfeit trinity separates us from God through the "respectable sin" of overwork that leads us to neglect our fellowship with God, or through "gross sins" such as financial fraud or sexual immorality, the ultimate, infernal goal is achieved: grieving the Holy Spirit through the disruption of our love for God.

---

*T*he enemy's strategy in temptation is not to get us to break a law but to break a heart—God's heart.

Some people view God as keeping a scorecard on our individual sins, as if he were scouting us for a team of supersaints: "Let's see, Doug's good on fielding temptations to pride, but he's a little sloppy in the temper department. Better get him in some extra training. . . ." I'm not trying to say that our individual sins aren't important, or that, in human terms, all sins have equal consequences. Obviously, murder has more severe consequences than making a misleading comment to protect your reputation. But the fact that we so often miss is that *love is at the heart of it all.* "Against thee, thee only, have I sinned," confessed David, in deep anguish (Ps. 51:4, RSV). When we begin to see sin in terms of love instead of legalism, we begin to tap a new reservoir of resolve to resist temptation and preserve our fellowship with God.

*W***hen we begin to see sin in terms of love instead of legalism, we begin to tap a new reservoir of resolve to resist temptation and preserve our fellowship with God.**

We agree with God that we were made for a better, more fulfilling life. At the very least, sin is like consuming junk food that feeds an appetite without providing any nourishment. At its worst, sin is like subjecting ourselves to dangerous levels of radiation; it produces cancer that consumes our very lives for its own sake.

Guidelines for Battling Temptation
One of the greatest deceptions of sin is that we are powerless against it. How often I have said, and heard others say, "I was overcome. I just couldn't help myself."

I remember one time when I lost my temper with one of our

children, the child shot back at me, "You can't get mad at me; you're a pastor!"

"And you're a pastor's kid!"

As we were struck with the humor of our conflict—and our anger melted into laughter—it struck me that our children were making assumptions that resisting temptation (in this case, anger) should be easier for me since I've gone to seminary and spent half my life preaching. Wrong! We all battle temptation. The only defense is continual reliance upon the Lord and a deepening awareness of our areas of vulnerability.

In our conflict with sin, I would suggest that we use three primary sources as aids to examine our consciences and to make us aware of our most vulnerable places. The first is the Ten Commandments. The second is Jesus' teaching in Matthew 5–7, the Sermon on the Mount, which includes much of his own commentary on the Ten Commandments. The third is the list of the seven deadly sins that provides a comprehensive inventory for us.

The seven deadly sins are gluttony, greed, sloth, envy, wrath, pride, and lust. Such lists were developed in various forms in the early church in order to instruct people in the most common pitfalls of sin. Gregory the Great (A.D. 540–604) described these as "a classification of the normal perils of the soul in the ordinary conditions of life."9

The question for us is: Can spiritual exercises really help us stand against sin? The answer is an unequivocal yes. Since I began this section of the book with the story of Steve, let's see the role of the disciplines in helping him stand firm. Following my conversation with Steve, I wrote down the ideas that had come to me as we spoke. It was one of those times like James chapter 1 speaks of when the Lord gives us wisdom. Steve and I saw that there were five "lines of attack and resistance" for him to take in facing this temptation.

Renew His Vision for Loving His Wife More

Using the *discipline of study,* we went through the Scriptures that warn against adultery and call for faithfulness "to the wife of your youth" (Prov. 5:3-23; Mal. 2:13-16). Steve wrote these down for reading each day. As we read, he shared that what surprised him most was the fact that he was *not* dissatisfied in their marriage. In fact, he was quite happy. But he knew he had been taking so much for granted. He had lost his vision for what a marriage was meant to be. He hadn't been enjoying his wife and appreciating the privilege of sharing life with her. God's Word encouraged him to think about how to express affection and attention to Jenny. "If it matters that much to God," he said, "I guess I'd better take it more seriously!" The best defense is a good offense, as they say.

Renew His Mind by Replacing Fantasies with Facts

As pleasurable as his fantasies of sex with another woman might be, Steve had to remind himself of the cold, hard facts about the devastating consequences sexual indiscretion would bring upon him, his wife, their marriage, all their relatives and friends, and his career, as well as the same concerns for the other woman. Again, we looked at the Scripture, this time at the story of David and Bathsheba. Nathan's rebuke of David brings home the fact that *even with repentance and forgiveness, sin committed sets terrible consequences in motion.* These consequences are often not reversed. For David, things were never the same. "The sword will never depart from your house," said the Lord—and that's what came to pass (2 Sam. 12:10).

The movie *Fatal Attraction* had not yet been produced at this time, but this movie (though I do not endorse its graphic sexual scenes and violence!) depicts what they call "the law of unintended consequences." What starts out as a careless tryst can become the stuff of nightmares—only worse, since we are already awake! Steve and I saw so clearly that victory over sin begins with a ruthless discipline of our minds to consider the consequences of sin.

Picture Temptation in a Negative, Even Repulsive, Light

Using a modified form of meditation, I had Steve take time to look at his temptations from a different angle: seeing the actions of this woman from God's perspective. Steve needed to picture this beautiful woman as a "temptress," (which she, in fact, was, in this situation). He had to see the temptress as negative, even repulsive, in the eyes of the Lord.

While we want to maintain a loving spirit toward even those who tempt us—for they, too, are being tempted by the evil one—we must be ruthless in our mental depiction of their role in our life. We need to counteract the idealization that so often occurs when we find ourselves attracted to someone who seems to be offering us a wonderful option and an exciting adventure.

Steve wrote a series of sentences such as "How dare she try to hurt my wife like this; it's a type of murder, causing us a pain that could be unbearable to live with. How dare she try to spoil the lives of our children; it's like letting her barge into our home and take them away." He also reminded himself that when he saw her, she was dressed in the best clothes, with her hair and makeup at their best for the business day. He tried to picture her in crummy clothes, with no makeup, and greatly aged. That was a fantasy slayer!

Anticipate Dangerous Situations

The exercise of preview helped Steve to be proactive in anticipating the situations that could cause the greatest concern. He scanned his daily routines and his past experiences with the woman and asked himself, *What would Jesus do?*

Steve realized he had to guard against flirtatious language and nonverbal signals. He also planned to always have someone around or be in a public setting whenever he and the woman had to work together. And no more lunches with just the two of them! He also planned to leave office parties early "to get home to the family." He was even willing to leave work and come home immediately if the situation got too intense.

Pray
Steve began, and poured out his heart, which by this time was broken by the situation but also greatly strengthened by our time together. Then I prayed a strong prayer of intercession for Steve and Jenny and for the woman, who also was trapped in temptation's web. Steve actually voiced forgiveness of her and prayed for her to find Jesus Christ and a relationship where godly love could be shared.

Last, he carried my home and church phone numbers with him so he could call me anytime, day or night.

As I already shared, it worked! Yes, we put in a tremendous amount of effort that evening, but I am convinced that it was worth every moment. Think of the countless *years* of agony that tens and possibly hundreds of people were spared because Steve was equipped to battle temptation.

Other sins can be confronted by using this model. Different disciplines are appropriate for different situations, but many overlap. Here are some of my suggestions:

GLUTTONY: *fasting, disciplines of self-care*
GREED: *stewardship, disciplines of community*
SLOTH: *vision, disciplines of purpose*
ENVY: *simplicity, solitude*
WRATH: *disciplines of character*
PRIDE: *confession, silence, and solitude*

In spite of all this, however, we will fall into temptation. I will discuss how to handle our failures and imperfections in the chapter "How to Lead an Imperfect Life." But the main point to remember here is that *when we fall, we fall to our knees.* We invoke the grace and mercy of God and begin again.

We can also develop what I call a "rapid-response strategy." Even as police, fire, and military groups have specific plans to respond immediately and effectively to catastrophic threats, so we can develop such plans for the places and times we are most vulnerable to the enemy's attacks.

A Rapid-Response Strategy

Somewhere recently I heard that it is possible to escape from quicksand. I had always thought that once you fell into it that was it—the end. But I've heard that there is a way out. (I hasten to add that you'd better confirm this for yourself before you test it in the jungle.) The first step is to stop struggling. Struggling causes you to sink more quickly into the sand. When you stop moving, you may stop sinking and may "float" in the quicksand, suspended at the point you've reached. The second step is to tilt your head back and lift your eyes to the sky. This creates a bit broader surface area to slow your sinking. It also keeps your mouth and nose free for breathing. The third step is to take deep breaths. These will expand your lungs and add buoyancy to your body. Even as pumping air into a balloon under water causes it to rise, expanding your lungs should help to bring you up.

I see the spiritual principles here for a rapid response to temptation.

Stop doing whatever you're doing. First, realize that whatever you are currently doing has gotten you into the quicksand. *Stop doing it!* Instead, call a friend, get up and go to a different place—anything that interrupts the temptation cycle will slow the sinking.

As someone has said, the first step to getting out of a hole is to stop digging.

Look up. What a beautiful image. Turn your attention to the Lord. Put on some Christian music; read through your journal or personal planner for the vision and goals you have for yourself. Revisit memories of spiritually powerful times. Remember other people who have triumphed during times like the one you're facing now.

Take deep breaths of prayer. The Jesus Prayer, "Lord Jesus Christ, have mercy on me," can become an empowering petition, especially if it has become a deeper part of your life through the discipline of unceasing prayer.

Of course, the surest way to get out of quicksand is to have someone nearby on safe ground who can help you out! That is one of the primary purposes of intercessory prayer. While our study thus far has focused primarily on the individual, we live and grow in the community of faith. One of the central fibers of our life together is prayer, especially for one another.

PRAYER FOR SPIRITUAL BATTLE

Prayer is our primary weapon in spiritual warfare. After describing the complete armor of God, Paul offers this blanket exhortation, "Pray at all times in the Spirit, with all prayer and supplication" (Eph. 6:18, RSV). Prayer keeps the communication and supply channels open to sustain us in the battle. Without it, we are sure to fall. With prayer, God makes us stand.

In a previous chapter, we considered prayer as an exercise for making the connection with God's presence. At this time, we want to look at the role of praying for one another through intercessory prayer. It is the means of releasing the power of God into others' lives.

My wife, Sarah, struggled for a number of years with anxiety and depression. Such problems are very complex, involving a number of personal, physiological, and family factors, along with a dose of mystery. Through counseling and prayer, Sarah and our family members began to make changes in our life together, developing skills of thinking and behavior that led to a measure of relief. Still, Sarah had some rough times. Finally, she asked her friend, Melanie, and another friend, Ginny, to pray with her for relief. They met for prayer a few times. Melanie and Ginny would call Sarah periodically to see how she was doing. One morning, Melanie called early to see how Sarah felt. Sarah said she felt much better than she had in a long time. Melanie was thrilled to hear that God was answering their prayers. After hanging up from talking with Sarah, Melanie called Ginny to tell her the great news. Ginny was so excited that she screamed with joy. Later that evening, Melanie called back to tell Sarah how Ginny responded and how thrilled they were. Sarah was so deeply touched by their love and support that she wrote the following poem and sent it to them the next day.

Angel Friends
by Sarah Rumford

Do you believe in angels
—those who guard us and rejoice
and care about all that we do?
God has convinced me many times,
but most recently through you.

I cry and smile and feel so loved,
when I see the picture God's given me:
of friends shouting for joy in my brighter day,
watching as Jesus brings healing in his gentle, sweet way.

And then setting their task to encourage with hope,
with laughter
and prayers
and pictures from Jesus.

You're giving me Spirit gifts
woven with love,
threads of gold from angels sent from above,
to assure me that Jesus is holding me tight
—mending me
—filling my darkness with light.

May I be ready to fly with the angels
—doing my work for the Lord.
Always open to where I am needed,
desiring no hurt to go unheeded.
Imitating angels who've rejoiced over me.
Friends who are angels who want me to be free.

I love you, angel friends!

Out of this experience, Sarah gathered a small of group of women who felt called to pray for one another. They have grown into a ministry of intercession for other women, going to visit in their homes for intensive prayer ministry. Sarah has always called them her "Angel Friends," and that's how the group is known now. They are experiencing great joy in touching others with God's love, expressed through intercessory prayer.

Intercessory prayer is one means of fulfilling the exhortation to "bear one another's burdens, and so fulfill the law of Christ" (Gal. 6:2, NKJV). When we pray for each other, we take on the burden with the strength of love. We do not have to know exactly how to pray, but we carry their names before the Lord.

Guidelines for Powerful Prayer

Spiritual exercises equip us for the battles of life. They enable us to detach from the worldly power sources that will fail us in the fight. Instead, we tap into infinite and varied resources of the Lord, finding his power sufficient to overcome.

The Armor of God

One specific means of equipping ourselves for battle is taking up the armor of God described in Ephesians 6:10-18. Anyone who wishes to meditate on these verses would do well to invest in the Puritan classic *The Christian in Complete Armour* by William Gurnall.[10] This 1,189-page, double-columned tome is a priceless exposition of "the Saints' War against the Devil." John Newton said, "If I could read only one book beside the Bible, I would choose *The Christian in Complete Armour.*"

Ephesians 6:10-18 contains some of the most practical advice for standing against temptation from any source. As I was praying through this passage once, I had the delightful image of Christ buckling the armor on me. He was smiling and teasing with me in a way that surprised me, given the seriousness of armor and all.

"Oh," he seemed to say, "but this armor is a thing of joy. It shines with the light. And when struck, it rings a clear note of protection. When you go into battle, rejoice that you have this armor."

As I continued in this spontaneous meditation, he explained each piece of the armor. What I remember most was his joy and the fact that the armor was tailored perfectly for me. As I pray this prayer regularly, I am greatly enriched as I envision the Lord himself suiting me up for battle.

A Prayer for the Battle

Another resource for spiritual warfare is a prayer from the Middle Ages, and possibly much earlier, attributed to Patrick (c.

389–461), the missionary who brought Christianity to Ireland. This prayer, known as "St. Patrick's Breastplate," is an invocation of God's power against the power of darkness. I am struck by its theological grounding and scope. Its structure presents a model for warfare prayer:

1. The invocation of the triune God.   We admit from the start our allegiance to and our full dependence upon the Father, Son, and Holy Spirit. As Gurnall urges us to be strong in the Lord, he reminds us, "The Christian, when fullest of divine communications, is but a glass without a foot, he cannot stand, or hold what he hath received, any longer than God hold him in his strong hand."[11] Insights such as these drive us to grace.

2. The affirmation of the historical Incarnation and the resources of God in the church and the creation.   This section reviews major elements of the gospel message, reminding us of the importance of affirming the fact that Christ came "in the flesh" (1 John 4:2). It also reminds us that Christ has battled on this earth and won on our behalf. We are not alone in the fight. Nor do we cry out to a distant, unempathetic God. We cry out to "the pioneer and perfecter of our faith" (Heb. 12:2, RSV), who is coming again.

3. The affirmation of the attributes of God.   These affirmations give us confidence in the effectiveness of our prayers. The prayer reminds us of the infinite resources that are ours in Christ. We have the power, the Word, the wisdom, the sovereign governing, and the very angels of God Almighty!

4. A catalog of evils.   This representative list surveys the enemy's stratagems in terms of the world, the flesh, and the devil and his evil hosts. It awakens us to the manifold attacks evil will wage against us, body and soul. But note its place in the prayer, following the affirmations of the first sections.

5. Petition to cover all of life.   This passage, with echoes of Psalm 139, is one of the richest petitions in the literature of prayer.

6. Pronouncement of allegiance.   The prayer returns to its starting point, but with the rich meaning of what has been offered in the body of the prayer. I put the emphasis on this section as a pledge of allegiance. It is a confession of faith.

St. Patrick's Breastplate

(1)   I bind unto myself today
      the strong name of the Trinity,
      By invocation of the same,
      The Three in One, and One in Three.

(2)   I bind this day to me for ever,
      By power of faith, Christ's incarnation;
      His baptism in the Jordan river;
      His death on the cross for my salvation.
      His bursting from the spiced tomb;
      His riding up the heav'nly way;
      His coming at the day of doom;
      I bind unto myself today.

(3)   I bind unto myself today
      the power of God to hold and lead,
      His eye to watch, his might to stay,
      His ear to hearken to my need;
      The wisdom of my God to teach,
      His hand to guide, his shield to ward,
      the word of God to give me speech,
      His heav'nly host to be my guard.

(4)   Against all Satan's spells and wiles,
      Against false words of heresy,

Against the knowledge that defiles,
Against the heart's idolatry,
Against the wizard's evil craft,
Against the death-wound and the burning,
the choking wave, the poison'd shaft,
Protect me, Christ, till thy returning.

(5) Christ be with me, Christ within me,
Christ behind me, Christ before me,
Christ beside me, Christ to win me,
Christ to comfort and restore me,
Christ beneath me, Christ above me,
Christ in quiet, Christ in danger,
Christ in hearts of all that love me,
Christ in mouth of friend and stranger.

(6) I bind unto myself the name,
the strong name of the Trinity,
By invocation of the same,
The Three in One, and One in Three,
Of whom all nature hath creation,
Eternal Father, Spirit, Word.
Praise to the Lord of my salvation:
Salvation is of Christ the Lord.[12]

The spiritual disciplines of power unlock the chains that bind us to this world. As we draw near to the Lord, we find the freedom of relying on his strength without making alliances with this world. Writing of Paul in prison, William Gurnall comments, "He knew too much of another world, to bid so high for the enjoying of this."[13]

Somewhere I read that when a hawk is attacked by crows, he does not make a counterattack. Instead, he soars higher and higher in ever widening circles until his tormentors leave him alone. This is the way of the spiritual exercises the Lord has provided for our conditioning and training. We soar higher on the wings of prayer, catching the currents of God's Spirit.

This is the pathway of freedom, blazed by Jesus Christ and maintained by giving ourselves to the practices that call us back to the essentials of the gospel.

NOTES

1. Cited by David W. Phillips in "The Ultimate Sellout," a sermon preached in the Presbyterian Church of Old Greenwich, April 1, 1979.
2. Sun Tzu, *The Art of War,* trans. Samuel B. Griffith (London: Oxford University Press, 1988), 84.
3. Richard F. Lovelace, *Dynamics of Spiritual Life* (Downers Grove, Ill.: InterVarsity, 1979), 88.
4. Kenneth Leech, *Soul Friend* (San Francisco: Harper & Row, 1977), 128–129.
5. Ibid.
6. For a recent consideration of these temptations from the aspect of spirituality, see Henri J. M. Nouwen, *In the Name of Jesus: Reflections on Christian Leadership* (New York: Crossroad, 1989).
7. Augustine, *The Confessions of St. Augustine,* trans. Rex Warner, Book III, chap. 1 (New York: New American Library, 1963), 53 emphasis added.
8. Ibid., bk. II, ch. 3, 43.
9. Dallas Willard, *The Spirit of the Disciplines* (San Francisco: HarperSanFrancisco, 1988), 160.
10. William Gurnall, *The Christian in Complete Armour* (Carlisle, Penn.: Banner of Truth, 1974).
11. Gurnall, I:19.

12. Translated by Mrs. C. F. Alexander, *Eerdmans' Handbook to the History of Christianity* (Grand Rapids, Mich.: Eerdmans, 1977), 212.
13. Gurnall, I:10.

SOUL-SEARCHING

Questions for Reflection and Discussion

1. What are the three fundamental sources of temptation? Can you give examples of how each has affected you?

2. How was Jesus tempted? What resulted from these experiences?

3. What is the difference between temptation and testing? Why is this distinction important?

4. Consider the temptations you face most frequently. Use the Ten Commandments (see Exodus 20) or the seven deadly sins as tools to help you examine your conscience.

   a) What troubles you the most?
   b) What do these temptations tell you about yourself?

5. When are you most vulnerable to temptation? Are there certain "seasons" (times, places, situations) in which you are most vulnerable? Why?

6. What specific "rapid-response strategies" could you develop to resist a fierce temptation? Write your thoughts in your journal, where they can be reviewed frequently.

7. What is one of the toughest battles you are facing right now? In what specific ways could the resources of this chapter (or book) give you strength?

8. Who's praying for you on a regular basis? If no one is, whom could you ask? Take time to share your hopes for intercession with one person and agree to pray for him or her.

9. Pray through the prayer of "St. Patrick's Breastplate" several times. Feel free to rewrite portions of it in your own words.

PART **FIVE**

Making a Difference: A Life of Purpose

SOULSHAPING AT A GLANCE

Exercises That Increase Our Awareness of God's Presence

- Repentance
- Confession
- Preview
- Review
- Prayer
- Worship

Exercises That Help Us See Life with an Eternal Perspective

- Bible study
- Meditation
- Spiritual reading

Exercises That Free Us from Evil's Power and Connect Us to God's Resources

- Fasting
- Silence
- Solitude
- Battling temptation
- Prayer for spiritual battle

Exercises That Direct Our Lives toward Kingdom Purposes

- **Building character**
- **Building relationships**
- **Spiritual direction**
- **Spiritual friendship**
- **Stewardship**
- **Spiritual service through spiritual gifts**

On Thursday, April 23, 1987, I turned on the television at the end of one of our delightful, sun-drenched vacation days in Florida, to hear on the news of the collapse of L'Ambiance Plaza, a thirteen-story building under construction in Bridgeport, Connecticut—about four miles from our home at the time. Of the seventy men working at the site, twenty-eight were missing under the tons of concrete and steel.

We returned from Florida on Monday. I joined the pastoral care team immediately at the L'Ambiance disaster site to be available to the families, construction workers, police, firefighters and medical personnel. By Wednesday, they had recovered sixteen bodies and were still searching for the remaining twelve.

My shift was from 9:00 P.M. to 2:00 A.M. I was troubled not only by the catastrophe but also by feelings of my own helplessness and unimportance as I stood at the edge of the pit. They had located four more bodies, but it would be hours before they could get to them. What could I do? I remember feeling intimidated by the workers who could use the heavy equipment and provide practical help.

I was talking with one of the union bosses who'd been there from the very beginning. He was a rough, burly guy. I doubt if we would have had much conversation if we had met outside of these circumstances. As we talked, I expressed my appreciation for all he and his men had done. Many of them were doing this physically grueling, emotionally stressful work of recovery with minimal sleep.

"I only wish I could do more," I said.

"You're doing enough" he said, "I am so glad you pastors

come here. This place is like hell—and you keep reminding us that God's still around."

GETTING BEYOND OURSELVES: SPIRITUALITY LEADS TO A LIFE OF PURPOSE

On countless occasions I remember the comment by that union boss: "You keep reminding us that God's still around." While I could not dig through concrete, operate an acetylene torch, or provide medical care, I *could* be there as a visible representative of Jesus Christ, his presence in the midst of tragedy.

When the world looks at us, are we, in fact, such a reminder? Do we live to reveal the presence of Christ—not only in crisis but as a quiet conscience in times of decision, a persistent influence in leadership and service, a model of hope in times of discouragement, and a testimony to recovery in times of brokenness? Unless we are rooted in Christ, the world may not be reminded.

The spiritual director François Fénelon (c. 1651–1715) warns that "a persuaded mind and even a well-intentioned heart is a long way from exact and faithful practice. Nothing has been more common in every age, and still more so today, than meeting souls who are perfect and saintly in speculation."[1] The spiritual life is not an escape from life but the preparation for encountering life in this world. "True spirituality is not a leisure-time activity, a diversion from life. It is essentially subversive, and the test of its genuineness is practical."[2]

---

*T*he spiritual life is not an escape from life but the preparation for encountering life in this world.

Spiritual exercise and practice can seem self-centered if we focus on God's presence, the renewing of our mind, and the increase of our own spiritual power—yet go no further. Spiritual health and vitality, in addition to bearing the many fruits of fulfillment in our lives on a personal level, have the ultimate goal of bringing about God's kingdom here on earth. Unless we stand on the disaster sites of life, reminding the world that God does exist and that this makes a difference, our personal fulfillment and spiritual power fall sadly short of God's purposes for his people.

Spiritual exercises are not ends in themselves. While we may think of them as retreats from life, they actually fit us for service. God has much for us to do in bringing the world to a redeeming knowledge of himself. But we must be connected to God, filled with the mind of Christ, and empowered by the Holy Spirit in order to accomplish what God intends.

FOLLOWING THE RHYTHM OF JESUS' LIFE

There is a rhythm to the healthy, active spiritual life. We see it most clearly in the life of Jesus. His life was marked by involvement and solitude, action and reflection, engagement and withdrawal. His powerful ministry was energized by his time apart with the Father. His time with the Father was informed and directed by the issues he was contending with in his active ministry (see Matt. 11:25-27). He kept a balance between gathering strength and wisdom and then applying them to the situations around him. This is a rhythm we would be wise to follow.

We are developed spiritually—our souls are shaped—in this arena called the world. While we may have countless questions about the suffering and trials of this life, there are aspects of our spiritual growth that can happen only in the contests of these difficult days. In vivid images, Forbes Robinson says that, far from being a hindrance, life in this sullied world is a matter of privilege and potential that could be fulfilled in no other way.

> I think I have told you of my father's words spoken during his last illness: "If I had a thousand lives I would give them all, all to the ministry." You will not regret your decision. If angels could envy, how they would envy us our splendid chance, to be able, in a world where everything unseen must be taken on sheer faith, in a world where the contest between the flesh and the spirit is being decided for the universe, not only to win the battle ourselves but also to win it for others! To help a brother up the mountain while you yourself are only just able to keep your foothold, to struggle through the mist together, that surely is better than to stand at the summit and beckon. You will have a hard time of it, I know; and I would like to make it smoother and to "let you down" easier; but I am sure that God, who loves you even more than I do, and has absolute wisdom, will not tax you beyond your strength. . . . I'll pray for you, like the widow in the parable, and I have immense belief in prayer. . . . You remember what was said of Maurice, "He always impressed me as a man who was naturally weak in his will; but an iron will seemed to work through him." That will can work through you and transform you, but for God's sake don't trust to your own will.[3]

Though written to one who has decided to serve God through the ordained pastoral ministry, this counsel applies to any person who decides to serve the Lord. In fact, I find it even more stirring when applied to those who serve God as laypeople in the varied arenas of life. Their task is to balance multiple demands, often at greater sacrifice than those of us who serve God's people with the gracious provision of financial remuneration for our service. No matter what our vocation, however, we are all embroiled in "the contest for the universe." In this contest, spiritual exercises not only address the weaknesses of our own inner lives, but they also release that "iron will"—the truth, grace, and power of God—to work through us.

The practical nature of the spiritual life is measured by our role of being "in the world but not of it." The focus of the chapters in this section is on our role in the world. How are we to conduct ourselves in the midst of the daily pressures and expectations of life?

We operate in the world through who we are (as we develop Christlike character); through the quality of our interaction with others (relationships); through the use of our material resources, especially money (stewardship); and through Christ's work, made possible by our spiritual gifts (service). The following four chapters explore how we can be spiritually fit in these areas.

NOTES

1. François Fénelon, *Christian Perfection* (Minneapolis: Bethany House Publishers, 1975), 3.
2. Kenneth Leech, *True Prayer*, quoted in Postema, *Space for God*, 155.
3. George Christian Dieffenbad and Christian Müller, *Evangelishes Brevier* (Gotha: Gustav Schloessmann, 1869), 416f, in *Ministers's Prayer Book*, ed. John W. Doberstein (Philadelphia: Fortress Press, 1986), 203.

CHAPTER SEVENTEEN

Cultivating a Character You Can Count On

🌿 BUILDING CHARACTER

MY friend Gary and I were talking over coffee about a colleague who had left the ministry because of sexual misconduct. As in so many of these situations, this news had surprised and saddened us. It also raised the troubling paradox of an obviously gifted pastor who had been caught in the trap of leading a secret life for years. He had inspired many people to commit their lives to Christ. He was an effective communicator and had discipled many others in the ways of Christ. Yet he had fallen prey to dark desires, hurting countless others in the process. Why? How did this happen?

Gary took the napkin (one of his favorite writing surfaces!) and a felt-tip pen and drew two lines, as on a graph. The first line gradually sloped upward. The second line, just above it, started to slope upward slowly, then shot up dramatically, leaving a huge gap between the two.

"The line with the gradual slope," said Gary, "is the 'character line.' The second line is the 'gift line.' His gifts in ministry promoted him to a place that couldn't be supported by his character. His opportunities outgrew his character. That's what makes many people so vulnerable."

A character gap develops when we allow activity in the outer world to distract us from the daily business of bringing our attitudes, desires, words, and behavior under the sanctifying power of the Holy Spirit. Character is like physical exercise or any form of learning; you cannot "cram," hoping to do in a day or week what can only be accomplished by months and years of consistent practice.

The character gap is a weakness that will one day become apparent, when the circumstances or stresses of life converge and reach a breaking point. We may be able to coast for a while, and we may feel quite secure. But raw talent, personality, and fortunate circumstances cannot substitute for the forging of inner holiness, resilience, and the convictions that comprise integrity of character.

Raw talent, personality, and fortunate circumstances cannot substitute for the forging of inner holiness, resilience, and the convictions that comprise integrity of character.

Character is not developed in a vacuum. I can tell myself, in the sanctuary of silence and solitude, that I will control my temper, but it is not until I have been insulted and have returned a blessing that I have taken a step in character development. "But solid food is for the mature, *who by constant use have trained themselves to distinguish good from evil*" (Heb. 5:14, italics added).

Our character develops as we become increasingly aware of the complexity of life and wrestle with specific decisions we have to make. It also develops as we connect up the various parts of our lives into an integrated whole and have some sense of where we have come from, where we are now, and where we are heading.[1]

My personal definition of character is captured in the affirmation "You can count on me." You can count on my word to be honest and direct, you can count on my promises to be kept, you can count on me to admit my mistakes and ask forgiveness, and you can count on me to act with integrity when I am away from you. Those simple words carry a tremendous amount of power. Say them, and see what I mean.

Godly character is a prime ingredient of spiritual vitality. As we envision what character looks like in our lives, we feel the energy and joy rise within us. When we have character, we have the confidence of honesty, the power of self-control, and the freedom of never having to hide, dodge, or deny.

Godly character shares the fruit of spiritual discipline with the people around us. They have the privilege and, we hope, the inspiration, of harvesting from the seeds of life that God has sown in us. In our marriage, for example, my wife reaps the honor of purity in our relationship as well as in the eyes of the community. In a business, the firm reaps the benefits of a trusted, conscientious worker or the security of integrity in leadership.

THE ART OF ARTS

The process of character transformation, which encompasses all of life, is truly the "art of arts." Change in other areas of life can pale in comparison with the complexities and dynamics of dealing with the human heart. Gregory of Nazianzus was an Eastern church leader and theologian who lived from A.D.

330 to 389. A champion of orthodoxy at the Council of Constantinople in 381, he also understood the practical difficulties of working with fallen human beings.

> Guiding man, the most variable of creatures, is the art of arts. Pastors have been called the "physicians of souls," and compared with physicians who treat the body. But as difficult as treatment of the body is, it pales in significance when compared with soul work.
>
> Physicians work with bodies and perishable, failing matter. Ministers work with souls that come from God and partake of heavenly nobility.
>
> Place, time, age, and season are the subjects of physicians' scrutiny. They prescribe medicines and diets, and guard against things injurious. Sometimes they make use of the knife or of severer remedies. But none of these are so hard as diagnosis and cure of our habits, passions, lives, and wills.[2]

From the beginning, we are wise to cultivate realistic expectations based on a clear understanding of the natural resistance of our hearts. As Jeremiah 17:9 says, "The heart is deceitful above all things and beyond cure. Who can understand it?" This does not mean that we abandon our efforts. But we undertake the task with realistic expectations and in full reliance upon the Lord and his resources. As Jeremiah proceeds to say, "I the Lord search the heart and examine the mind" (Jer. 17:10). As the Lord leads us, step-by-step, his Spirit transforms us into the likeness of Christ.

CULTIVATING CHRISTLIKE CHARACTER: THE FRUIT OF THE SPIRIT

A primary theme in Christian character is "the imitation of Christ," best articulated by Thomas à Kempis (1379/80–1471).

In more recent times, Charles Sheldon's book *In His Steps* has presented a picture of what this could look like in everyday life. Imitation should not be taken in the sense of mimicry, merely going through the outward motions. Nor should the imitation of Christ be reduced in any way to a denial of God's grace at work in and through us. Martin Luther was especially concerned with such confusion, warning people against any presumption that our imitation of Christ could secure our salvation. He said, "It is not imitation which brings about our sonship of God, but our sonship which makes possible imitation."[3]

The idea of imitation includes our conscious effort, combined with the indwelling power of the Holy Spirit, to manifest the qualities of Christ in our lives. We look to passages such as Colossians 3:9-10: "Do not lie to each other, since you have taken off your old self with its practices and have put on the new self, which is being renewed in knowledge in the image of its Creator." Also, we have the words of Jesus: "I tell you the truth, anyone who has faith in me *will do what I have been doing*. He will do even greater things than these, because I am going to the Father" (John 14:12, italics added).

The simple questions "What would Jesus do in this situation? What would Jesus say?" can have a profound effect by shifting our frame of reference from a worldly point of view to a heavenly perspective. They can broaden our repertoire of responses from our natural instincts to include our spiritual instincts. As we look to the Lord, our pioneer (Heb. 12:1-3, RSV), our hope awakens, our creativity stirs, and our courage increases.

We can't reduce the Christlike character to a simple list of traits, but Scripture does give us some overviews as guidance, such as that found in Galatians 5:22-23: "But the fruit of the Spirit is love, joy, peace, patience, kindness, goodness, faithfulness, gentleness and self-control." Meditation on each of these character qualities leads us into countless implications for char-

357

·
·

acter development. For instance, "goodness" and "self-control" encompass such traits as moral purity or business integrity. With the help of the mind of Christ and the searching and wisdom of the Holy Spirit, we can meditate on the qualities named in Scripture and bring them to focus on more specific aspects of character.[4]

WITH CHARACTER COMES AUTHORITY

As God shapes our character, we will discover a new sense of authority in Christ. Authority is the force of presence, not the presence of force. Authority is not a matter of position but a matter of person. Our authority grows out of our integrity. Without integrity, we are never more than placeholders; with integrity, we can be life shapers. By authority, I mean the freedom to take the initiative and influence others for godly purposes, the confidence to face intimidating circumstances, the ability to stand against sin and wickedness, and the ability to stand firm against evil.

---

*A*uthority is the force of presence, not the presence of force.

I have learned to look for the authority of character in places I never expected to find it. John worked in automobile repair for most of his life. Anyone who shook hands with him couldn't help but notice the grease embedded in every wrinkle and crack of those hardworking hands. His dirty hands, however, were good, very good. He wasn't much for talking, and he wasn't at all comfortable on church committees. But you could count on John. If your car had a problem, he told you exactly what it needed—never more, never less. There were many times he'd spend a few hours on a car and not charge, especially elderly customers on fixed incomes. "I have all I need," he would say. But more than these things, John developed a ministry that you'd never expect: a ministry of letter writing.

I got my first letter from John on a day I was really struggling. It was one of those days when you'd like to roll the clock back and just start over. The late afternoon mail came, and there was John's letter:

> Dear Doug,
>
> Jesus is pleased with you. I know you already know that, but the Lord told me to tell you again. You may not feel you do enough for God, or that you don't do all the right things, but that's not what God is looking for. He just wants your love—that's all.
>
> I try to remember this when I'm fixing cars. I do the best I can, but I know that what people want most is an honest man they can trust. So, if I don't do it right the first time, I just apologize and do it again for free. They like that. I tell them that's what love is all about.
>
> We love you. If there is anything my wife and I can do for you, just call us. I'm not the type to get up in front of groups, but I love being backstage. I pray for you every day when I unlock my shop. As I open that door, I thank God that I opened the door of my heart to him, and I pray that he will use you as a key for others to unlock their hearts.

John wrote with authority. That letter renewed me for days and weeks. His simple exhortation, "Jesus is pleased with you," was like a warm, healing hand reaching right into my heart, relieving much of my burden. The impact lay in John's clear grasp of

Christ and his unwavering commitment to honoring Jesus in his life and work. How he did what he did made the difference.

HOW DO WE BUILD OUR CHARACTER?

Character is formed by faithfulness in the little things. While we may be tempted to think of it as the ability to pass the big tests, it is truly formed in the "little quizzes" we're given each day. Charles Spurgeon's advice to young preachers is apt for us all:

> Let us so act that we shall never need to care if all heaven, and earth, and hell, swelled the list of spectators. . . . Take care of your life, even in the minutiae of your character. . . . We cannot afford to run great risks through little things. Our care must be to act on the rule, "giving no offence in anything, that the ministry be not blamed."5

Whenever you are faced with a choice, character is on the line. Each choice shapes us. Every action bends us in a certain direction, toward or away from the light, toward or away from qualities we may consciously reject or embrace. C. S. Lewis used the image of a "central core" of personality within each of us that is being formed and molded by the daily decisions of life. At the end of life, we will see the results of our efforts.

> People often think of Christian morality as a kind of bargain in which God says, "If you keep a lot of rules I'll reward you, and if you don't I'll do the other thing." I do not think that is the best way of looking at it. I would much rather say that every time you make a choice you are turning the central part of you, the part of you that chooses, into something a little different from what it was before.

And taking your life as a whole, with all your innumerable choices, all your life long you are slowly turning this central thing either into a heavenly creature or into a hellish creature: either into a creature that is in harmony with God and with other creatures, and with itself, or else into one that is in a state of war and hatred with God, and with its fellow-creatures, and with itself. To be the one kind of creature is heaven: that is, it is joy and peace and knowledge and power. To be the other means madness, horror, idiocy, rage, impotence, and eternal loneliness. Each of us at each moment is progressing to the one state or the other.[6]

It's a sobering image. It begs each of us to consider how the choices we make today are shaping us for eternity. Our choices do not put our eternal salvation in question if we have put our faith and trust in Christ, but they will affect us:

For no one can lay any foundation other than the one that has been laid; that foundation is Jesus Christ. Now if anyone builds on the foundation with gold, silver, precious stones, wood, hay, straw— the work of each builder will become visible, for the Day will disclose it, because it will be revealed with fire, and the fire will test what sort of work each has done. If what has been built on the foundation survives, the builder will receive a reward. If the work is burned up, the builder will suffer loss; the builder will be saved, but only as through fire. (1 Corinthians 3:11-15, NRSV)

In other words, some of us may arrive in heaven smelling of smoke!

Guidelines for Building Character

Building character is based on developing an awareness of the character issues we face, especially in our daily choices and temptations. Then we make a plan for developing the character traits we believe the Lord most desires to nurture in us at this time. It's best if we focus on one trait at a time, though life has a way of frustrating such neat divisions!

This "plan" has three primary steps.

1. Cultivate vision for what our new attitude and behavior would be like. We have seen how vision, rather than willpower, is the best catalyst for unlocking the energy of change. Take some time to formulate a sense of the new person you know God is calling you to be. The visioning process has two aspects. First, you will want to study and meditate on Scripture that applies to your particular need. A concordance or Bible dictionary can lead you to passages on most any character trait you may want to consider, from anger to zeal, from contentment to commitment, from gentleness to boldness. Look at the biblical characters and see how they model these qualities. Second, you will need to study your own life. What in your lifestyle and circumstances is most in need of transformation? How would "the new you-in-Christ" respond differently? Picture this as vividly as you can.

2. Confess and repent of the negative trait. I have listed this as second because our new vision helps us understand the way in which the negative trait has cheated God, others, and ourselves. It makes us more eager to be free from that which compromises our integrity and weakens our discipleship. You may want to record a specific prayer in your journal in which you release your guilt to God and receive his forgiveness in Christ. This can be an ongoing source of encouragement and incentive.

3. Develop a plan for implementation and accountability. For example, if you have a problem with anger, you can plan how to cultivate patience, gentleness, and kindness. You may want to envision situations in which you typically lose your temper and prayerfully invite Jesus to show you how to respond. More than that, you may invite Jesus to help you experience *the feeling* of responding as he would in such situations.

I know a man who was counseled to keep an anger log. He wrote down the situations that triggered his anger and how he expressed it. This discipline forced him to interrupt his impulsive response by writing down his trigger points and responses. This helped him make significant progress because it broke his habitual response cycle. He is learning to control his anger through the spiritual disciplines.

Physical Exercise and Self-Care

Our character involves the whole person, including the body. The affirmation and care of the physical body has often been neglected in the pursuit of spirituality. This has roots in the "taming of the flesh" which lies behind many ascetic practices. But the true purpose of spiritual disciplines is not to devalue the material world as evil in and of itself but to focus more fully on the things of God.

Our bodies are the temple of the Holy Spirit (1 Cor. 6:19). The care of this temple is not to be taken lightly. If we abuse or neglect our bodies, we not only hurt ourselves, but we also devalue the priceless gift God has entrusted to us. Physical stewardship is more than a matter of moral purity. Physical exercise honors the body God has entrusted to us.

The Link between Physical and Spiritual

Physical stamina and vitality can be key elements of spiritual health. What we diagnose as a spiritual malaise may be the result of being physically out of condition. Our sedentary habits work against the natural processes of physical energy. This affects the way we think and our emotional moods, making us especially susceptible to mild depression and lethargy. I have found regular aerobic exercise to be an important part of my spiritual stamina. Physical health is also a matter of responsible living.

Physical exercise is good training for other spiritual exercises. Because so much of spirituality is intangible and subjective, physical actions provide concrete expression and feedback that can help us a great deal. Illustrations from our physical experience, such as the training effect,[7] give us insight into the dynamics of spiritual life. The physical discipline of exercising and seeing the progress can be a powerful incentive to pursue similar goals in the spiritual life. For example, in exercise the key to strength gain is pushing yourself just far enough so that muscle tissue bursts. This tissue then receives a greater blood supply and grows stronger. The determination to grow physically fit, pushing yourself (safely!) farther than you thought you could go, can help you learn how to push for strength in other areas.

As an amateur, I cannot offer specific advice on exercise. But I can share my own experience and goals. About seven years ago, I began exercise "whole hog," spending nearly one and a half hours at least three days a week at the gym. I would do an aerobics class, then specific exercises with free weights and weight machines, on a schedule set up by a trainer. That lasted for about eight weeks. It was thorough, but the demands of family and work, as well as the fact that "the spirit is willing, but the flesh is *weak*," led to my slacking off. I went back sporadically for several years but felt too discouraged to continue. If I couldn't do it properly and regularly, I didn't want to do it at all.

Then, several years ago, I changed my thinking. First, I clarified the fact that my goals are basic health and physical stamina. I want to have the energy to do all I want to do with an active family and ministry. I am not personally interested in much greater strength. I want energy and muscle tone. This insight helped me develop a realistic goal, freeing me from the expectations that had consumed so much time. I made a fundamental commitment to cardiovascular training by running for one half hour on a treadmill two to three mornings a week, as well as a fifteen-minute weight circuit for the upper body. This type of regimen is "the bare minimum" that's recommended—and that's OK![8] I have been able to do this for more than a year and see no reason I would stop. I have adjusted to running early in the morning, and I enjoy the stamina that has come from my exercise. One other insight that has helped me stay with it this time is a simple phrase that gets me up and out in the early morning: "Discipline weighs ounces; regret weighs tons." I have never regretted exercising!

There are numerous other areas of self-care, including nutrition, rest, and developing a pace of life that leaves us free to respond to God. Each person, as a steward of God's temple, is wise to embark on the adventure of discovering how best to manage his or her life. Above all, remember that we are finite beings, "earthen vessels." The amount of energy and time we have is limited. As we release our anxious schedules to God and care for ourselves, we will be replenished with joy. Instead of grinding resentfully through obligations, we go forward with appreciation for our part and place in life.

NOTES

1. Robert Banks, *Redeeming the Routines: Bringing Theology to Life* (Wheaton, Ill.: Victor Books, 1993), 137.
2. Gregory of Nazianzus, "In Defense of His Flight to Pontus," cited in *Leadership* (summer 1984), 22–23.
3. Gordon S. Wakefield, *The Westminster Dictionary of Christian Spirituality* (Philadelphia, Penn.: Westminster Press, 1983), 209.
4. Deeper issues of character may require ministries such as counseling and healing prayer. A person can be

discouraged by expending efforts to correct a problem that needs more specialized care. A spiritual friend, pastor, or spiritual director can guide in this area.

5. Charles H. Spurgeon, *Lectures to My Students* (Grand Rapids, Mich.: Baker Book House, 1981), 17.
6. C. S. Lewis, *Mere Christianity* (New York: Macmillan, 1943), 86–87.
7. Used for my illustration of "The Delay Factor" in chapter 4.
8. See Kenneth H. Cooper, *Aerobics* (New York: Bantam Books, 1968).

SOUL-SEARCHING

Questions for Reflection and Discussion

1. Are you more of a reflective person or an active person? How has your basic orientation to reflection or action affected your approach to spirituality?

2. What was the rhythm of Jesus' life? In what specific ways was this important?

3. What are some examples of character gaps you have seen in public figures? Do not necessarily name names (if you're discussing this in a group), but describe situations where a person's opportunities outgrew his or her character. What happened? How do you think it might have been prevented?

4. "Authority is the force of presence, not the presence of force." What is meant by this statement? Have you seen examples of this? Explain.

5. How would you like people to describe your character? You may want to use the fruit of the Spirit described in Galatians 5 to guide you. Is this description true of you now? What traits need the most attention?

6. If you have a particular trait you wish to cultivate, take time to review the guidelines for building character, and develop a vision and a plan in your journal.

CHAPTER EIGHTEEN

Better Together than on Our Own

🌿 BUILDING RELATIONSHIPS
🌿 SPIRITUAL DIRECTION
🌿 SPIRITUAL FRIENDSHIP

IN 1979, I had the privilege of meeting with Bishop Festo Kivengere and his associate, John Wilson. They ministered in Uganda at the height of Idi Amin's brutal dictatorship. Ironically, in this time of intense persecution, the church in Uganda had witnessed a forty-year revival. When I asked if, in addition to the sovereign grace of God, there were any special characteristics of the revival, Festo said, "We guard our relationships. If an issue is causing division or anger, we face it immediately so that our fellowship is unbroken. A community of Christian love draws others to it. We cannot afford to tolerate alienation."

The Bishop told countless stories of conflicts that arose in the community of faith and that were dealt with immediately and effectively. That requires discipline. As we practice it, we learn that love is the soil of vitality and revival.

The spiritual life is not a solo quest. It is intimately tied to our relationships with others.

> The community is the first place where you will make God's kingdom incarnate. . . . The quality of your community does not depend on age or numbers. The only thing that counts and will bring you a blessing is that you should be always seeking each other in the Spirit of Jesus. From Him alone comes salvation.[1]

Fellowship with people does much to make God more real in our lives. Jesus called twelve to be *with* him. Following Jesus' ascension, his followers stayed together in the upper room, forming a waiting, praying community that was filled by the Holy Spirit. The early church was, first and foremost, a caring fellowship, as evidenced especially in Acts 2 and 4: "All the believers were one in heart and mind. No one claimed that any of his possessions was his own, but they shared everything they had. With great power the apostles continued to testify to the resurrection of the Lord Jesus, and much grace was upon them all" (Acts 4:32-33). There was a direct correlation between the elements of unity, power in testimony, and great grace. A study of Jesus' prayer in John 17 reveals that these are the very qualities he most earnestly desired among his followers. Their unity would be a testimony to the world. And it would release grace among and through them.

Guidelines for Building Relationships in the Body of Christ

The subject of community is much broader than what we can cover in this brief overview, but there are a number of practices that can mark our involvement with each other. These are spiritual exercises in the sense that they are "policy decisions" we make by virtue of our faith in Jesus Christ and our commitment to love others as he has loved us. A policy decision is a choice made in advance concerning how we will respond to a particular matter. When policies such as these are woven into our lives, our relationships can operate with real spiritual energy.

Be Available

We must discipline ourselves to be available—physically and emotionally—to one another. In our fast-paced lifestyle, we so often hear, "I hate to bother you, but . . ." or, "I know you are busy, but . . ." Most relationships feel like intrusions or interruptions instead of being enjoyed as gifts or, even more, being celebrated as one of life's highest purposes. If we are too busy for people, especially the special people in our lives, we are too busy! No system of spiritual exercise can substitute for love!

Recently, I went through a period of reevaluating my commitments. I concluded that I was overinvested in areas outside my gifts and interests at the expense of availability to my family. I went through the initially painful process of finishing out my terms on several boards, reducing my participation in other activities, and saying no to several pending requests. It felt great to have some extra evenings at home and less pressure on my daily schedule.

But my "free time" soon began to fill. It wasn't long—you guessed it!—until I was overcommitted doing things I value! I was seduced this time by projects and opportunities I most enjoy. I was not pressured by others' expectations but by my own unmonitored desires. My family was again paying the price— only this time I had only myself to blame. I was not available to them emotionally, even when I was physically present. Once again, I had to go to prayer and to my journal to think through my priorities. I made some more hard phone calls, made some more apologies, and worked to get my schedule in order so that

371

I could be interruptible without becoming resentful, and available without being anxious. I know this is an area I must monitor continually. That's why I have made myself accountable to some other men; the development of some disciplines requires support from others.

A few years ago, our young family, with four children under the age of ten, was preparing to leave for vacation. We were borrowing a station wagon to drive from Connecticut to Florida to enjoy time with Sarah's parents. As I was making comments about the twenty-four-hour drive that lay ahead of us, an older woman in our congregation said, "I envy you! You are going to have a wonderful time together. Even the noise. Just remember, you can never replay that music." The loud "music" of our children, the soft melodies of special loves, even the jarring disharmonies—these are notes on the score of life that are only played once, never to be repeated. We don't want to miss them because we weren't available.

Show Others Their Value

One of my most vivid memories from elementary school years is of my parents building a new home. They brought home the plans from the builder and showed me the blueprint for my room. They then asked if I would like to figure out how my furniture should be arranged in the room. Dad explained the scale drawing and helped me make scale cutouts of my furniture. I placed them in the room in various ways until we found the best fit. I then did that for other rooms in the house. When the movers brought our furniture in, I was right there to tell them where each piece went. I'm sure they appreciated my supervision! My parents' request for my participation made me feel that I played a significant role in our move into a new home.

We value others most through involvement and association. We may be tempted to do a project ourselves, but we will be

prompt calls (usually on the same day as the problem) and his nondefensive approach bring understanding and reconciliation.

Learn to Forgive

One of the most delightful and meaningful stories of forgiveness I've read comes from Peter Gillquist. He tells of a time when their four-year-old, Wendy Jo, kept jumping on the bed. Marilyn, Peter's wife, warned her to stop jumping. A few minutes later, the jumping resumed. This time the instruction was much more specific. "If I have to tell you again," Marilyn told Wendy, "you will get a spanking. Besides, Mommy's favorite lamp is on the table next to the bed, and I'd feel terrible if anything were to happen to it. Now be quiet and go to sleep." The story continues:

> The lamp on our bedside table was one of the prettiest we had ever seen and was just right for the room. It had come from a large, stately home on the North Shore in the beautiful Chicago suburb of Winnetka. We were always sure to have it aglow when guests came to call.
>
> Back in the kitchen for the third time, Marilyn thought she heard the sound of a bouncing child. Just before she reached the bedroom there was a distinct crash. After the execution of the spanking, Marilyn took Wendy in her arms, hugged her, and said, "I spanked you because you bounced on the bed after I told you not to." Marilyn then proceeded to sweep up the remains of the shattered lamp. Wendy watched with dismay. When all the pieces were removed from the floor and the lamp was solemnly discarded in the trash box, Marilyn told her, "As far as the lamp is concerned, Mommy loves you and forgives you, and I'll never mention it to you again."
>
> The next day Marilyn was walking through the apartment and inadvertently stepped on one of Wendy's toys and

smashed it. She felt terrible. Wendy ran over and picked it up and said, "Mommy, I forgive you for that and I'll never ever mention it to you again."[2]

Perhaps there is no more important discipline than releasing the power of forgiveness into our relationships. Forgiveness is so central to spiritual health that it is singled out from all the petitions of the Lord's Prayer for special comment (Matt. 6:14-15). When people ask me if a lack of forgiveness puts their eternal destiny in danger, I refocus them on their earthly destiny. This much is clear: Our *experience* of forgiveness now is directly related to our *expression* of forgiveness toward others.

Forgiveness releases us from the chains that would hold us in bitterness and bondage. It may be helpful to consider the difference between forgiveness and reconciliation. As David Stoop clarifies:

> Forgiveness is unilateral: It is something I can do all by myself. Reconciliation is bilateral: It is something both parties must do together. If you have hurt me, and we are estranged as a result, I can forgive you on my own, without your permission, without your even knowing about it. But we are not reconciled until we sit down and take mutual action together.[3]

Practically speaking, this means that we take care of our own "stuff" concerning what others have done against us. We do not allow it to accumulate, blocking the flow of living water from our own hearts. "If it is possible, *as far as it depends on you,* live at peace with everyone" (Rom. 12:18, italics added). This is truly an area of discipline as we exercise the deliberate choice to obey God, often in spite of our feelings. As we put forgiveness in this light, we find hope for freedom from the paralysis of anger and the resentment of bitterness that drain our spiritual energy.

Confession and Restitution

Generally speaking, the circle of the confession should only go as far as the circle of the offense. But restitution may also be called for. If we have done something that can be repaired or replaced, the honorable choice is to do whatever we can to set the situation right. When Zacchaeus received Christ, he not only repented but also made a promise of restitution, "Look, half of my possessions, Lord, I will give to the poor; and if I have defrauded anyone of anything, I will pay back four times as much" (Luke 19:8, NRSV). Such restitution went beyond what could normally be expected. It conveys his immense gratitude for the riches of salvation in Christ. It may also indicate Zacchaeus's personal integrity. Even though tax collectors were viewed with disgust as yes-men of the occupying Roman government, Zacchaeus may well have maintained his integrity in a vocation riddled with corruption. Otherwise, such fourfold restitution would not have been possible.

The goal of discipline in our relationships is best presented by Thomas Kelly:

> Can we make all our relations [to others] relations which pass *through Him?* Our relations to the conductor on the trolley? Our relations to the clerk who serves us in a store? . . . For until the life of men in time is, in every relation, shot through with Eternity, the Blessed Community is not complete."[4]

Viewing each relationship through Christ moves us to a different level of interaction. At the least, it interrupts our often careless attitude towards others so that we value each person not only for themselves but for the Lord. "Inasmuch as ye have done it unto one of the least of these my brethren, ye have done it unto me" (Matt. 25:40, KJV).

SPIRITUAL DIRECTION

Spiritual direction is a term that may be foreign to some of us, but it has a long tradition among God's people. It is defined as "the pastoral guidance of souls by counseling and prayer through the illumination, grace and power of God the Holy Spirit."[5] A more contemporary term that may feel more appropriate is a *spiritual mentor*. The role is a combination of counselor, teacher, confessor, cheerleader/booster, and friend.[6] The director asks questions such as that of John Wesley, "How goes it with your soul?" He or she helps us look at our activities and relationships from the soul's perspective. A director listens to our life stories and asks, "What is God doing or saying in this situation?" Their role is not to be the voice of God, but to help us listen and discern God's voice. The director also asks us the tough questions, exposing the rationalizations that undermine our obedience and challenging the assumptions that limit our growth.

George Niederauer defines spiritual direction as "the relationship between a mature Christian and younger Christian wherein help in prayer and assistance in discerning the activity of the Holy Spirit takes place. The mature Christian serves as a pilgrim-companion to the younger Christian."

> "Spiritual direction is unique most of all because it is a 3-way conversation; the third party—the always central third party—is Jesus the Lord, and it is the directee's prayerful dialogue and growing relationship with Jesus Christ which the director helps along."[7]

Spiritual direction is different from counseling in that the focus is on the spiritual movements of life, the activity of God, and the life of prayer. If issues emerge that require counseling, the spiritual director will refer the person to a qualified counselor.

In my own experience, a spiritual director has helped me look at life through heaven's eyes. He has helped me discern the presence and activity of God in my life. Spiritual direction has helped me understand the place of silence and solitude and how to make decisions concerning God's will. I have learned better how to lift the curtain of the ordinary and see the workings of God behind it all. I have chosen to place the subject of spiritual direction here because the key to its effectiveness is our relationship of love and trust with the spiritual director, and the freedom to be honest about who we are.

A Light and a Mirror

It may help to think of a spiritual director as bringing additional illumination to our path. This doesn't replace God's Word, nor does it relieve us of our responsibility to discern what God is saying or what steps we must take. Still, the wise counsel of a spiritually mature friend or mentor can bring greater clarity and courage as we seek God's will. The experienced director has seen many of the problems that arise on the journey of faith. He or she can offer assurances that we are on the path or provide specific correction to guide us back onto the way.

A spiritual director is also a mirror in which we can see a more accurate reflection of our beliefs about God and our discipleship. In one of my first meetings with my spiritual director, I was confronted with my impoverished view of grace. I was having a difficult time discerning God's will for a particular decision because, believe it or not, it seemed too good to be true. As I shared this, my director asked me to explain my concepts of call, grace, and obedience. I was professing to believe in God's grace, yet I was operating on the assumption that, when given a choice, God's call is to the hardest, most uncomfortable place. As my director pushed me on the biblical concept of the grace and goodness of God, I could see that my unconscious assumption that God prefers my misery was truly a distortion of all God had taught me and done in my life. "Doug," my director said, with a hearty laugh (we laugh a lot!), "you have the theology right in your head, but your heart resists accepting it!"

My exercise for the next time was to search the Scriptures and my experience for all the evidences of God's abundant grace and goodness to his people. My "recovery" is still "in process," as they say, but I have moved significantly because of a courageous, gracious spiritual director.

I heartily concur with the advice "He who really desires to give himself to God, should weigh well the advantages of having guidance from another, because the best and wisest men are blinded as to their own inward life, and the holiest and best fitted to direct others would not effect to direct themselves."[8] Even those who are skilled in counsel and guidance of others cannot take a self-guided tour through their own spiritual landscape. We too easily miss the nuances of the Spirit and are blinded by our strengths and weaknesses. Even as you wouldn't consider doing your own surgery, you cannot always penetrate beyond the forces of your own spiritual history and personality to discern the movements of darkness and light in your soul.

The guidelines for spiritual direction are largely determined by your director and yourself; it is a unique process that grows out of the personalities and gifts of the two people involved. If you are interested in investing yourself in this type of relationship, you can inquire through churches and seminaries in your area. Pray for God's guidance as you consider this possibility and as you meet with potential spiritual directors.

SPIRITUAL FRIENDSHIP

Spiritual direction may strike you as too formal. Or it may not be readily available to you at this time. But one discipline that can definitely be pursued along these lines is that of spiritual friendship. A spiritual friendship is an intentional relationship between two people, founded in Jesus Christ, in which they focus alternately on the nurture of each other's spiritual life. The expectation is not that you be experts but that you come together as spiritual peers who commit themselves to growing in Christ.

The key words are "intentional" and "alternately." The discipline comes in keeping the primary focus of the meeting on the spiritual aspects of life—all of life. You choose to open up to each other by the regular commitment of time together and in preparation for your meetings. These times aren't casual conversations, though that is a part of the friendship. They are times when you set aside all the distractions of life and look at its inner workings. That takes effort! And then mutuality is maintained by alternating the focus on each other. There may be times when one person stays "in the spotlight" because of major crises or deep concerns. But that is the exception.

In a helpful overview of spiritual friendship, Tilden Edwards presents a catalog of characteristics gleaned from interviews with leaders involved in spiritual formation and direction. These qualities include:

- personal spiritual commitment to Jesus Christ, supported by an active discipline of prayer/meditation
- experience in one's own life of moving from despair to grace
- knowledge of God's Word and the ministry of the Holy Spirit in a believer's life
- discernment in noticing the movement of the Spirit, and of providing an environment out of which the person can pay attention and allow this intuitive noticing to become an important part of his/her life
- humility, especially shown in the capacity to be caring, sensitive, open, and flexible with another person, not

    projecting one's own needs or fostering long-term
    dependency
- freedom rooted in having no expectation or anticipation of
  where a person should go. The friend says, "Not my will but
  Thine be done."9

The common theme of these descriptions is awareness of the
grace and activity of God in people's lives. Such friendships and
direction nurse an expectant faith, a watching faith, a searching
faith, looking for the fingerprints of God. Regular conversation
along these lines does much to develop our awareness of the
Lord in times when we're apart. We learn how to look for his
presence, to take the time to interrupt our habitual reactions in
order to test for the movement of God. We learn to alter our negative belief system, replacing thoughts of unbelief and practical
atheism with affirmations of biblical truth and memories of
God's grace throughout our lives.

Guidelines for Developing a Spiritual Friendship

To take the first step, many people invite another person to
become a prayer partner. When we think of this work as "the help
one Christian gives to another to help that person become himself
in faith,"10 we see that we are all on the journey together. There is
no set formula. We are each handcrafted treasures. The joy is in
helping one another grow up to be all that God created us to be.

    I suggest your first two meetings be devoted to sharing your
spiritual journeys with each other, one at one meeting, the other
at the next one. An interesting way to do this is to chart your spiritual autobiography, using key words, symbols, a graph, or colors
to present the highlights (and lowlights!) of your spiritual life.
Try to discern the major themes and questions that charac-
terized the various periods of your life.

The emphasis in this sharing is not on the historical facts of your lives but on the spiritual impressions and dynamics of God's presence and work (or the apparent lack thereof). What did God teach you in these different times? How did you grow? Why did God seem so distant? How did you resolve that? Questions such as these help you get beneath the simple chronicle of the events. After you have completed your sharing, the one listening responds with comments of appreciation for the person's life. Then, close in prayer, with the emphasis on thanksgiving.

You might begin your subsequent meetings with silence and meditation on Scripture. This may be uncomfortable at first, but it will prove to be a valuable means of reminding yourselves that the One who is your best Spiritual Friend is present with the two of you. The silence is also a tangible "buffer," marking this time as different from standard appointments and conversation.

There is no set agenda for your conversation, but it may be helpful to share what you have been writing in your journal. In fact, your spiritual friendship can be a catalyst for the spiritual exercise of reflection through journaling. The time in conversation can flow back and forth, but it is wise to maintain mutuality by giving each other equal attention. The exception, of course, is when one is in a place of special need, either celebrating God's goodness or seeking God in a dark or confusing time.

An important aspect of spiritual friendship is accountability for fulfilling specific goals for other spiritual disciplines. As commitments to growth or change arise out of the conversation, determine appropriate responses to weave them into your life. Agree to measurable goals and agree to check in on one another between meetings. This can mean the difference between growth and stagnation for both the individuals and the relationship. The contact between meetings reawakens the resolve first stirred at the meeting, grounding that resolve in a new way in the thick of things.

A way of keeping the friendship fresh is by reading books in areas of particular interest and sharing your reactions to the reading. This reading is not meant as an academic exercise but along the lines of the discipline of spiritual reading.[11]

A pastor in a non-American culture once said to a visiting missionary, "For you Americans, life is 80 percent work and 20 percent fellowship. For us, life is 50 percent fellowship and 50 percent work." Given all the Bible says about our fellowship with one another and with God, this pastor's culture was probably closer to the mark! We will be amazed at how much richer our souls become when we make fellowship a more intentional and integral part of life.

NOTES

1. *Rule for a New Brother* (Springfield, Ill.: Templegate Publishers, 1976), 10.
2. Peter Gillquist, *Love Is Now* (Grand Rapids, Mich.: Zondervan, 1970), 31–32.
3. David Stoop, *Making Peace with Your Father* (Wheaton, Ill.: Tyndale House, 1992), 234–235.
4. Thomas Kelly, *A Testament of Devotion* (New York: Harper & Row, 1941), 88.
5. Gordon S. Wakefield, *The Westminster Dictionary of Christian Spirituality* (Philadelphia, Penn.: Westminster Press, 1983), 114.
6. The fiction of Susan Howatch (*Glittering Images, Glamorous Powers, Ultimate Prizes, Scandalous Risks, Mystical Paths, Absolute Truths*) provides a remarkable study in the process of spiritual direction, including the fact that even spiritual directors need spiritual direction from another and they themselves can make a mess of their own lives!

7. G. Niederauer, "Spiritual Direction," *Theology News and Notes* (Pasadena, Calif.: Fuller Theological Seminary, March 1979), 5.

8. Wakefield, *Dictionary*, 114,

9. Tilden Edwards, *Spiritual Friend* (New York: Paulist Press, 1980), 126–127.

10. Father Damian Isabell, in G. Niederauer, "Spiritual Direction," *Theology News and Notes* (Pasadena, Calif.: Fuller Theological Seminary, March 1979), 6.

11. For further resources on developing a spiritual friendship based on prayer partnerships, see David Mains and Steve Bell, *Two Are Better than One* (Portland, Oreg.: Multnomah, 1991).

SOUL-SEARCHING

Questions for Reflection and Discussion

1. How would you describe your relationships? Are many of them built around spiritual issues? Do certain relationships enhance your walk of faith? Do others detract from it?

2. How important is community to you? What are the specific evidences of this in the way you spend your time?

3. Festo Kivengere spoke of the importance of guarding relationships. What does this mean? Have you practiced this principle yourself? Why or why not?

4. There are a number of "policies" suggested for building relationships. Which of these interests you the most? How could you begin or continue to practice it more fully?

5. What is spiritual direction? Do you think it is an exercise you want to undertake at this time? Why or why not?

6. Spiritual friendship can be one of the most revitalizing steps you can take for your spiritual life. What is spiritual friendship? How could you develop such a friendship? If you are interested in starting one, make a list of two or three people, and pray over the list daily for seven to fourteen days. Then, approach your first choice and explain the concept.

CHAPTER NINETEEN

Money: From Root of Evil to Fruit for Good

🌿 STEWARDSHIP

A MAN came into a large sum of money. He didn't trust banks, so he kept all the money at home. At first, he was quite happy, but then one day he heard about a robbery in his neighborhood. He became anxious. The next morning he hid all his money in a special hiding place. As a result, he was a few minutes late to work. The second morning he decided he'd better use a different hiding place—just in case someone had seen him. This made him about a half hour late to work. The third morning he divided his money into three equal amounts. It was harder to find three good hiding places, but he finally did. He went to work two hours late. This pattern continued so that he missed more and more work. He also stopped going out evenings and weekends.

His friends grew concerned at his continual refusal of their invitations. Finally, one beautiful autumn Saturday, he yielded to their invitation to go on a picnic. He had to admit that it felt great to be in the sunshine, to savor the crisp air and beautiful colors of autumn. Most of all, it was a delight to be with his friends.

When he came back home, he went immediately to his hiding places. When he looked in the first one, it was empty! He rushed to the second—empty! With heart pounding and hands trembling, he raced to the third. In the place where the money should have been, he found this note:

> *You have hidden much more than your money.*
> *You've been robbed, but not by thieves.*
> *For you have loved that which could not love you back,*
> *and yourself, not your Lord, you have pleased.*
>
> *Signed,*
> *The Safecracker*[1]

> *And Jesus said, "Do not lay up for yourselves treasures on earth, where moth and rust consume and where thieves break in and steal, but lay up for yourselves treasures in heaven, where neither moth nor rust consumes and where thieves do not break in and steal. For where your treasure is, there will your heart be also. (Matt. 6:19-21, RSV)*

Jesus knew that our attitude toward money and our use of it are deeply spiritual concerns. Money is one of the most "spiritual" substances in the world; it becomes the vehicle that moves us toward or away from a deeper knowledge of God. I have heard that 25 percent of Jesus' teaching dealt with money. While it is clear that it was a significant subject,[2] I have been unable to confirm this specific percentage through my own research. It is fascinating to see how Jesus consistently used money in his parables and other teachings. In the Sermon on the Mount, he speaks directly to the wickedness of "mammon" as a competitor with God for our loyalty. In the account of Judas's protests at the anointing of Jesus, we see how greed corrupts (John 12:4-6). Jesus also used money in his parables as a symbol for the most important aspects of life: responsibility (the talents), commitment (the pearl of great price), and forgiveness (two debtors), to name a few.

The spirituality of money is also highlighted by Paul. First Timothy 6 is the classic passage: "For the love of money is a root of all kinds of evil" (1 Tim. 6:10). This generalization does not cover every expression of evil (jealousy of a lover, for example, may have nothing to do with financial concerns), yet it sounds the alarm to how corrupting money can be. Money is a powerful force. Handled carefully, it can accomplish great things. But handling money carelessly is like juggling with vials of nitroglycerin!

MUTINY WITH THE BOUNTY?

Use your imagination for a moment: The world is a vessel laden with priceless treasures destined for the shores of God's eternal kingdom. We are the deckhands, responsible for maintaining the vessel and seeing that its treasures are used properly. But there's a critical problem: The deckhands have revolted against the captain and seized the treasure for themselves. We've committed mutiny with the bounty! It's time to acknowledge the Captain and submit the treasures again to his control.

If we understand the spiritual aspect of money, we can begin to see how to use it as a discipline for spiritual maturity. My own studies have led me to see three primary purposes that money serves in our spiritual lives.

The First Purpose of Money Is to Test Our Loyalty to God and Our Dependence on Him.

In the parable of the rich fool (Luke 12:16-21) Jesus tells us of a man who expected money to do what it could never do. He had come into a great deal of money and decided to use it to build more barns. But he died the next morning, before the blueprints were even drawn up! In contemporary terms, we might say that the man invested his windfall in a diversified portfolio for long-term appreciation, but God came to him and said, "You fool. Don't you appreciate the fact that your windfall can turn into a hurricane and sweep you away?" This man had intended to use his money as a hedge against death. It is more important to prepare for your death with your money! Money has limits.

> *Money will buy a bed, but not sleep;*
> *Books, but not brains;*
> *Food, but not appetite;*
> *Finery, but not beauty;*
> *A house, but not a home;*
> *Medicine, but not health;*
> *Luxuries, but not culture;*
> *Amusements, but not happiness;*
> *Religion, but not salvation—*
> *A passport to everywhere but heaven.*[3]

Money is one of the most tangible evidences of our priorities. You can fake many things but not how you use your money. Money is a matter of the heart. This helps us make sense of the account of the rich young ruler in Mark 10:17-31. When he asked Jesus what he could do to inherit eternal life (note the term "inherit"!), Jesus advised him to sell *all* that he had, give it to the poor, then follow him. Jesus did not respond this way to all who were wealthy. In this case, he discerned that money held the central place in this man's heart. Money was his source of security, his motivation in life, and the primary concern of his days. God couldn't compete with it! Therefore, the rich man had to let go of the money clenched in his fist so that he could take hold of God.

The Second Role of Money Is to Allow Us the Privilege of Responsible and Meaningful Contributions to God's Work.

The offerings of the Old and New Testaments were frequently associated with a joyful outpouring for the opportunity to serve the Lord. "The people rejoiced at the willing response of their leaders, for they had given freely and wholeheartedly to the Lord" (1 Chron. 29:9. See also Exod. 35:20-29). Whether we give small or large amounts, we are able to advance the kingdom of God through the stewardship of our gifts. Our money can enable people to go where we cannot go, and to do what we cannot do.

The Third Purpose of Money Is to Shape Us for Greater Responsibilities.

In the parable of the talents (Luke 19:11-27), the stewards' management of the master's material resources determined their destinies. Jesus uses money, which we consider a major responsibility, as a training ground for service in the kingdom. The way we handle money reveals much about how we handle our lives.

STEWARDSHIP: COMMITMENT LIVED OUT

Our stewardship begins with an unwavering commitment to God. "They gave themselves first to the Lord and then to us in keeping with God's will" (2 Cor. 8:5). Money cannot bribe God. Rather, it expresses the condition of our allegiance to him. Seen in this light, the most common financial discipline is tithing. The tithe (one-tenth of your income) is a confession of faith. First of all, you don't give that kind of money to something you don't believe in! And if you do believe, it is difficult to see how you could give less. When we give a tithe or more, it represents the fact that we would give anything the Lord asks of us.

When I was a fledgling author, one of my personal heroes was Charlie Shedd. When he spoke at a church conference, I met him afterward and explained my interest in writing. He invited me to breakfast with him the next morning. I was thrilled to have an hour or so with this pastor-author who had touched so many lives through *Letters to Karen, Promises to Peter,* and his many other books. We had a stimulating conversation, including his brief review (and redlining!) of a manuscript I was working on. Then he said, "Doug, I want to challenge you not only to be a good writer, but also to be a great giver." He proceeded to tell me that he gives 50 percent of his royalties to mission projects around the world. That has added up to a significant sum of money over the years. Countless lives have been blessed.

Another fascinating story is that of Ken Taylor, translator of *The Living Bible.* His first "break" in getting exposure for *Living Letters* (which was the only portion then translated), came when Billy Graham asked to use it as a gift for anyone who requested it from his television audience. Ken readily agreed and said he didn't want a royalty. He didn't think it was appropriate since, as he said, "I had a strong conviction that the ability to write *Living Letters* was a special gift from God, and, because it was His Word, He should get all the royalties."[4] The Graham Association insisted on a royalty, however, so they settled on five cents per copy. Ken still felt uncomfortable, so he set up the Tyndale House Foundation to receive the royalties for all the segments of *The Living Bible* as well as *The Living Bible* itself. While Billy Graham expected to give away up to fifty thousand copies, resulting in a royalty of twenty-five hundred dollars (which was significant in the early 1960s), they were all stunned when the more than six hundred thousand requests poured in, resulting in royalties of thirty thousand dollars! God has blessed the venture such that, to date, the Tyndale House Foundation has distributed millions of dollars for Bible translation and other missionary projects!

Stories such as these broaden our horizons in the discipline of giving. Those who have taken a step of faith in commitment have found God faithful beyond what they could ask or imagine. The return may never be financial prosperity, but there are treasures of the soul that are priceless.

Guidelines for Stewardship

As in any other spiritual exercise, we begin with a plan, we practice it, and we make adjustments until we know we can stick with it consistently and bring about good results. Here are some suggestions for a workable plan.

Determine that all you have belongs to God.   The first step, as they say, is the hardest. But it also sets you on the road to the greatest satisfaction in life. Affirming God's ownership of all resources puts everything in a different light. We receive all things from God's hand and make them available for his service. We enjoy them and use them with gratitude and responsibility.

Make a commitment to God based on percentages of income, not specific dollar amounts.   Percentages are a more accurate indicator of the level of sacrifice you are making. You may not be able to jump from your current level to a 10 percent figure immediately. This is an area in which I believe God regards the spirit of our giving, not the amount (2 Cor. 8:12 and 9:5-7). Begin with an increase of one percent and add a percent every year as you are able. I know of several families who have done this and have reached percentages far beyond the tithe.

Stretch yourself, especially in an area of additional income.   This was the practice of Charlie Shedd and Ken Taylor. Their particular projects were not their "bread and butter" careers, so they exercised more freedom and adventure in their commitments. Their testimonies proclaim God's faithfulness in pouring out blessing beyond comparison.

Involve your loved ones in the decision making as appropriate.
Teach them the rationale of giving out of love and loyalty rather than out of the law of giving a certain amount. Let them see your contentment and gratitude for what you do have.

Make prayer a priority, especially when your commitment is heavily tested—as it will be—by financial pressures.   Continually affirm your faith in God's provision.

When giving is viewed as a spiritual discipline, we quickly move through many of the details that would otherwise confuse and distract us. For example, whether you tithe on gross or net income is a matter between you and God, to be decided in a spirit of grace. When there are difficult seasons in which you have to adjust your giving for special circumstances, the condemnation of the law is lifted, leaving you free to do what you can. After all, God provided for a reduced offering of two doves or pigeons for those too poor to afford a lamb (Luke 2:24). When money is transformed by the Midas touch of grace, we receive riches that are riches indeed.

NOTES

1. Written by Douglas J. Rumford.
2. James S. Stewart, *The Life and Teaching of Jesus Christ* (Nashville: Abingdon Press, n.d.), 128–129.
3. "Voice in the Wilderness," quoted in *Leadership* 5, no. 2 (spring 1984).
4. Ken Taylor, *My Life: A Guided Tour* (Wheaton, Ill.: Tyndale House, 1991), 283.

SOUL-SEARCHING

Questions for Reflection and Discussion

1. The "parable of the safecracker" presents a progression of steps as money takes greater control over a person's life. How would you summarize these steps?

2. How would you describe your attitude toward money?

   a) I think about it frequently but not in anxious ways.

   b) I am a contented person. I see money simply as the means to reasonable comfort.

   c) I worry frequently about having enough money.

3. What are the three primary purposes of money in the spiritual life? Which of these strikes you as most important? Can you add other purposes? Use Scripture to support your additions.

4. What decisions have you made about your discipline of giving? Have you grown in this area? What struggles have you faced in fulfilling your financial commitment?

5. If you feel that God is leading you to take a new step in financial discipline, review the guidelines and record your decisions in your journal. Remember to involve appropriate family members (such as your spouse, if married) in your decision.

CHAPTER TWENTY

Putting Our Gifts to Work

SPIRITUAL SERVICE THROUGH SPIRITUAL GIFTS

ONE of the goals in our summer ministry for training college students (called NetWorkers) is to develop an instinct for service. Several weeks into the summer training, we had the seven NetWorkers over to an adviser's house for our regular training meeting. This time, however, the room was not set up. We also didn't interrupt them during refreshments to call them to gather in the living room. As time passed to ten minutes, then fifteen minutes into our meeting time, Cam, one of the NetWorkers, came over and said, "Hey, can I help you set up the chairs?" He started rearranging the furniture the way we had set it up for our other meetings. As the others saw him, they pitched in and helped us finish up.

When we began our meeting, we asked them what they had noticed when they walked into the house. All admitted they really hadn't noticed anything. We then asked when they became aware that things needed to be done. All said, "When

Cam started moving the chairs." That led to a discussion of observation as a fundamental principle of ministry.

One of our central concepts in the NetWorkers and in our congregation is "Be a host." There are two types of people in the world: guests who expect to be taken care of and hosts who are willing to welcome and care for others. Each of us makes a basic choice as to how we will live in this world—either as a guest or as a host. Most of my life, I confess, I have lived as a guest. I'm the youngest child, the little brother, and I know how to let myself be cared for! The concept of being a host has changed the way I interact with people.

When I traveled, for example, my tendency was usually to hang back in a new setting until I was invited in. Now I take the initiative to introduce myself and open the way for others to introduce themselves. One of the ways we could think about lavishing Christ's love on one another is to say that we will treat each other, and all whom God brings to us, in the way a gracious host or hostess would treat an honored guest.

When our expectations are shaped around observing what needs to be done to welcome and care for others, our entire attitude toward service changes. Instead of focusing on tasks, which vary in their desirability, we focus on the people who are being ministered to in the process.

OUR CONDITIONS—OR GOD'S?

One of the greatest temptations in service is to establish criteria or conditions that must be met before we will serve. When David Livingstone was working in Africa, opening the interior of that vast continent to the gospel of Jesus Christ, a group of friends wrote him: "We would like to send other men to you. Have you a good road into your area?" According to a member of the family, Dr. Livingstone sent this reply: "If you have men who will only come if they know there is a good road, I don't want them. I want men who will come if there is no road at all."

Part of the discipline of service is submitting ourselves to the constraints of the situation. We make up our minds to be available for whatever is needed. One couple, the parents of teenage boys, has chosen to serve in the church nursery so they can support new parents. They often go beyond Sunday morning, offering to help in other ways. A good friend of mine is retired and loves to garden. One morning, on my day off in the late fall, he drove up unannounced. He didn't come to the door but began looking over our rose bed.

"What are you doing here, Ivan?" I asked, going outside to meet him.

"Oh, I didn't think you'd be home! I just drove by here the other day and noticed you hadn't had the chance to trim your rosebushes for winter. Thought I could help you out."

He trimmed not only our bushes but took care of our neighbor's bushes, too!

Another friend, a leading businessman with literally worldwide influence, walks across the street from our church each Sunday morning to Hope Manor, a care facility for the elderly. He picks up Dwight and brings him to church. Their hundred-yard walk takes ten to fifteen minutes, but there is never a sense of hurry. Sam is eager to serve Dwight because Dwight has served literally thousands of men as one of the founders of the Rescue Mission.

Service not only helps others, but it is also one of the most effective means of cultivating humility. As we learn to surrender our pride and prerogatives, we find a quietness and calm entering our souls. The need to impress, to be noticed, and to be insulated from difficulty are sources of turmoil and discontent. But service is a concrete way of surrendering these things to the Lord.

Our spiritual gifts determine an important aspect of our service to others.

CONTINUING CHRIST'S WORK IN THE WORLD— GIFTS OF THE SPIRIT

When I was a child, I remember my mother taking me to the store to buy a birthday present for one of my older brothers. We picked out a nice gift, and then Mom said, "Now, this is your gift for your brother."

"But how can it be from me?" I asked. "I didn't pay for it."

"Because I'm giving it to you to give to him," she replied.

Now, you're right, I did for a moment think, with my selfish little mind, *Well, if this is a gift to me first, why can't I just keep it?* But, of course, I knew that we wouldn't have gone shopping in the first place if my parents didn't want to get the gift for my brother.

Too often, we have thought of spiritual gifts primarily as gifts God has given to us for our own benefit. When seen in this way, they become "options" or "luxuries" for our own enjoyment. Consequently, we have either neglected them or used them according to our whims instead of under the discipline of service.

Our spiritual gifts are the gifts God gives us to give to others. Said another way, the spiritual gifts are the gifts God gives others through us. "Now to each one the manifestation of the Spirit is given *for the common good*" (1 Cor. 12:7, italics added). The gifts entrusted to us belong to the community. What is "the common good"? Continuing to do Jesus' work in the world.

The subject of spiritual gifts has stirred great controversy and a lot of debate, but I have yet to hear it discussed under the subject of spiritual exercise or the spiritual disciplines. Yet the gifts are at the heart of our call to serve Christ. They also play a significant role in our spiritual maturation.

WHAT IS A SPIRITUAL GIFT?

What do we mean by *spiritual gift?* Why are such gifts given to us? How does a spiritual gift differ from natural talent?

The word for gift, *charism,* is from the same Greek root as grace, *charis.* It is something freely given in love. God gives us certain abilities out of his grace, to be used to express his grace to others. The biblical passages describing the gifts—Romans 12, 1 Corinthians 12, and Ephesians 4—call attention to our use of the gifts for others. One author writes that a gift *(charism)* signifies "the call of God, addressed to an individual, to a particular ministry in the community, which brings with it the ability to fulfill that ministry."[1] God gives us the gift in order to give it to others through a particular ministry. A gift is not meant to draw us into ourselves but is given to equip us to serve others.

How many gifts are there? Some merge the lists of the gifts in Romans 12, 1 Corinthians 12, and Ephesians 4, claiming they are the official, exhaustive catalog of gifts. A careful study of each list, however, reveals that they are meant to be representative. Each list highlights the gifts that are most appropriate to the context of each epistle.

The flexibility among the lists themselves gives us reason to think that there's more to God's creativity in equipping us for his service than what we see in the brief lists in Scripture. I believe a more expansive approach to the gifts awakens us, as Christ's disciples, to reevaluate *all* our skills, interests, activities, and responsibilities in a new light.

The concept of *charism* plays a central role in the life of each individual, as well as in that of a congregation. We have the incredible privilege of being partners with the Lord in and through the gifts, or *charisma.*

> For Paul, to have charisma means to participate for that very reason in life, in grace, in the Spirit, because *a charisma*

is the specific part which the individual has in the lordship and glory of Christ; and this specific part which the individual has in the Lord shows itself in a specific service and a specific vocation. For there is no divine gift which does not bring with it a task, there is no grace which does not move to action. Service is not merely the consequence but the outward form and the realization of grace.[2]

A gift is a God-given ability for us to play a role in Christ's continuing work on earth. The Holy Spirit has given us a role in reaching and transforming this world in the name of Jesus Christ. Seen in this light, our gifts need to be submitted to the exercise of responsible stewardship. Their neglect, misuse, or even their overuse have implications, not only for our lives, but for the kingdom of God.

The followers of Jesus offer themselves "as living sacrifices to God" (Rom. 12:1), viewing every talent, capacity, and personal resource as spiritual in the sense that it is yielded to the Holy Spirit. In this way, every action is empowered and directed by the Lord. When a person takes this approach, the question of whether an ability comes out of the human personality or out of supernatural empowerment recedes into the background. The focus is on the activity accomplished through the Holy Spirit to the glory of God and the fulfillment of God's will. Robert Banks further develops this thought when he writes

Paul's language about "gifts" should not be taken to rule out altogether their connection with natural capacities, implanted by the prior creative activity of God, or by social advantages conferred by the circumstances of life. . . . Such abilities are renewed (passing through their own "crucifixion" and "resurrection") along with all other aspects of the personality, as well as activated by the Spirit to achieve their full potential when there is a service to be performed.[3]

This view does not mean that we equate every natural talent with a *charism*. One writer has explained the difference this way:

> Charism is different from a gift for music or mathematics, for example, which one either "has" or does not have. Charism is bestowed, assigned, distributed not on one's own behalf, but on behalf of others; it is not a natural talent, but a call of grace, a call to service. In this sense, of course, even natural talents can become charisms. . . . From this viewpoint we can see why Paul can so easily transfer from talking about the apostolate and public functions in the community to talking about private virtues when he is listing various charisms (cf. 1 Cor. 12:28-30; Rom 12:6-8). Charisms are potentialities which are appealed to, aroused and created by the spirit of God.[4]

ENERGY POINTS: HOW OUR DESIRES POINT TO OUR SPIRITUAL GIFTS

There are a number of helpful inventories that can assist you in discovering your spiritual gifts.[5] I would encourage you, however, to begin the process by prayerfully considering this question: "When have I felt the greatest energy and satisfaction in serving the Lord?" Our primary call is to fulfill the design God has woven into our hearts. God has given us the gifts that fit that call. Consider these words from Psalm 37:4: "Delight yourself in the Lord and he will give you the desires of your heart."

---

*O*ur primary call is to fulfill the design God has woven into our hearts.

403

What *are* the desires of your heart? The answer will reveal the deepest longings of your life in a number of areas. I had an enlightening exercise in this respect. My spiritual director was leaving for the Holy Land. As we were talking about his activities there, he explained the practice of praying before the Wailing Wall in Jerusalem. The Wailing Wall is the only remnant of the temple the Romans destroyed in A.D. 66. They left the wall standing as a testimony both to the grandeur of the temple and to their own power in destroying it. The custom arose over time of praying before the wall and of putting prayers on tiny slips of paper and stuffing them into the cracks between the massive stones that comprise the wall. My director invited me to put my heart-desire prayers on a single, tiny slip of paper, promising to pray for me and put it in the Wailing Wall. The exercise of searching my heart and distilling my deepest desires into so few words had a powerful effect of clearing my mind and clarifying my vision.

Among the prayers I wrote were two concerning my deepest desires for service to the Lord and his kingdom. I found myself gaining great energy just thinking about the desires God had placed within me.

Those desires are the clues to our gifts. I believe our heart desires are the allurements of God, coaxing us to a life beyond what we could ever ask or imagine. As we serve God out of our desires, we find a fulfillment and satisfaction like we've never known. Yes, it's true that we are all called to do some tough things, things we don't like to do, if we want to follow Jesus. Sacrifice and obedience are not easy. But our primary call in life is to live out of those desires that really give us enthusiasm—what I like to call our energy points.

An energy point is an idea that taps your joy and stirs you into action. You may be tired, but when an "energy point" thought comes to mind, you're up and at it. I use the term "energy point" because it describes the process of tapping the energy reserves that God has woven into our hearts and character. The person who lives in trust of God and out of the desires of his heart savors the joy of serving God, even in the midst of trying, sacrificial circumstances.

Psalm 37 shows us the practical use of a spiritual energy point in overcoming several very common problems. In this psalm, David shows us that the answer to fretfulness and envy is getting in touch with and acting upon the desires or passions of your own life. When you do this, you have no envy for others because you are so thrilled to be doing the things that fit you perfectly. Envy is a sign that you either haven't given yourself the permission to be the person God calls you to be or you don't yet know who that person is.

How do you get in touch with your energy points? You take inventory, searching your past for the times you felt most energized. When did you undertake a project and lose all track of time? What have you done that you would gladly do again? In his book *What Color Is Your Parachute?* Richard Bolles outlines a basic exercise: Take ten sheets of paper and write one of your ten most satisfying experiences on each sheet of paper. Then take each sheet of paper and write single words and phrases that describe what you enjoyed about each experience. For example, if one of your favorite experiences was writing for the church newsletter, was it because of the creativity involved, the opportunity to meet new people in the process, or the challenge of designing a piece of paper in a way that effectively communicated information in an attractive manner? If it was solving a particular problem, was it because you like a challenge, the opportunity to learn more and apply what you are learning, or the satisfaction of fixing something? Your responses are windows to your gifts.

I once heard Lloyd Ogilvie ask of us, "If you had no fear of failure, what would you attempt for God?" We could add questions like, If resources were no object, what would you love to do? At the heart of this process is this fundamental question: Who has God recreated me to be as he shapes me into the image of Christ?

Write in your journal all the instances of being inspired by your desires, and review them for significant patterns. Do you get energized by certain age groups, such as children and youth? Do you enjoy serving quietly or having the opportunity to make decisions and lead? Have your most satisfying times involved large groups, smaller groups, or individuals? Are you asked to do your most satisfying ministries frequently?

The discipline of spiritual gifts involves discovery, development, and making your gift available. It's a discipline to say, "Yes, I have a gift; I will make it available to you." It is also a discipline to use your gift "decently and in order" (1 Cor. 14:40, NRSV). The way you use your gift is to be a blessing to others; the disorderly use of gifts can bruise people.

Guidelines for Discovering and Using Your Spiritual Gifts

1. Read and study the primary Scripture passages on the gifts: Romans 12, 1 Corinthians 12, and Ephesians 4. Notice the similarities and differences in the lists. Why do you think they were presented in this way in each book? Which gifts interest you the most? the least? Why? From your reading and reflection on your own experience, what gifts have you used most frequently, and when?

2. If possible, complete one of the inventories mentioned earlier. These should not be taken as infallible guides, but they are extremely helpful in giving you a general profile of your mix of gifts.

3. Discuss your self-assessment with a spiritual friend. No matter how honest we try to be with ourselves, we cannot be objective. There may be more wish than gift in our conclusions. We may have desires that do not match our "track record." A good friend can offer us feedback, provided we welcome his or her honest response.

4. Prayerfully seek an opportunity to exercise your gift.   This is the most exciting step, as you open yourself to God. "Lord, if you have prepared me for using this gift, now prepare a place or situation in which I can use it." Such a prayer is an invitation to see God's direct leading. This is another place in which the disciplines of preview and review can be powerful exercises for supporting the fulfillment of our desires. We take time to envision a situation in which we can exercise our gift. When we review our day, we may discern instances of exercising our gift we hadn't noticed at the time.

5. Evaluate your experience.   How did God open the door for the use of your gift? Were you ready or resistant? Why? Was the use of your gift as you hoped and expected it would be? What went well? Were there any difficulties you hadn't anticipated? In what ways do you better understand your gifts now? In what ways would you like to grow? If you feel as if you really missed it—that this particular gift is not, in fact, your gift—what is your next step?

6. Develop your gift through a consistent cycle of prayer, study, and service.   My strong sense is that the gifts are part of a dynamic process, not static possessions. In other words, they are given by God to be used, not to be put on a shelf. Continue to work with your gifts. You will most likely go through seasons in which your gifts are used intensively; then they may "lie fallow" for a time. Reviewing your journal will help you see the pattern of the seasons.

MAKING A DIFFERENCE

We have been given the privilege of participating with God so that his kingdom may come and his will be done, "on earth as it is in heaven." The disciplines of purpose equip us to make a difference in the lives of those near and far. And that difference may happen simply because of our availability, not our ability.

George was at work one day when he heard on the radio that an explosion at an industrial plant had killed one of his close church colleagues. He and another friend immediately called the minister to see how the widow and her son were doing. Then they drove to visit her. They were so shook up that they sat outside in the car for about ten minutes, debating whether or not to go in. Finally, they did.

They shared in her sorrow and made themselves available to help in any way. Primarily, they answered the door and phone to relieve her of that stress. Then they checked in every day to see how they could serve. This man told me, "I realized that it wasn't how much or just what we could do that mattered; it was the fact that we got involved, that we were concerned and available. At first it seemed a lot easier to send a card or flowers. I mean— what do you say? But I think getting involved was one of the greatest experiences of my life."

As we enter into life more fully and intentionally, we discover the power and purpose of our spiritual gifts. They inform our service, and our service drives us into deeper dependence upon the Lord. Each aspect of life is supported by the other. As George MacDonald says:

> The words of the Lord are the seeds sown by the sower. Into our hearts they must fall that they may grow. Meditation and prayer must water them, and obedience keep them in the sunlight. Thus will they bear fruit for the Lord's gathering.[6]

NOTES

1. Hans Kung, "The Continuing Charismatic Structure," *Theological Foundations for Ministry,* ed. Ray S. Anderson (Grand Rapids, Mich.: Eerdmans, 1978), 486.

2. E. Käsemann, *Essays on New Testament Themes* (Philadelphia: Fortress Press, 1982), 65. Quoted in Hanson, *The People Called* (San Francisco: Harper & Row, 1986), 443, emphasis added.

3. Robert Banks, *Paul's Idea of Community: The Early House Churches in Their Historical Setting* (Grand Rapids, Mich.: Eerdmans, Reprinted 1988), 100.

4. Hans Kung, "The Continuing Charismatic Structure," in *Theological Foundations for Ministry,* ed. Ray S. Anderson (Grand Rapids, Mich.: Eerdmans, 1978), 82.

5. Below is a sample of various spiritual gifts surveys:
    - Bruce L. Bugbee, *Networking Assessment Booklet* (Pasadena, Calif.: Charles E. Fuller Institute, 1989).
    - *Heights Spiritual Gifts Survey* (Pasadena, Calif.: Charles E. Fuller Institute, Fuller Evangelistic Association, 1991).
    - Kenneth Cain Kinghorn, *Discovering Your Spiritual Gifts* (Grand Rapids, Mich.: Francis Asbury Press, 1981).
    - *Wagner-Modified Houts Questionnaire* (Pasadena, Calif.: Charles E. Fuller Institute, 1978).
    - *Wesley Spiritual Gifts Questionnaire* (Pasadena, Calif.: Charles E. Fuller Institute, Fuller Evangelistic Association, 1983).

6. George MacDonald, *Life Essential,* quoted in Ruben P. Job and Norman Shawchuck, *A Guide to Prayer for Ministers and Other Servants* (Nashville: The Upper Room, 1983), 325.

SOUL-SEARCHING

Questions for Reflection and Discussion

1. Describe the two "basic types" of people discussed toward the beginning of this chapter. Which are you most likely to be? How does this affect your spiritual life?

2. What conditions are you likely to put on serving the Lord?

3. Explain the meaning of "spiritual gift" in your own words. What role do spiritual gifts play in our own spiritual development? What role do they play in others' lives?

4. What are some of your "energy points"? In other words, if God allowed you to fulfill the desires of your heart, what would you do in his service?

5. What are your "Top Ten Favorite Experiences in Service"? Write each one on a separate sheet of paper and then jot down what made that experience special for you. Look over the sheets to see the pattern of gifts that seems to emerge. Does the pattern fit any of gifts listed in the Bible passages referred to in this chapter?

6. For further growth, do the exercises presented under "Guidelines for Discovering and Using Your Spiritual Gifts."

Conclusion

We are human becomings. No, that's not a typo-
graphical error. We really aren't so much human
beings as human *becomings*. Every day we are becoming the person we will be. Some people will become
less than they are now by this time the next week,
the next year, and the next decade rolls around. But
most of us want to become *more*.

TIM HANSEL, *Holy Sweat*

The greatest tragedy in life is that most people
spend their entire lives *indefinitely preparing to live.*

PAUL TOURNIER

CHAPTER TWENTY-ONE

How to Lead an Imperfect Life

I T'S a great thing to learn how to stay spiritually fit. It's wonderful to apply tried-and-true spiritual principles to our neglected souls until they become healthy and thriving. In the beginning, the principles and spiritual exercises discussed in this book can seem to be too much to think about or remember. But after a while, when you've become more practiced in one area, you move on to something else; in spiritual growth, we add on bit by bit. God is pleased with our gradual progress! In fact, the Lord Jesus is cheering us on, even as we move forward, suffer setbacks, and try again. This is called *growing*. It is also called *learning*.

Even knowing this, most Christians are unprepared when they are faced with failure or a loss of vision. Just one of these can be enough to slow or stop our progress altogether. We need to be prepared with spiritual wisdom where these things are concerned.

Soul growth is not a straight journey from weakness *to* power, but a journey in both weakness *and* power. "In our moments of enjoyment we feel as if we can do anything. In times of temptation, we think we can do nothing. And both ideas are wrong."[1]

We sustain our spiritual vitality not by achieving success, but by focusing on growth, even in the midst of discouragement. There is a nobility in life that is only possible this side of heaven. In some sense, our present experience is like high-altitude training for an athlete. The athlete who exerts herself at seven thousand feet develops a capacity to process oxygen more effectively than one who trains at lower elevations. At sea level, she will have greater stamina and endurance. At the high altitude of worldly pressure, we develop the lungs of faith to breathe the sparse quantities of spiritual air, and our hearts grow stronger in love for God, while as yet we cannot see him. Above all, our wonder at his mercy grows with each passing moment.

OF EXPECTATIONS AND EARTHEN JARS

The study of spirituality can be overwhelming. It may raise issues we never intended to deal with, or uncover old wounds we haven't learned to process. We see how far short we fall of the ideals of holiness and wholeness. At this very point we need to embrace again the gospel of grace.

As we search our souls, we must remember who we are and how we are made. "As a father pities [has compassion on] his children, so the Lord pities those who fear him. *For he knows our frame; he remembers that we are dust*" (Ps. 103:13-14, NKJV, italics added). In another place we read, "But we have this treasure in earthen vessels," or "in jars of clay" (2 Cor. 4:7). There is a built-in tension in God's design. It is a tension we must not fight. It is a tension essential for the synergy of growth in grace. By "synergy" I mean that the energy generated by the interaction of the different forces creates a whole that is greater than the sum of the parts.

This dynamic interaction between the ideal of the gospel treasure and the practical, God-designed limitations of being human actually generates spiritual vitality. The fact that we are "dusty people" does not devalue the human person; rather, it magnifies the treasure and the glory of God being able to use us. The treasure inspires our vision and our hope. Though we are fallible human beings, we are entrusted with the priceless gospel. We know that "with God nothing [is] impossible" (Luke 1:37). We see evidence from the stories of Scripture and the accounts of God's people across the centuries that God uses ordinary people in extraordinary ways. John Woolman (1720–1772), a Quaker tailor, single-handedly influenced all Quakers to release their slaves prior to the War Between the States. I've seen this grace in Mary, who has opened her home for more than twenty years for a neighborhood Bible study through which literally hundreds of families have been touched. I've seen it in a lawyer who began a soup kitchen and works in it weekly, and in a physician who tutors immigrants. Both of these men have quietly inspired many other members of their professions to serve alongside them.

On the other hand, the fact that we are earthen vessels or jars of clay calls us to "sanctified realism" and faith. There is no place for pride or self-reliance. We respect our limitations and are not surprised by our failures. When a child falls learning to ride a bike, we do not criticize the child. We get him back on the seat and run alongside him a little longer this time. Likewise, the Holy Spirit, God alongside us, runs with us as we learn to balance on the wheels of faith.

Instead of being a liability, our weakness can even be said to attract God. E. M. Bounds shares the following story to illustrate the point.

A dear friend of mine who was quite a lover of the chase, told me the following story: "Rising early one morning," he said, "I heard the baying of a score of deer hounds in pursuit of their quarry. Looking away to a broad, open field in front of me, I saw a young fawn making its way across, and giving signs, moreover, that its race was well-nigh run. Reaching the rails of the enclosure, it leaped over and crouched within ten feet from where I stood. A moment later two of the hounds came over, when the fawn ran in my direction and pushed its head between my legs. I lifted the little thing to my breast, and, swinging round and round, fought off the dogs. I felt, just then, that all the dogs in the West could not, and should not capture that fawn after its weakness had appealed to my strength." So is it, when human helplessness appeals to Almighty God. Well do I remember when the hounds of sin were after my soul, until, at last, I ran into the arms of Almighty God.[2]

Human limitations are not a source of shame; they are a greater avenue for grace. We find great freedom and joy as we accept the fact that God created us with both potential and limitation. Both are to be managed in and through the Holy Spirit. We are not to let weaknesses or failures disqualify us nor discourage us from making an effort in the first place. Our attitude is not "If we try harder, we will never fail." Rather, we say, "Though I may fail in the attempt, I will go forward." We know that God uses each failure to bring us new growth, with his grace and acceptance undergirding us.

A physical body is not expected to have perfect health at all times. Its vitality is seen even in sickness, as it mounts the battle of overcoming infection, repairing broken bones, or healing wounds. This self-repair is itself a sign of life and health.

A live body is not one that never gets hurt, but one that can to some extent repair itself. In the same way a Christian is not a [person] who never goes wrong, but a [person] who is enabled to repent and pick himself up and begin over again after each stumble—because the Christ-life is inside him, repairing him all the time, enabling him to repeat (in some degree) the kind of voluntary death which Christ Himself carried out.[3]

As earthen vessels, we can still play an active part in preparing ourselves to become vessels God can use. "In a large house there are utensils not only of gold and silver but also of wood and clay, some for special use, some for ordinary. All who cleanse themselves of the things I have mentioned will become special utensils, dedicated and useful to the owner of the house, ready for every good work" (2 Tim. 2:20-21, NRSV). Central to the process of preparation is growing in our understanding of our particular weaknesses. Where are we most vulnerable to temptation? What are the primary sources of our resistance to spiritual things? What incorrect theological assumptions have we made that deter—or detour—our progress?

GET TO KNOW YOURSELF—AND HELP OTHERS IN THE PROCESS

You are a living laboratory of faith and life. Study yourself and you will be studying the lives of others: what you embrace, what you resist, what helps you learn, and what trips you up. As these are handled with Christ, they become the materials of your growth and the resources of your ministry and service.

By grace, even our failures and struggles aren't wasted. God uses them as signposts and lifelines for others on the journey. People respond when we put into words what we have been experiencing. They find encouragement as we share our defeats and victories on the walk of faith. This is a primary reason for keeping a spiritual journal. It helps you pay attention to what God is doing in your life, redeeming your mistakes. It also provides a record of God's work in our lives, showing us the patterns of his grace with us. Honest reflection with a "safe" person is another tool for developing this quality. Several questions that are helpful in journaling or conversation are: What has happened in my life today and how have I felt about it? What lessons have I learned about life in Christ today? What mistakes have I made? How will I avoid repeating them? To be more effective, I need to . . . (complete the thought).

KNOWING YOUR "RESISTANCE POINTS"

We will grow best when we have realistic expectations and when we recognize and deal with unrealistic expectations effectively.

Realistic expectations begin with an understanding of our resistance points. Resistance takes many forms, some of which are difficult to recognize. That which looks good may undermine our long-term spiritual vitality. What are our primary places of vulnerability on the spiritual journey? In what ways are we likely to be deceived, distracted, or diverted from the way of Christ? I suggest that there are five primary areas of resistance, the five most predictable problems that interfere with spiritual growth.

A Noble Temptation

Not all temptations prickle with danger or trouble us with twinges of conscience. Some positively sparkle with the appearance of virtue. Some temptations hide behind high ideals and noble images.

A number of noble temptations, such as workaholism,

codependency, and legalism, lead us into spiritual dryness and soul neglect. These temptations do not appear to be dark and evil; they spring out of the best, even if misdirected, motives. But their striving after perfection in this life will wear us out and discourage us.

Perfection seems to be a righteous expectation. After all, if we go back to the Sermon on the Mount, Jesus says, "Be perfect, therefore, as your heavenly Father is perfect" (Matt. 5:48). What can be more clear? Jesus seems to be saying that we should never have a moral failure. We must achieve a state of moral perfection in which there are no lapses in thought, word, or deed. Yet Jesus had just taught that anger is equivalent to murder, and lust to adultery. Who is capable of meeting such a standard?

A careful study of this passage, however, reveals a different intent behind Jesus' words. The Greek word translated as "perfect" is *teleios:* "You must be *teleios* as your heavenly Father is *teleios.*" *Teleios* means "the goal, the consummation, the final purpose" toward which we are moving. It originally meant "the turning point, hinge, the culminating point at which one stage ends and another begins."[4] From this, it came to mean "maturing" or being at the proper stage at the proper time. This nuance of meaning helps us understand that the journey, not just the arrival at the goal, is what matters to God. As such it means fulfilling the intended purpose for a particular stage in development. The concern is not that we've arrived but that we continue to face in the right direction and move in that direction.

For example, in the central valley of California, you can drive the Blossom Trail in springtime, when all the trees are in full bloom. It is a glorious, fragrant ride. As you drive along the Blossom Trail, you could say, "Those trees are *teleios;* those trees are perfect." They are right where they are supposed to be at this season, at this time in their life stage. Granted, mature fruit is not yet on the trees, but the conditions are right *at that stage of blossoming* for fruit to be produced in time. If you drove the Blossom Trail in the summer, you would see the fruit just beginning to take shape. It hasn't ripened yet, but you could still say, "That is *teleios* fruit." Why? It's not ripe yet, but it's perfect for the season.

Until we moved to California, I'd never seen citrus trees. At our new home, we had two citrus trees in our backyard. I was so excited that I would check them weekly. One day I saw green fruit taking shape. I went in the house and said, "Sarah, we have lime trees!" I don't like limes that well, but I still thought it was exciting to have lime trees. After a few weeks, I picked one from the tree and cut it open. There was just a little bit of pulp and a whole lot of skin. It tasted worse than I could have imagined. "Oh well," I said, "there must be some trick to caring for these trees to get good fruit. I'll leave them on the tree and see if they get any better." A month later my "limes" turned orange! And they tasted really good!

When the oranges were green, they were still perfect for where they were supposed to be. I, as a "rookie grower," had improper expectations—but that did not affect the condition of the fruit. I had to learn what was appropriate at each stage in growing citrus. Likewise, we can be *teleios,* maturing, even when we are green in the practices of spiritual living. When we fall, we fall to our knees, and that's an evidence of maturity.

When we fall, we fall to our knees, and that's an evidence of maturity.

The spiritual journey is grace from start to finish. The greatest sin is not our failure; it's our presumption that we can succeed without full dependence on Christ. His goal is our maturing, until we attain "the whole measure of the fullness of Christ" (Eph. 4:13). And as mature disciples, we learn to make profitable use of our imperfections. We see that even our failures become avenues to God's love and deepest treasures. P. T. Forsyth writes:

> Perfection is not sinlessness. The "perfect" in the New Testament are certainly not the sinless. And God, though He wills that we be perfect, has not appointed sinlessness as His object with us in this world. His object is communion with us through faith. And sin must abide, even while it is being conquered, as an occasion for faith. Every defect of ours is a motive for faith. To cease to feel defect is to cease to trust. To cease to feel the root of sin would be to have one motive the less to cast us on God for keeping. Every need is there in order to rouse the need for God. And we need God chiefly, not as a means to an end, not to satisfy earthly need, to keep the world going, to comfort us, or to help us to the higher moral levels. We do not need God chiefly as a means even to our own holiness. But we need God for Himself. He Himself is the end. We need chiefly communion with Him; which is not confined to the perfectly holy but is open to all in faith, and possible along with cleaving sin. To treat a living person as an end, to seek him for himself, has but one meaning. It is to love him, to have our desire and energy rest in him, to have our personal finality in him. So it is that we need and seek God, not His help nor His gifts—even of sanctity, but Himself. His great object with us is not our sinlessness but our communion. "Give me thy heart." He does not offer us communion to make us holy; He makes us holy for the sake of communion. It has pleased God to leave us *in* our sin (though not *to* our sin) that we may be driven to seek more than His help, namely Himself.[5]

Though a noble goal, then, perfection is not for this life. Striving for perfection can be counterproductive, turning our attention from the Lord and from our need for continual reliance upon grace. God did not save us so that we could gain perfection in this life but so that we could experience the joy of his power overcoming our imperfection.

The Burst and the Burnout

"If you could change one thing about your walk with the Lord, what would it be?" The most common response I hear consistently is, "Have a regular quiet time, or devotional time, with the Lord." Yet the average person can only sustain that practice for a short time before failing again.

Inspiration and enthusiasm are wonderful traits, but they are often short-lived. When we begin the disciplines of the spiritual life, we often start strong but fade with the passing of several weeks or a month. The starting burst soon fizzles.

There are numerous reasons for falling away. You develop a routine that gets interrupted by travel or special circumstances, and you never restart. You come to the end of the book or Bible study guide you were using and have made no plans for the next step. You fall into temptation and are too ashamed and discouraged to begin again. You may even find a mild depression setting in. You get tired of the discipline, having lost sight of the vision.

As I've said earlier, the most important source of motivation is not willpower but the power of a vision, an image of who God is calling us to be in Christ. Thomas Kelly counsels us, "Don't grit your teeth and clench your fists and say, 'I will! I will!' Relax. Take your hands off. Submit yourself to God. Learn to live in the passive voice—a hard saying for Americans—and let life be willed through you. For 'I will' spells not obedience."[6] As we begin, we shape a vision and review it each day. We change it, add to it, rephrase it, allow it to grow with us. But the key is keeping our eye on the goal (see Phil. 3:12).

Another principle for sustaining our commitment is to release the guilt and self-accusation that compound our failure to maintain our discipline. In his book *A Testament of Devotion*, Thomas Kelly encourages us to react lightly to ourselves when we slip.

> The first days and weeks and months of offering total self to God are awkward and painful, but enormously rewarding. Awkward, because it takes constant vigilance and effort and reassertions of the will, at the first level. Painful, because our lapses are so frequent, the intervals when we forget Him so long. Rewarding, because we have begun to live. But these weeks and months and perhaps even years must be passed through before He gives us greater and easier stayedness upon Himself.
>
> Lapses and forgettings are so frequent. Our surroundings grow so exciting. Our occupations are so exacting. But when you catch yourself again, lose no time in self-recriminations, but breathe a silent prayer for forgiveness and begin again, just where you are. Offer *this* broken worship up to Him and say: 'This is what I am except Thou aid me.' Admit no discouragement, but ever return quietly to Him and wait in His Presence.
>
> Once having the vision, the second step to holy obedience is this: Begin where you are. Obey *now*. Use what little obedience you are capable of, even if it be like a grain of mustard seed. Begin where you are. . . .
>
> If you slip and stumble and forget God for an hour, and assert your old proud self, and rely upon your own clever wisdom, don't spend too much time in anguished regrets and self accusations but begin again, just where you are.[7]

This is wise counsel to those who are likely to be overwhelmed by failure. The tragedy is that the sensitive conscience can be incapacitated in the very act of seeking God.

Being Intimidated by the Extraordinary

Maybe you're not plagued by the ideal of perfectionism. Yet you are tormented by comparing your journey with one that seems much more extraordinary. The reported experience of others is often taken as the model we should adopt. The classic example of this is the standard for prayer that is often advocated from Martin Luther's practice. This exceptional servant of God is reported to have said, when most pressed with his gigantic toils, "I have so much to do that I cannot get on without three hours a day of praying." I have read somewhere the added statement, "And when especially pressed, I must pray four hours."

That is an overwhelming ideal! I do not doubt Luther's devotion; nor do I mind others setting such a goal for their own devotional lives. But I have seen countless people give up altogether because they felt like failures, unable to sustain such an ideal in the pressures of daily life.

When our children were small, Sarah was discouraged because she couldn't have a regular quiet time. With four children under the age of six—is that any wonder?! I tried to help, but we weren't able to make it work. Then she read of a woman who set the alarm to awaken her at 3:00 A.M. so she could have uninterrupted time with the Lord. Sarah did that for several nights in a row but found the fatigue overwhelming as dinnertime approached. She concluded that this was one discipline she couldn't keep—but she had to work through the guilt and regret she felt at not attaining the ideal.

One of the most common tendencies is to idealize others' experience. We see other people who seem happy and assume that they have few problems. We hear speakers talk about love and assume they have no interpersonal conflicts. We read about spirituality and assume that the writers have a hot line to heaven. Wrong! We don't see them when they are alone, afraid, and discouraged because their experience falls far short of their knowledge. We also forget that what we often hear or read about may be the one high point out of months or years of struggle and failure.

Nip idealization in the bud before it bears the bitter fruit of competition. There is no basis for comparison because the Lord meets each of us in a way that's unique to our history and personality. Think of the differences between Jeremiah and Ezekiel, Paul and Timothy, John and Mark! No comparisons are possible.

Choose a single discipline that touches the need of your soul at this time. It's a matter between you and God. As God restores your soul, you will find yourself freed from the temptation to compare yourself with others. You will celebrate your unique walk with God.

Getting Caught Up in the Program instead of the Person

A man once told me, "When I was having my quiet time one morning, our toddler came in. I was so frustrated at being interrupted that I took the child into our bedroom, woke up my wife, and said, 'Here, you take care of her—I'm trying to pray!' In a few minutes, I calmed down. *Wait a minute,* I thought. *Why am I praying in the first place?* He saw that he'd put his personal program ahead of the qualities that such a program is meant to inspire and sustain. He went back to the bedroom, asked his wife's forgiveness, took his little daughter into his lap, and they prayed together. "It was one of the most tender times of prayer I've ever had," he said.

Getting preoccupied with the program is yet another resistance point to real spiritual growth. Our children have a young friend who began to exercise and work out to get in shape for

425

sports. He decided he was going to be a healthy eater, so he cut down on snacks and fatty foods. Then he decided he would be more healthy if he ate less. Soon he became so preoccupied with limiting his food intake that his health was in serious danger.

Ironically, spiritual activity can become an end in itself rather than the means to God's presence, perspective, power, and purpose in our lives. Spirituality is a fascinating area for study and reflection; a lifetime is too short to read and experience a fraction of what is available on the subject. We can be like children at a huge amusement park, wanting to ride every ride, eat every food, and see every show. The result is exhaustion—or worse. A type of spiritual greed and gluttony can seduce us. We seek experience for experience's sake. We can be fascinated by the new discoveries we make, such as in the realm of meditation, without seeing the link to fellowship with God and obedience in discipleship. We can be consumed with exploring the nature of various ascetic practices, looking for things that make us feel better instead of seeking practices that make us more aware of the Lord. We can get caught in the maze of feeling compelled to do a certain number of exercises or we feel guilty. In short, we get caught up in the program instead of in the Person.

The remedy for this problem is to ask ourselves frequently: "Why am I doing this?" If the practice is not translating into life change, we need to reexamine our purpose. I'm thinking of the times when I've tried to have family devotions, only to become irritable at the lack of participation by our children. The program was not fulfilling the goal of drawing us together into God's presence. My commitment to a particular type of devotional program had to yield to the higher purpose of that program.

The Good Distraction

We've often heard it said, "The good is the enemy of the best." Nowhere is this more of a problem than in serving the Lord.

We can so easily be consumed by the things that need to be done that we neglect the one thing that is needful (see Luke 10:38-42).

When we say yes to good things that crowd spiritual disciplines from our lives, we've given ourselves a "holy escape clause." "I'm doing God's work," we say. But God will not allow us to sustain ourselves forever. The time will come when we drop our bucket into the well and come up dry. We need a clear focus on the necessary priorities, resisting the pressure to do all the good things that are possible. *Don't equate activity with effectiveness.*

The Next Play

All of our children have played soccer. They play with intensity and a desire to win. One of the biggest problems they have faced is becoming frustrated and even angry with themselves when they "muff" a kick or miss a pass. Their attitude would distract them through the sets of plays that followed. The result was that their own mistakes would take them out of the game more effectively than any opponent. I asked one of the coaches how they could overcome this self-defeating behavior.

"The point I want to teach these kids is that they learn from their mistakes, brush them aside, and get on with the game. We don't have instant replay here. We just need to focus on the next play."

"The next play"—that became our code phrase for letting go of the mistake and getting on with the game. "Don't punish yourself by letting that last play mess up future plays. Let it go and go on." In time, the idea took hold.

We all learned from that process. That phrase has helped me when I fall to temptation or when I fail to keep up my own spiritual exercises. I have realized that brooding about mistakes gives them additional power to generate more mistakes.

MAKING MISTAKES WORK FOR US

What are some of the profitable uses of imperfections? First, our imperfection discloses our helplessness apart from God. "I am the vine, you are the branches. Those who abide in me and I in them will bear much fruit, because apart from me you can do nothing" (John 15:5, NRSV). Augustine said that the saints are not praiseworthy because they are sinless but because of their poignant awareness of their continuing sin. They're striving in hope for a perfection that will only become a reality after death. It takes incredible courage to keep running for that goal for a whole lifetime.[8]

Luther said, "Paul called Christians to be righteous and holy and free from sin not because they are but because they have begun and should become people of this kind by making constant progress."[9] He depicted a Christian as a convalescent, recovering from brokenness.

John Calvin said that "all Christians are partly unbelievers, and most therefore constantly flee to Christ for aid."[10] I love that image of fleeing to Christ. Calvin believed that the highest perfection of the godly in this life is that earnest desire to make progress. When we break, we break open, not down. That's what the Holy Spirit seeks to do in our lives.

God did not redeem us so that we could make ourselves holy apart from him. He redeemed us so he could reveal his grace in our lives from start to finish. God always measures us with the yardstick of grace. In living the imperfect life we learn to know the perfect grace of God.

In living the imperfect life we learn to know the perfect grace of God.

A second use of imperfection is to cultivate an honorable humility. There's no room for excessive pride in our lives. I have had some very difficult years of ministry. At one point, I seriously considered leaving the pastoral ministry. In the process, God showed me my limits and the necessity of relying on him more. I came to know in my experience what I had always affirmed in my theology: that apart from the Holy Spirit working in my life, I can do nothing. Nothing. That is the ground of humility.

Humility is not thinking less of yourself; it's thinking more of God and of others. We are able to take our proper place in the scheme of things. Humility is not becoming a doormat; it is becoming a doorway. We enable others to enter into the joy of affirmation and the blessing of being served.

A third use of our imperfection is to stimulate our patience and gentleness with others. This flows right out of humility. When you're broken and humbled, you're more tender with others. Every person is carrying a heavy load. As we acknowledge our imperfections and learn patience and compassion for ourselves, we are better able to show compassion to others.

Finally, our imperfections drive us into the arms of grace. When the woman washed Jesus' feet with her hair and then anointed him, he said, "She loves much because she's been forgiven much." It wasn't that she had more of which to be forgiven than others; she was simply aware of her sin. The secret to handling imperfection, then, is to acknowledge it, to release it, and to move on. Again, quoting P. T. Forsyth:

> The saints, in the New Testament, are not always the saintly but the believing. What Christ always demanded of those who came to Him was *not* character, not achievement, but faith, trust.
>
> His standard was not conduct; it was not character, it was not creed. It was trust, and trust *not* in His manner but in

his message, His gospel. That was the one demand of God; and to answer it is perfection.[11]

GETTING STARTED

We now have the information we need to undertake an intentional commitment to soulshaping. Now we need a specific plan, developed through honest reflection and the guidance of the Holy Spirit. I would like to conclude this chapter by presenting the steps for developing your own plan for the restoration and the holy shaping of your soul.

Soul-searching. We can begin at any number of places, but I find that it's most effective to pay attention to what is already stirring in our heart. Where do you *want* to start? What has stirred your heart as you've read this book? Why? What seems most intriguing or meaningful to you?

Come up with a vision. What is one step to "glory" you believe God would like you to make? Picture yourself with this change. How would your attitude, behavior, knowledge, or skills be affected? How would your schedule adapt to allow this? What would be different by next week? What could be different in your life in the next eight weeks?

Select a spiritual exercise. With this vision clearly in mind, what discipline(s) would best help you move forward toward this vision? Look over the following list and prioritize the ones you want to practice.

🌿 Keeping a Spiritual Journal

Exercises That Increase Our Awareness of God's Presence
🌿 Repentance
🌿 Confession

❧ Preview
❧ Review
❧ Prayer
❧ Worship

Exercises That Help Us See Life with an Eternal Perspective
❧ Bible study
❧ Meditation
❧ Spiritual reading

Exercises That Free Us from Evil's Power and Connect Us to God's Resources
❧ Fasting
❧ Silence
❧ Solitude
❧ Battling temptation
❧ Prayer for spiritual battle

Exercises That Direct Our Lives toward Kingdom Purposes
❧ Building character
❧ Building relationships
❧ Spiritual direction
❧ Spiritual friendship
❧ Stewardship
❧ Spiritual service through spiritual gifts

Why have you chosen the exercises you have? What specific soul needs will they address? How? Is there a particular symptom of soul neglect that you hope to remedy? Considering all these questions moves you to a different level of awareness, commitment, and motivation. If you neglect this diligent work at the outset, you will most likely find yourself in the situation of the starting burst that soon fizzles.

What additional information or resources do you need to initiate this discipline? For example, buy your spiritual journal today and write your vision and initial plan. Go to the bookstore and select the book you will use for spiritual reading. Or call your friend and arrange to meet to discuss a spiritual friendship. Start a personal prayer guide (I prefer the word *guide* to *list*, since it sounds more open and free; *list* has the ring of fulfilling a mechanical obligation). Immediate action will help cement your intention.

Make tangible commitments. Someone has said, "Performance has more to do with commitment than with competence." When we make commitments, our hearts, minds, souls, and bodies join together to bring them to fulfillment. Add to this the gracious power of God and we will make great progress. Make a simple plan of commitments to yourself. Set specific goals or commitments for time. Each day I will_____. [Number of] times per week I will_____. Each month I will _____. Each year I will_____.

One practice that has helped me a great deal is to prepare the night before for the day ahead. I lay out my exercise clothes, wallet, keys, and club card so I don't have to rummage around for them in the morning. Knowing everything is ready when the alarm rings is a significant incentive.

In the same way, having the desk cleared, with your journal and Bible open, removes one of the most common obstacles to a disciplined quiet time. When you decide to have a quiet time and sit down to a messy desk with bills, phone messages, and advertisements strewn across every bare space, the soul is unsettled, and the mind is distracted. You are already several steps behind and will have to work all the harder to center your attention on the Lord and his Word.

Make yourself accountable. How will you handle accountability? It may be enough to log your goals and plans in your personal calendar or daily planner. A simple check chart may be enough. On the other hand, most people benefit from the support and encouragement of another person. Many players have natural ability, but a coach is necessary to get a person to invest the effort to move from talent to skill. When we ask someone to hold us accountable, we are inviting them to be our coach and hold us to our commitments.

Your life *will* be imperfect. But imagine what it would be if you did nothing at all! You know too much now to simply allow the world to shape your soul according to the current whim or evil. When you see the vision of what you can become in Christ and determine to move ahead, depending on God's grace, the Holy Spirit will indeed shape your soul, even with the ups and downs, the failures and slumps.

How will you know when your soul is getting healthy? In chapter 1, we discussed the symptoms of soul neglect. For our conclusion, let's look at the vital signs of a healthy soul.

NOTES

1. François Fénelon, *Let Go* (Springfield, Penn.: Banner Publisher, Whitaker House, 1973), 40.
2. E. M. Bounds, quoting A. C. Dixon in *The Necessity of Prayer* (Grand Rapids, Mich.: Baker Book House, 1976), 9.
3. C. S. Lewis, *Mere Christianity*, (New York: Macmillan, 1943), 64.
4. R. Schippers, *"Telios*, Goal" in *The New International Dictionary of New Testament Theology*, vol. 2, ed. Colin Brown (Grand Rapids, Mich.: Zondervan, 1971), 59.
5. P. T. Forsyth, *Christian Perfection* (Edinburgh University Press, 1899), 11–13.
6. Thomas Kelly, *A Testament of Devotion*, (New York: Harper & Row, 1941), 61.

7. Ibid., 39, 60–61.
8. Donald G. Bloesch, *Essentials of Evangelical Theology,* vol. 2 (San Francisco: Harper & Row, 1978), 48.
9. Ibid.
10. Ibid.
11. Forsyth, *Christian Perfection,* 83.

SOUL-SEARCHING

Questions for Reflection and Discussion

1. Read 2 Corinthians 4:1-12. What is the primary purpose of our being "jars of clay"? In what ways does acknowledging that we are "earthen vessels" affect our spiritual lives?

2. Explain the meaning of the statement "Human limitations are not a source of shame; they are a greater avenue to grace." Has this been true in your experience? Explain.

3. What are five resistance points (or predictable problems) that interfere with spiritual growth? Which of these most troubles you? Are there any you would add?

4. How do you handle failure, especially in your spiritual life?

5. What are some of the ways we can make mistakes work for us? In what specific ways have you found these principles relevant to your life?

6. Reread the process described in "Getting Started." What is God saying to you at this time about taking care of your spiritual life?

CHAPTER TWENTY-TWO

The Vital Signs of a Healthy Soul

W HEN Julie came to see me, she said, "I think I have every addiction there is." She was, in fact, in support groups for substance abuse and for eating disorders. She was a beautiful young woman; you'd never suspect by her appearance how deeply troubled her soul was. But God was stirring her heart. She had made an initial commitment to Christ and wanted to lead a life that would please him. But she was over-whelmed by the abuses she had suffered, the mistakes she had made, and her powerlessness to make substantial changes. "How can God really love me?" she asked in deep anguish. "I don't know if I'll ever get my life together. I feel better now, but how do I know it will last?"

Normally, I would have used the analogy of a loving father or mother as an image to help her understand the unconditional love of God, but Julie had never known such a father or mother. She, like so many—*so very many!*—knew parents as unpredictable people who could smother you with love one minute and turn on you with vicious anger the next. She had witnessed her own father pull a knife on her mother in a threat so real Julie still has nightmares. Where do I find a reference point for one who has never known even a trace of unconditional love in her life?

"Julie, God loves you right now. He's going to continue to love you *before* you can do anything more to get or keep your life together. He brought you here because he wants to show you."

"Show me?"

"I could take time to go through the Scriptures again [since we'd done that in a previous session], but I have a strong sense that God wants to touch you now. Let's pray and ask the Lord, very simply, to touch you with his love." I then guided her into a time of prayer ministry. I invited Julie to ask the Lord for whatever he had to give her. She sat quietly for a few moments, then a tear began to trickle down her check. After more time had passed, I quietly asked her to share what was happening.

"I was in my bedroom in the house where I lived in the third grade. My parents were fighting and I was curled up in bed, trying to get away, to feel safe. And I felt the Lord come into my room. He sat on the bed with his hand on my head and began to sing very softly. As he sang, I couldn't hear my parents arguing any more. It was so sweet . . ." and Julie couldn't say another word as the tears flowed freely down her beaming face. She had been touched by grace. She had come with the question: Will it last this time? Could the spiritual renewal begun in her result in lasting change and continuing refreshment? She left feeling a deeper assurance.

We have come to the conclusion of a thorough study of the specific means for "sowing to the Spirit," or for what we could call "training in godliness." We now have a clear idea of specific steps to take in order to care for the priceless soul God has entrusted to us. And I make the point again that I've made repeatedly throughout this book: This kind of care for ourselves is not selfish! The care of your soul is one of the greatest things you can do, not only for yourself, but for the welfare of others. We've seen the many symptoms of soul neglect that result from ignoring or shortchanging our souls.

There are a variety of dams and leaks in our inner "soul reservoirs." Some block the flow of refreshment and energy into our lives, while other things drain us. The goal of soulshaping is to keep the streams of living water flowing into and out of our lives to refresh others.

Now, we need to be reminded again of the purpose of spiritual vitality: the glorious enjoyment of God in the midst of life. We may step apart from the world for a time, but only so that we can enter fully into life as people who can make a difference. A life marked by spiritual vitality shines, radiating hope and purpose in a dark and confused world. I think of John-David, my spiritual director, whose eyes dance with joy, whose full-bodied laugh infects all around him with joy, whose integrity gives him great confidence in the face of opposition, and whose love for Jesus is as real as any passion in life.

VITAL SIGNS OF SPIRITUAL VITALITY

So how do you know if your soul is healthy? What does spiritual vitality look like in the "dailies" of life?

A Continuing Experience of Grace

We begin with grace, and we will conclude with gratitude. These are the brackets of a life that is life indeed. The deepest joy in life springs from the assurance of being known and loved *just as we are.*

I can't explain what happens in prayer experiences such as I had with Julie, but I've seen it many times: the fresh touch of

God's grace in a weary, life-worn heart. His gracious love is there for the asking when we turn to him in prayer—prayer not just as a one-way conversation, but prayer as an encounter with the living Lord. Julie is truly a different woman, as are countless other people who have had such a touch. She's different because she experienced unconditional love, the assurance that God was with her in all things. She experienced grace.

Grace is the richest term in the vocabulary of faith. We've already explored this term in some depth, but we can never spend enough time contemplating it. If we compare life to a race we are running, we are tempted to think that performance is the key and only one person wins. But the race of life is far different. *Love is not the reward at the finish line after a person has run a race that impresses God. Love is given at the starting line, winning before the race even begins.*

The daily experience of living in grace means telling ourselves every morning and throughout the day:

> I am accepted.
> I am loved.
> I am called to live in the power of the Lord today.
> Nothing good I can do today will make God love me more.
> No sin or failure will make God love me less.

Spiritual vitality is not blind to the heartbreak of sin or to the reality that this is a fallen world. Spiritual vitality is realistic, living life with eyes wide open. But it also sees that life is shot through with God's mercy at every turn. It looks for this mercy, developing spiritual instincts and intuition for discovering the Father's fingerprints. Every activity is seen through "resurrection eyes."

When we live our lives expecting and depending upon the undeserved grace of God's love, we find that its clear, fresh waters bubble up in the most unexpected times: reminding us that we are royal children when someone tries to attack our integrity; filling us with confidence when we would normally shrink from responsibility; comforting us with assurance when nothing around us looks promising; giving an unsought moment of joy in the midst of mundane duty; washing away the dirt of life in this dusty world. A vital life is rooted in grace. No other soil will bear lasting fruit.

A **vital life is rooted in grace. No other soil will bear lasting fruit.**

Expectancy That Is Rooted in Faith

When we begin with love, hope follows right on its heels. Hope gets us out of bed and into the heart of life. Those who hope see the coming kingdom of God, while others see only the sad disorder and destruction of this world. An expectant spirit is fueled from within, from the inner reservoirs of vision and faith. It is realistic, but also optimistic.

My most vivid image of expectancy came from our daughter. When Kristen was around three years old, we drove past Binney Park in Old Greenwich, Connecticut. We loved to feed the ducks that lived around the pond in the center of the park. Because of a long dry spell, however, the water level was so low that the ducks sought "wetter pastures." Kristen really missed the ducks, so she asked if we could pray for them to come back to Binney. I thought this was a great idea; so I closed one eye as I drove (I wanted her to learn this basic habit of prayer!), and together we prayed, "Dear Lord, send the ducks back to Binney Park." "And remind them how to get here in case they've forgotten," chimed in Kristen. "Amen!" As soon as we said amen, Kristen started to wiggle out of her car seat, trying to stand up. "Where are the ducks? Where are the ducks?" she said, as she looked at the pond!

Kristen expected an answer—immediately! I was convicted. I realized I didn't have such high expectations. I was curious to see what God would do, but I was not burning with the excitement that gripped my daughter. I guess you might credit her faith for the fact that several days later we had a major rainstorm. The day after the storm, Sarah, Kristen, and I took a walk to the park. Kristen was sitting straight up in the stroller as we came through the tunnel, turned the corner, and saw the pond. "There are the ducks! I knew it!" she exclaimed. "There are the ducks Dad and I prayed for, Mom!"

Expectancy looks for God to work even though reason and common sense counsel us otherwise. It is the force that enables us to stand firmly in unsettling circumstances. A woman shared with me about having a group of women over to her house for bridge. "Now, I want you to know most of these women claim to be Christians. They are active in their churches. But all they did was grumble and worry about the world situation. Not one of them talked about their faith in God! So you know what I did?" she asked me. Before I could respond, she said, "I let them have it! 'Aren't we people of prayer? Don't we believe God is in control? Can't we begin to trust Christ and give him our prayers and begin to believe that God will work all of this out?'" Talk about playing a trump card! Patty did what few people have the courage to do because she nurtures a vibrant expectancy every day.

We are able to appreciate God, ourselves, and others when we cultivate expectancy through a heavenly perspective. We can do this very quickly, by the way, if we're in a tough situation. Do what parents do with their young children: Take a time-out. I heartily recommend it for adults. Take a time-out to pray, to read a brief passage from the Bible or a section of inspiration from a

Christian book, to write in your journal, to listen to a favorite song, or to jot a note of encouragement to a friend. You can do this in a variety of settings. A few moments focused on the right things can change your outlook for the rest of the day.

Two specific qualities tell us how much progress we are making in this area. The first is this: When we are able to respond to life without an undue magnification of the problems, we are developing faith to see life from God's perspective. One of my problems is compounding—I take the responsibilities I have today and then add to them the responsibilities I will have tomorrow; and then I think about the responsibilities of the next day and the next day and . . . and pretty soon I'm carrying the entire year on my back! Compounding smothers our joy, draining our energy to carry burdens we were never meant to bear. "Your strength will equal your days" (Deut. 33:25). When we spend more time dwelling on the details of the problem than on the dimensions of God's promises, we have shifted our focus to that which can overcome us. When we turn our attention to the Lord, we've taken the essential step to overcoming all problems. The following questions help us test for the undue magnification of problems:

---

*W*hen we are able to respond to life without an undue magnification of the problems, we are developing faith to see life from God's perspective.

- How big is this problem really?
- What are the worst consequences that are likely to flow from it?
- What difference would the response of faith make in my response?

The other quality that indicates a low level of expectancy is the trivialization of blessings. When you see something great happen, you may thank the Lord, but then you're on to the next thing. You have just trivialized a blessing. Caring for your soul enables you to celebrate. Take time to celebrate. If somebody does something really special, take the time to savor it by writing them a letter. A moment spent in this way freezes time. If you meet a goal, take time to thank God and give yourself a little gift of self-care. You may want to call a friend or make plans for something you can look forward to or buy something you've been hoping to get. You may want to take time for a prayer meditation or to write a psalm of thanks. The point is, take time to celebrate throughout the day.

So often I get myself all worked up over something I can't control and which, in the light of eternity, isn't that important anyway. And that's a sign of losing perspective. The practices of soulshaping help us hold up a mirror to our lives so that we can begin to see where things belong and how they fit in.

Resilience

A third vital sign of spiritual vitality is resilience. This is the ability to recover from misfortune or to adjust to change. I like to think of someone who is buoyant, unsinkable. When life pushes them down, they pop up somewhere else, bouncing as joyfully as ever.

Most people I know who have this quality of resilience are not naive. They do not deny the problems and struggles of life. They are wise. Their strength comes from the fact that they have not given control of their lives to outer circumstances or to other people. They've decided that in Jesus Christ they can do all things. If somebody insults them or disparages their reputation, they turn it over to God. That takes courage, strength, and confidence in Christ.

One of the most touching and powerful stories of resilience comes from one man's response to very difficult circumstances. Robertson McQuilkin, the beloved former president of Columbia Bible College, faced a major decision when his wife, Muriel, began suffering from the advanced ravages of Alzheimer's disease. He was urged by many to provide the best care possible for her but continue in his ministry. In March 1990, however, Dr. McQuilkin announced his resignation in a letter with these words:

> My dear wife, Muriel, has been in failing mental health for about eight years. So far I have been able to carry both her ever-growing needs and my leadership responsibilities at CBC. But recently it has become apparent that Muriel is contented most of the time she is with me and almost none of the time I am away from her. It is not just "discontent." She is filled with fear—even terror—that she has lost me and always goes in search of me when I leave home. Then she may be full of anger when she cannot get to me. So it is clear to me that she needs me now, full-time.
>
> Perhaps it would help you to understand if I shared with you what I shared at the time of the announcement of my resignation in chapel. The decision was made, in a way, 42 years ago when I promised to care for Muriel "in sickness and in health . . . till death do us part." So, as I told the students and faculty, as a man of my word, integrity has something to do with it. But so does fairness. She has cared for me fully and sacrificially all these years; if I cared for her for the next 40 years I would not be out of debt. Duty, however, can be grim and stoic. But there is more; I love Muriel. She is a delight to me—her childlike dependence and confidence in me, her warm love, occasional flashes of that wit I used to relish so, her happy spirit and tough

445

resilience in the face of her continual distressing
frustration. I do not *have* to care for her, I *get* to! It is a high
honor to care for so wonderful a person.[1]

Spiritual maturity gives us an entirely different perspective on
life and love, on commitment and priorities. It generates an
inner strength that finds God's glory where others can't find a
trace of good.

Resilience is a quality of character that's in short supply in our
day. We have become people who expect instant gratification.
When we make a phone call and are told the person is not available, we're likely to feel insulted and put off. We don't like the
busy signal. We don't want to stand in lines. We don't like incon-
venience. Soulshaping helps us refocus our attention on Christ's
resources and gain an inner strength—strength and patience for
lines, busy signals, and all sorts of things that impinge on us.
And we take this strength to the deeper levels of stress and strain
and difficult relationships, thwarted dreams, and the more
severe frustrations of life.

Persistence and perspiration may look good on paper, but
they make up a lifestyle that we don't anticipate with joy! But
when God reveals his plan to us in our quiet fellowship with him,
we gain a confidence that is not easily shaken. There are times
when we may cling to him as one aboard ship lashes himself to
the masts as they go through the storm rages. Yet we know we're
going to get through the storm. The assurance of grace and a
hopeful expectancy nourished on God's Word and presence are
key sources of resilience. We can endure some hard times if we
have a vision that we're going to get through it. Resilience comes
from a deepening knowledge of our Lord and of his resources.
We learn to pray and to enjoy him; above all, we gain that deep
assurance the Bible often says is beyond understanding.

Resilience comes only from being tried time and again and

coming through in the power of God. Resilience taps the springs of memory. Unlike the Lethe, the river of forgetfulness in Greek mythology, we drink from the strengthening waters of God's faithfulness. Resilience comes from having dwelt with Christ. As we cultivate his presence and perspective, tap his power, and follow his direction, we gain a deep, unshakable confidence that he is in control and can sustain us. We see the effectiveness of promises such as, "Be anxious for nothing, but in everything by prayer and supplication, with thanksgiving, let your requests be made known to God; and the peace of God, which surpasses all understanding, will guard your hearts and minds through Christ Jesus" (Phil. 4:6-7, NKJV). I like to picture angels marching around my heart, keeping watch over it. This peace is like a Patriot Missile. When an incoming rocket is threatening, this missile is fired to destroy the rocket in the air before it hits the target. The peace of Jesus Christ, likewise, keeps guard over your hearts. It may not prevent the incoming threat, but it intercepts it.

Compassion

Mother Teresa, perhaps the best-known model of compassion in our day, prays the following daily prayer. Listen to the soulshaping of this woman:

> Dearest Lord, May I see you today and every day in the person of your sick. And whilst nursing them minister unto you. [Comment: Immediately she has broken down the barrier between Christ and others. This is not a mystical violation of Christ's transcendence but a fuller understanding of his imminence, his permeation of Creation—as clearly stated in Matthew 25:40]. Though you hide yourself behind the unattractive disguise of the irritable, the exacting, the unreasonable, may I still recognize you and say, "Jesus, my patient, how sweet it is to serve you."

Lord, give me the seeing faith, then my work will never be monotonous. I will ever find joy in humoring the fancies and gratifying the wishes of all sufferers. O, beloved sick, how doubly dear you are to me when you personify Jesus. And what a privilege is mine to be allowed to tend you. Sweetest Jesus, make me appreciative of the dignity of my high calling and its many responsibilities. Never permit me to disgrace it by giving way to coldness, unkindness, or impatience. O, God, while you are in Jesus my patient deem also to me to be a patient, Jesus. Bearing with my thoughts, looking only to my intention, which is to love and to serve you in the person of each of your sick. Lord, increase my faith, bless my efforts and work, now and forever.

That's a prayer to begin a day and sustain a day.

Compassion is definitely a vital sign of a healthy soul. When we better know and love our Creator, we learn to value the creation. We learn to love what God loves. We learn to see people through his eyes. We gain a greater appreciation for the complexity and wonder of the human being and a deeper sense of the heroism of the human soul.

Have you ever thought about the heroism of the ordinary human being? Each morning we awaken to the mystery and demands of a new day. Each day we are asked to say yes again to the responsibilities God has given us in our homes, our work, our communities, and beyond. We are asked to bear the anxiety of a world with desperate needs and seemingly diminishing resources. The normal support networks of family and community have been weakened. The moral consensus that once set the boundaries and established the expectations of relationships is no longer accepted. Is it any wonder that people are more than ever "like sheep without a shepherd"? We may not encounter the mythical dragons of fairy tales, but we face threats of every kind every day. Each person who tries to live with integrity and responsibility is a hero.

This burden is intensified by the two-edged sword of the media. Those very powers that put us in touch with the world seem to demand that we do something about what we learn. Famine, orphans, political and social injustice, ethical dilemmas—these issues bombard us and take a toll on the heart that cares. So it's not enough to worry about what's happening in your own community. You've got to know about the problems facing your state or province, nation, neighboring nations, and world.

It can cause what some have called "compassion fatigue." We become aware of problems we can't solve, yet we feel responsible for them. Our concern and guilt work on us, draining our energy. Then the time comes when we switch off.

> Massive exposure to human misery often leads to psychic numbness. . . . It can also lead to hostility. . . . "When I can't do anything about it anyhow, why do you bother me with it!" Confronted with human pain and at the same time reminded of our powerlessness, we feel offended to the very core of our being and fall back on our defenses of numbness and anger.[1]

Spiritual exercises reorient our attitude toward the world and our sense of responsibility. We hear the voice of God, which calls us to action *and* calls us to rest and trust him. We are not driven by the needs of the world; we are called by the voice of God to meet particular needs by his strength.

With this kind of spiritual maturity comes a deepening sense of empathy. We can never fully experience what another person is experiencing, but we can gain a new sense of respect and appreciation as we listen and care. What did Jesus do on many occasions? He wept. He wept with Mary and Martha when Lazarus had died. He wept in the Garden of Gethsemane. He wept many silent tears the Gospels do not exploit. We learn to weep. We have a new compassion for ourselves and for others. Compassion replaces our anger and resentment at being surrounded by needy people and a hurting world. We accept others in their pain and seek to show the love of God to them. Soulshaping enables us to be truly human. We become more sensitive; we hurt more deeply; *however,* we experience the joy that accompanies God's supernatural love lived out through us.

We also gain a deepening sense of the vast potential in each person; we begin to see what God could do if he really got hold of a person. Spiritual energy and motivation become the wellspring of social action. The artificial division between the social gospel of compassion and the evangelical gospel of conversion is not biblical. It's not one or the other; it's got to be both. If we have compassion without Christ, we burn out and do not address the deepest, eternal need of the human soul. If we have Christ without compassion, we become condescending and self-righteous. But if we have Christ *and* his compassion we become a whole people in the service of others.

Zeal—Holy Energy

"H" is a man of zeal. He and his wife, Terry, moved from the suburbs into the heart of a tough downtown neighborhood. They are passionate about bringing the love of Jesus Christ to the streets, reclaiming neighborhoods for Christ, one block at a time. Early on Tuesday mornings, you will find him with several others who have also moved into the neighborhood, sharing and praying for themselves and their community. "These prayer times are one of the most important things we do. God revitalizes us so we can pour ourselves out for others."

Zeal is one of a healthy soul's most impressive vital signs because true zeal stands apart from mere enthusiasm or salesmanship. When Jesus said, "Zeal for your house will consume me," he was drawing energy, power, and commitment from God. We are inspired with energetic devotion to Christ's priorities because of our fellowship with Christ. Zeal is not fanaticism—fanaticism is zeal without a rudder. Zeal is a passion that is inspired by and surrendered to the Lord.

Zeal is not fanaticism—fanaticism is zeal without a rudder. Zeal is a passion that is inspired by and surrendered to the Lord.

When Jesus spoke of zeal, he combined the ideas of prayer and purity. He cleared the temple of the money changers because their business transactions had polluted the temple worship, distracting people from the focus on prayer. Zeal is a burning passion for honoring God and fulfilling his purposes in life.

Zeal is the fruit of God's presence. The spark of zeal is kindled from the altar of worship and will soon die if it is not fueled by continually dwelling near the flame. David was zealous for the Lord. His zeal flagged in his middle years but then revived in his later years as he gathered the materials for the temple.

Paul was a man of zeal. His intense commitment to spreading the gospel to those who had never heard it led him to adventures such as few have ever known.

The Spirit of God kindles a zeal within us which, when tended prayerfully, grows in intensity. It is the passion for being all God created you to be. God created you as you to do what only you can do. When a person taps into that purpose, it is like tapping a deep well of energy. One of the secrets of spirituality is the stewardship of our energies. As we grow in our love and trust and ability to communicate with God, our worry power is transformed into kingdom power—into a holy zeal. As we allow God to establish the purpose and direction of our lives, we give our attention to the important rather than to the urgent.

There is also a zeal that arises from seeing the needs of human beings, such as a zeal for justice—mentioned above under the subject of compassion. This kind of zeal will also dissipate unless it is fueled by God's resources. Zeal can be quiet, but it is intense. It is energy that is focused for a good purpose.

Paul describes this in 1 Corinthians 9:16: "I am under compulsion . . ." and 2 Corinthians 5:13-14: "for the love of Christ controls us . . ." (NASB). Zeal is that burning flame of love for God that leads to commitments to serve him. Maturing zeal is like the burning embers of a fire, giving off intense heat without a lot of fuss. They can ignite at any moment, when fresh fuel is placed on them. And they will rarely burn out, being tended by the Master's hand.

Zeal should not be confused with emotionalism, extroversion, or even with frenetic activity. It is better described as an unwavering confidence that results in a steady application of the truth of God in life. The person with zeal frequently steps back for renewal and then steps out in quiet boldness—to share her faith, to stand firm against the temptation to compromise, to go the extra mile when the road is tangled with brambles and brush.

We may expect to receive strength before we begin a task, but the actual dynamic works in the opposite direction. Strength comes with the doing of the task. In physical exercise, when you lift weights, the body demands more blood supply to the area where the demand is made. In the process, new circulation routes form, supplying more blood—which means more strength to the area. But if no demand is made, no strength is supplied! If you want to experience spiritual vitality, put yourself in a place where a demand is made upon you. For example, bring Jesus Christ into your conversation; say yes to mentoring a young child who has just begun walking with Jesus; reach out to a neighbor in need; pray with a person for healing. Until you step out in faith, your faith will not grow. When you do step out, you will be amazed at the experience of God's presence. It may not—in fact usually does not—come in a dramatic way. But there is a solid peace and confidence that you've done the right thing and God is pleased.

Integrity

This vital sign is the fruit of spiritual vitality translated into daily life. It's the collective sign of the fruit of the Spirit. *Integrity* means "integrated, unified around a central, controlling purpose." Integrity means that there is continuity between profession and performance. We do what we believe, and we believe in what we do. It means that our core values guide our decisions and guard us from words and deeds that would dishonor us. Integrity is congruence between heart purpose and life actions.

We usually connect integrity with honesty. But integrity goes much further than that. Integrity is the ability to count on yourself. Integrity is what you are when nobody's looking or when the lights are off. We demonstrate integrity toward ourselves by making good choices. We show integrity to others by honoring them with respect, fairness, and honesty in all of our dealings. Integrity is demonstrated in our faith as we strive continually to apply the principles of God's Word to our lives. We seek God's strength and power to live above compromise.

Gratitude

We begin with grace, and we conclude with gratitude. As I said before, these are the brackets of spiritual vitality. If everything in life falls within these boundaries, we will tap into the wellsprings of energy, purpose, and power for nearly all situations.

A grateful person takes nothing for granted. We develop a continual spirit of appreciation for the gifts of life. Even in the heartache and pain, there can be gratitude for a God big enough to lead us through it and wise enough to use it for the transformation of our lives.

A grateful person lets go of striving and scorns this world's empty promises. We release our insatiable greed for the satisfaction of our egos and appetites, for the accumulation of knowledge, experiences, reputation, pleasures, and possessions.

The soul that receives God's perspective looks not only toward the horizon of ideals but also at the beauty of that which is not yet finished. Gratitude teaches us to receive every piece of life as if it were the whole. We live most of our days with unfinished business. We learn to be thankful for the pieces. When one thing goes right, praise God! Stop and thank him. Allow that gratitude to permeate your soul.

Thanksgiving is not so much a response to the gift as to the giver. It sees not the object but the fingerprints on the object. That's why a mother and a father treasure even the wrapping of a gift received from a little child. The imaginative labor of those little not-so-nimble fingers working with that not-so-cooperative paper, crumpling corners here and slapping tape there—that paper is treasured as much as the gift inside. That wrapping paper can often bring a tear and a smile long before the treasure is ever revealed. And that's how we need to see each day.

As we go about the business of shaping our souls, we learn to become aware of the small things and receive them with great big gratitude. One of the ways to rest our hearts and minds is to be thankful. Be grateful for what God has done. We live in a world that has forgotten gratitude because we overemphasize achievement. The Scriptures call us to cultivate the "rejoice reflex" that praises God out of a vision of what God is achieving inside us.

AN ADVENTURE OF LOVE

One of the great sea navigators of the last century faithfully delivered his ship's cargo in excellent condition and on time all around the world.

He was often asked the secret of his ability to navigate. He'd reply, "Well, I go up on the deck at night and look up at the stars; I smell the wind and feel the way that it's blowing; I feel the pitch and roll of the waves and then I set my course."

Word came to the owners of the captain's ship that the insurance company would no longer insure any ships that were not using the most modern scientific methods and instruments of navigation.

So, after thirty years on the sea, the captain went back to school. He worked hard and graduated in the top of his class.

Now, when someone asked him how he navigated, he would say, "Well, I go down into my cabin and get out my charts and compass. I get my readings and do all my calculations. Then, I go up onto the deck. And I look up at the stars. I smell the wind and feel the way that it's blowing; I feel the pitch and roll of the waves—and then I correct my calculations!"

There's a time when, in spite of our careful analysis and reasoning, we must listen to our hearts and go by instinct.

Spiritual vitality cannot be reduced to systems and methods. It is an adventure of love. Even as we grow in our knowledge of the spiritual exercises available to us, we can never substitute them for the natural interaction of our relationship with the Lord.

Lasting vitality is like lasting love: It is carefully nurtured day by day with little courtesies, frequent affirmations, and a delight in the beloved. It looks more carefully and closely at the qualities of the beloved and remembers more clearly the gracious acceptance that the beloved has shown over the years.

God is at work, shaping us for all eternity. We are his beloved children, and he longs for us to love him and to be transformed by his love for us. Have your way, almighty Potter, Shaper of our souls! Have your way.

NOTES

1. Quoted by R. Kent Hughes in *Disciplines of a Godly Man* (Wheaton, Ill.: Crossway Books, 1991), 35–36.
2. Donald P. McNeill, Douglas A. Morrison, Henri J. M. Nouwen, *Compassion: A Reflection on the Christian Life* (New York: Image Books, 1982), 54–55.

SOUL-SEARCHING

Questions for Reflection and Discussion

1. What is your definition of *grace?* You may want to write your own definition, draw a picture, create a story, or share an experience from your life.

2. In what ways does expectancy mark your life? In what area(s) would you like to have a more hopeful, expectant outlook? What specific steps could you take to cultivate confidence and faith for these things?

3. How do you relate to the twin problems of the "undue magnification of problems" and the "trivialization of blessings"? Which area needs the most attention at this time? What spiritual exercises could help you develop in this area?

4. What is a picture of resilience for you? When have you shown resilience? Where do you need soul power for resilience at this time?

5. Think of someone who needs your support at this time. In what ways could your spiritual exercises help you support this person? What do you think God would like to do for them and in them? How might the Lord be calling you to be part of the process?

6. When you think of zeal, who comes to mind? How would you rate your level of zeal? Were there times in your life when you were more zealous? Less zealous? Why?

7. Understanding that integrity is a process, in what areas do you feel grateful for the integrity God is shaping within you? What areas need attention? What specific step can you take now to establish integrity in one area?

8. Count your blessings, one by one!

SELECTED BIBLIOGRAPHY

Augustine. *The Confessions of St. Augustine.* Trans. Rex Warner. New
  York: New American Library, 1963.

Baillie, John. *A Diary of Readings.* New York: Scribner's, 1955.

Banks, Robert. *Redeeming the Routines: Bringing Theology to Life.* Wheaton,
  Ill.: Victor, 1993.

Barna, George. *The Power of Vision.* Ventura, Calif.: Regal, 1992.

Blackaby, Henry, and Claude V. King. *Experiencing God: Knowing and
  Doing the Will of God.* Nashville: Lifeway Press, 1990.

Blamires, Harry. *The Christian Mind.* London: SPCK, 1966.

Bonhoeffer, Dietrich. *Life Together.* New York: Harper & Row, 1954.

Bounds, E. M. *The Necessity of Prayer.* Grand Rapids: Baker, 1976.

Brooks, Thomas. *Precious Remedies against Satan's Devices.* London: The
  Banner of Truth Trust, 1652.

Brother Lawrence. *The Practice of the Presence of God.* Mount Vernon,
  N.Y.: Peter Pauper Press, 1963.

Doberstein, John W., ed. *Minister's Prayer Book.* Philadelphia: Fortress
  Press, 1986.

Edwards, Tilden. *Spiritual Friend.* New York: Paulist Press, 1980.

Fénelon, François. *Christian Perfection.* Minneapolis: Bethany House,
  1975.

———. *Let Go.* Springfield, Pa.: Banner Publisher, Whitaker House,
  1973.

Forsyth, P. T. *Christian Perfection.* Edinburgh: Edinburgh University
  Press, 1899.

Foster, Richard. *Celebration of Discipline.* San Francisco: Harper & Row, 1978.

Griffin, Emilie. *Turning: Reflections on the Experience of Conversion.* New
  York: Doubleday, 1980.

Gurnall, William. *The Christian in Complete Armour.* Carlisle, Pa.: Banner
  of Truth, 1974.

Hallesby, O. *Prayer.* Minneapolis: Augsburg, 1931.

Hammarskjöld, Dag. *Markings.* New York: Alfred A. Knopf, 1964.

Heschel, Abraham. *The Sabbath: Its Meaning for Modern Man.* New York: Noonday Press, 1951.

Huggett, Joyce. *The Joy of Listening to God.* [city, pub., date]

Hughes, R. Kent. *Disciplines of a Godly Man.* Wheaton, Ill.: Crossway, 1991.

Job, Ruben P., and Norman Shawchuck. *A Guide to Prayer for Ministers and Other Servants.* Nashville: The Upper Room, 1983.

Kelly, Thomas. *A Testament of Devotion.* New York: Harper & Row,

Kepler, Thomas S., ed. *An Anthology of Devotional Literature.* Grand Rapids: Baker, 1947.

Krug, Ronald. *How to Keep a Spiritual Journal.* Nashville: Thomas Nelson, 1982.

Laubach, Frank C. *Letters by a Modern Mystic.* New York: Student Volunteer Movement, 1937.

Law, William. *A Serious Call to a Devout and Holy Life.* Grand Rapids: Eerdmans, 1966.

Leech, Kenneth. *Soul Friend.* San Francisco: Harper & Row, 1977.

Lewis, C. S. *Mere Christianity.* New York: Macmillan, 1943.

———. *Reflections of the Psalms.* New York: Harcourt Brace, 1958.

———. *The Screwtape Letters.* New York: Macmillan, 1961.

Lovelace, Richard F. *Dynamics of Spiritual Life.* Downers Grove, Ill.: InterVarsity, 1979.

Mains, David, and Steve Bell, *Two Are Better than One.* Portland, Oreg.: Multnomah, 1991.

McNeill, Donald P., Douglas A. Morrison, and Henri J. M. Nouwen. *Compassion: A Reflection on the Christian Life.* New York: Image Books, 1982.

Meisel, Anthony C., and M. L. del Mastro. *The Rule of St. Benedict.* Garden City, N.Y.: Image Books, 1975.

Mottola, Anthony. *The Spiritual Exercises of St. Ignatius.* New York: Image Books, 1964.

Murray, Andrew. *With Christ in the School of Prayer.* Old Tappan, N.J.: Fleming H. Revell, 1953.

Nouwen, Henri J. M. *In the Name of Jesus: Reflections on Christian Leadership.* New York: Crossroad, 1989.

———. *Making All Things New: An Invitation to the Spiritual Life.* San Francisco: Harper & Row, 1981.

———. *Reaching Out.* New York: Doubleday, 1966.

————. *The Genesee Diary: Report from a Trappist Monastery.* New York: Image Books, 1976.

O'Connor, Elizabeth. *Search For Silence.* Waco, Tex.: Word, 1972.

Packer, J. I. *Knowing God.* Downers Grove, Ill.: InterVarsity, 1973.

Peterson, Eugene H. *The Message: The New Testament in Contemporary Language.* Colorado Springs: NavPress, 1993.

Phillips, J. B. *Your God Is Too Small.* New York: MacMillan, 1958.

Postema, Don. *Space for God.* Grand Rapids: Bible Way, 1983.

Rule for a New Brother. Springfield, Ill.: Templegate, 1976.

Rule of St. Benedict, The. New York: Image Books, 1975.

Schaeffer, Francis A. *True Spirituality.* Wheaton, Ill.: Tyndale, 1971.

Smith, Hannah Whitall. *Christian's Secret of a Happy Life.* Old Tappan, N.J.: Flemming H. Revell, 1952.

Stahl, Carolyn. *Opening to God.* Nashville: The Upper Room, 1977.

Stewart, James S. *The Life and Teaching of Jesus Christ.* Nashville: Abingdon Press, n.d.

Stott, John R. W. *Your Mind Matters.* Downers Grove, Ill.: InterVarsity, 1972.

Strong, Mary, ed. *Letters to the Scattered Brotherhood.* New York: Harper & Brothers, 1948.

Taylor, Howard, and Mrs. Howard Taylor. *Hudson Taylor's Spiritual Secret.* Chicago: Moody, 1932.

Tozer, A. W. *The Knowledge of the Holy.* New York: Harper & Row, 1961.

————. *The Pursuit of God.* Harrisburg, Pa.: Christian Publications, 1948.

Traherne, Thomas. *Centuries.* Wilton, Conn: Morehouse Barlow, 1960.

Wakefield, Gordon S. *The Westminster Dictionary of Christian Spirituality.* Philadelphia: The Westminster Press, 1983.

Wells, Ronald V. *Spiritual Disciplines for Everyday Living.* New York: Character Research Press, 1982.

Whitney, Donald S. *Spiritual Disciplines for the Christian Life.* Colorado Springs: NavPress, 1991.

Willard, Dallas. *The Spirit of the Disciplines.* San Francisco: HarperSanFrancisco, 1988.

ABOUT THE AUTHOR

Dr. Douglas J. Rumford has pastored the 1,100-member First Presbyterian Church [PC(USA)] in Fresno, California, since 1988. He previously served congregations in Old Greenwhich, Connecticut and Fairfield, Connecticut. In addition to serving as a pastor for more than 18 years, he has written a number of articles for *Leadership Journal* and other leading evangelical publications. His first book, *Scared to Life: Awakening the Courage of Faith in An Age of Fear* (Victor Books), was featured for the "1995 50-Day Spiritual Adventure" of Chapel of the Air, directed by David Mains. *SoulShaping: Taking Care of Your Spiritual Life,* is a 1996 featured selection for the program.

Doug received his Doctor of Ministry degree from Fuller Theological Seminary. He earned his Master of Divinity degree from Gordon-Conwell Theological Seminary, and a Bachelor of Arts in English from Miami University, Oxford, Ohio.

Doug and his wife, Sarah, have been married more than twenty years and have a college-age daughter and three teenage sons.

His goal in writing is to touch hearts and minds with the truth, grace, and power of God: "As I serve Jesus Christ, my greatest joy is bringing ideas to life that can change others' lives."